TARGET 9 PRESENTS

IELTS

TREASURE

SPEAKING

Your ultimate guide to IELTS Success

FREEDOM PUBLISHING HOUSE

Publisher Address:

FREEDOM PUBLISHING HOUSE, SCF-32,2ND FLOOR, PHASE–5, Mohali, Pin-160059

For any suggestions, you can reach us at freedompressteam@gmail.com

Or visit – www.freedompublishing.business.site

TARGET 9
Check out candidate reviews and Testimonials by visiting:
Website – target9edu.com
Twitter - www.twitter.com/Target9Mohali
Instagram – www.instagram.com/target9educity
Facebook - www.facebook.com/target9educity
YouTube - https://www.YouTube.com/channel/UCl0oSaFn4gbM-kPZIzXjRRw/featured

2

Author's Word

I have been in the field of education from the past 9 years. I have the experience of training more than 10,000 students over a decade for IELTS exam.

I have collected the latest data by interacting with candidates that have taken the IELTS exam from all over India. With extensive research and foresight this book has been amassed for your help in the speaking module of IELTS.

Don't try to memorize the content. Try to learn from the ideas and use them while speaking practice.

I have compiled my experience of training from all these years and have locked in this book.

So, what are you waiting for? You have the key to this lock now. Open this book and share this knowledge with the world.

I hope this book helps you in achieving your goals.

Darshan Singh

Author | Speaker | Trainer

About the Book

This book is written after a thorough research in the field of IELTS Speaking Module. This book will offer you comprehensive variety of Topics that are asked by the examiners in the Speaking Test of IELTS.

This book contains more than 800 solved questions and answers for the follow-up round as well as Cue-card topics from the past exams. This book also contains expected topics for the year 2021.

This book includes five parts in which solutions are given for all the questions. This book should be read systematically in order to score high band score in your IELTS exam.

This book contains 1000 + useful vocabulary words along with speaking tips for the candidates. Read all those tips before taking the exams.

This book is a compilation of the most common and frequent questions and topics asked in the IELTS speaking test. This is entirely a guess work and shouldn't be considered as the final syllabus of the exam.

Table of Contents

42	A book you have read	77
43	An occasion when you helped someone	78
44	Something you planned to do but haven't done yet	79
45	An important letter you received	80
46	A time when you teamed up with an old person	80
47	A gift that made you happy	81
48	An achievement	82
49	Your ideal home	83
50	Your favorite sports	84
51	A product of your country	85
52	A big company/organization near you	85
53	A businessperson you admire	86
54	A holiday you enjoyed	87
55	A person you admire from a foreign country	88
56	An interesting place in your country that tourists don't know about	89
57	Your visit to a library	90
58	Visit to a museum	91
59	Describe a sports event you have seen	92
60	Describe a leisure activity near sea	93
61	Favourite newspaper	94
62	An international leader or politician you like	95
63	An English lesson	95
64	Describe a piece of art (a statue or painting)	96
65	Describe a time when you went to a crowded place	97
66	Favourite author	98
67	Something that you bought online	99
68	An important city	100
69	You were going on a tour and your vehicle broke down	101
70	A national building in your country	101
71	Favourite weather	102
72	A tranquil place you enjoy going to	103
73	A foreign dish you want to eat	104

	first time	
101	A time you had to search for information	127
102	Describe a building /structure in your city	128
103	Describe a water sport that you want to try	129
104	An advertisement you watched on TV recently	130
105	Describe a thing that has become a fashion or a matter of status nowadays	131
106	Describe certain laws of your country	132
107	Describe a historical event that you find interesting	132
108	An intelligent person you know	133
109	Describe a hotel you stayed at	134
110	Describe a pet that you have or once had	135
111	A part of your rituals or customs that you don't like	136
112	Any souvenir that you bought during your holidays	137
113	Describe a thing for which you saved money from a long time	138
114	A comic that you read in childhood	138
115	Speak about an interesting tour guide	139
116	Speak about a family that resemble yours	140
117	Speak about an aquatic animal	141
118	Speak about a time when you admired the sky	141
119	Describe a handcrafted item which you made yourself.	142
120	Describe a dish you like the most which is served during the festivals.	143
121	Describe a place full of colors	144
122	Describe a product or application which is based on Artificial Intelligence	145
123	A software that you use often	146
124	Something kind that someone did for you	147
125	Describe a time when you taught something new to an older person	148
126	Describe an instance when you solved a problem using the internet	149

9

159	Describe a piece of good news that you heard from someone	179
160	Your favorite magazine	180
161	A club that you have joined	181
162	An accident that you have seen	182
163	Favorite subject in your school	183
164	Tell about a subject you disliked in school	184
165	How do you utilize your free time?	185
166	An interesting old person you know well	185
167	A movie you watched recently	186
168	A time when you felt angry	187
169	Talk about an important photograph	188
170	Describe an old thing	189
171	First day at school/college/university	190
172	Birthday celebration you remember	191
173	An activity you find interesting	192
174	An activity you do to maintain good health	193
175	Speak about a room in which you spent a lot of time	194
176	A toy with which you played in your childhood	195
177	Speak about an adventurous person you know	196
178	Talk about your favorite restaurant	197
179	A person you know who is beautiful/handsome	198
180	Describe an important decision you made/ Decision you made with the help of someone	199
181	Speak about someone who is a good cook	200
182	Speak about something useful you learnt from the member of your family	201
183	Describe a stressful day at school/college/university	201
184	A place indoor or outdoor where you can study	202
185	A movie or TV show that made you laugh	203
186	Talk about a dish you know how to cook	204
187	A time when someone didn't tell you the whole truth	205
188	Tell about a party you went	206

189	Talk about something you taught to a teenager / Talk about something you taught to someone	207
190	When you found something that someone lost	208
191	A meal you enjoyed at a restaurant	209
192	Faraway place you would like to visit	210
193	Describe a beautiful home you have seen	211
194	A radio program you find interesting	212
195	A subject you did not like but now you find interesting	213
196	Something you bought but did not use	214
197	Time when you had to change your plan	215
198	A person you wanted to be like	216
199	Food that people eat on special occasions	217
200	An occasion when you bought/made a special cake	218
201	An aspect of modern society that you dislike	219
202	Describe a famous scientist/inventor you know about	220
203	Describe an exciting experience in your life	222
204	Describe a school you have studied in	223
205	Expensive clothing you have bought lately	224
206	Time when you had to take care of a baby	225
207	Job you think you would be good at OR Describe something you would like to do in the future	226
208	Something that you borrowed from your friend or family	227
209	Describe a shop or store you often go to	228
210	Describe a national day in your country	229
211	Describe your favorite flower	230
212	Describe an art and craft activity you did at school	231
213	Describe a noisy place you have been to	232
214	Describe a social networking website/platform you use	233
215	Describe a personal goal which you have not been able to achieve	234

216	Describe the politest person you have come across in your life	235
217	Describe a time when you received a good service from a hotel or a restaurant	236
218	A polluted city you have visited OR Describe a place you visited that has been affected by pollution	237
219	Describe a good law in your country	238
220	A talkative person	239
221	Interesting news you read in a newspaper	239
222	Talk about an instance when you invited a friend for a meal in a restaurant or at home.	240
223	Describe a meeting or discussion about fake news	241
224	Talk about a job one of your grandparents did	242
225	Describe a family business you know	243
226	Talk about your favorite movie star	244
227	Describe a period in your history that you would like to learn about	245
228	A person who has encouraged you recently	246
229	Describe a time when you were outside, and rain started	247
230	Talk about a practical skill you have	248
231	Describe an unusual vacation you had	248
232	Describe an irritating person in your neighborhood	249
233	Describe a surprise party you organized for your friend	250
234	Describe people who raise awareness about the environment	251
235	Describe an experience when children made you laugh	252
236	Describe the greatest success of your friend that made you feel proud	253
237	Talk about a situation when you complained about something and got good results	254
238	Describe an outdoor activity you did for the first	255

13

PART – THREE

14

35	Computer	296
36	Internet	297
37	Sky	297
38	Cars	298
39	Tourism	299
40	Crime	300
41	Health	300
42	Exercise	301
43	Foreign language	302
44	Space exploration	302
45	Future	303
46	Hotel	304
47	City village	304
48	Childhood	305
49	Jewellery	306
50	Songs/music	306
51	Art and craft	307
52	Parks	308
53	Book	308
54	Festivals	309
55	Accident	310
56	Politics	310
57	Children	311
58	Superstitions	312
59	Fashion	312
60	Gifts	313
61	Name	314
62	Nature	314
63	Shopping	315
64	Technology	316
65	bicycle	316
66	Work	317
67	Studies	318
68	Email	318

PART – FOUR

PART – FIVE

PART ONE

Introductory Questions and Answers

Introductory questions for IELTS (AC/GT)

What is your name?
My name is _____
How should I call you?
You can call me_____ OR You can call me by my name
_____

Tell me something about yourself.
I live in _____. I like playing cricket and football in my free
time. I also like reading books and newspaper. I have done (mention
your latest qualification). My biggest ambition is to settle in a foreign
country.
OR
Basically, I belong to _____, but nowadays I am living in
_____. I have done (mention your latest qualification). I love
reading books and listen to music in my free time. My dream in life is
to study abroad.

Speak about your family
I live in a nuclear family. There are four members, my mother, father
and brother. We live in house that has three rooms. My brother is
studying and he's younger to me. My father is a businessman, my
mother is doing a job.
OR
I live in a joint family. There nine members in my family. I am the
youngest one. The family consists of my mother, father, brother, his
wife and their two kids. My grandparents also live with us.

Where do you live?
I live in Chandigarh. It's a beautiful city with all the facilities. I was
born and brought up in Chandigarh. I did my schooling from the same
place. Our city is one of the cleanest and greenest cities in our
country.
OR
Basically, I belong to Amritsar but nowadays I am living in Chandigarh.
It's a beautiful city with all the amenities in it. I enjoy living here and I
think that it is one of the most beautiful cities that I have seen.

What do you like to do in your free time?

I like to play games in my free time. I like to play video games and cricket. I also like reading books and magazines whenever I get some time.

OR

I love watching television in my free time. I also like to browse the internet regarding latest trends and news.

Tell me something about your education qualifications.

I have passed 12th exams recently in commerce field.

OR

I have completed computer engineering from _____ University or college. **(If you are a graduate, never say I have done 10th from _____ school, then I did my 12th from_____. After that I completed my graduation from_____.)** Always mention about your current or the latest qualifications.

What is your plan for the next 5 years?

My plan for the next five years is simple. I want to complete my IELTS and then apply to a foreign college or university to get a degree. Then, I would like to settle over there.

OR

I would like to see myself doing a well-suited job for me on a good level. I will also try to buy a house for myself.

Why are you taking the IELTS exam?

It's the requirement of the embassy and the university that I clear my IELTS exam in order to get a visa and study there. This test is designed to test the English proficiency of a person.

OR

It's a mandatory language test that I need to pass to get a permanent residence visa. IELTS exam tests the capability of a person regarding English language.

What is the reason behind choosing Canada, Australia.......?

I have chosen Canada for myriad reasons. The first one is that many of my friends and relatives are already living there. Secondly, it's a beautiful country and people are very humble. The environment is fantastic and there are plenty of educational institutes and job opportunities.

Which course are you planning to study there? (Academic students only)

I am planning to study_____ (mention about the continuation of your current study. For example, if you have done Bachelor of Computers the you must say that I am going to take admission in Master of Computers)

There is no negative or positive effect of the answers of your IELTS interview on your visa. In IELTS test, they are only going to judge your level of English. Even if you haven't decided your course yet, you can speak about any relevant course.

It is recommended that you search for a course before going into IELTS exam as the examiner can also ask you few questions regarding that.

Why have you selected that course? (Academic students only)

I have done 12th in commerce so that's why I have chosen business course for myself. Moreover, it has a great scope in that country.

(You may speak about any course that relates to your current studies)

What are you doing currently?

Currently I am preparing to go abroad. Recently I have given my exams and I prepared for the IELTS as well. As soon as I get the IELTS result, I am going to apply in a foreign university or college. (*For Academic students*)

OR

Currently I am doing job in an IT company. I have applied for a job in the foreign country as well. Currently I am looking to get 8 Band in IELTS in order to apply for a Permanent Residence visa.

Where do you work presently?

I work in Chandigarh in an IT company. The name of my company is _____. I am working there as a software engineer.

How many hours do you work?

I work for eight to ten hours in a day. I feel that my working hours are a bit too much. If given a chance, I would like to reduce it in future.

What are your job responsibilities?

My primary responsibilities are to develop the software for any website or company. I also maintain and update software from time to time.

Is there anything that you don't like about your job?

I like everything about my job. The one thing that I would like to change is the working hours. Sometimes I work for more than 10 hours in a day. I feel that it can affect my health. If given a chance, I would like to work less and give time to other activities.

Speak about your daily routine.

I wake up early in the morning. After taking a nutritious breakfast, I get ready for my class. I study there for five to six hours. Then, I come back and take a nap. In the evening I go out and play or do cycling and exercise. I take my dinner as early as 7 PM. After taking my dinner, I like to spend time with my family members and then I go to bed at 10.

Is there anything that you would like to change about your daily routine?

I can't complain much about my daily routine. I have a balanced routine. But I wake up at 6AM. I wish that I could wake up at 5 so that I would have an hour extra in the day.

What are your hobbies?

I love playing video games and football. I also like to watch movies and documentaries of famous events and people.

OR

I am a big fan of watching cricket. I also play it with my friends. I am also fond of reading books and newspapers.

What will you do if you fail in the IELTS exam?

I think that I have prepared well enough to clear my IELTS exam. But, by any chance I fail in the exam, I will re appear and give my best.

Where would you like to see yourself in the next 10 years?

I want to see myself as a settled man/woman. I want to own a big house and would like to have a business of my own rather than doing job.

Describe your house?

I live in a big house as I am living in a joint family. There are six bedrooms and a big dining area where we have our meals together. There is a lawn at the front along with a driveway where we park our cars.

OR

I live in a small family hence my house is not that big. I live in an apartment which has two rooms with attached living room and a dining area. We live on the sixth floor of the building.

Do you like flowers?

Yes, I like flowers as I am the kind of person who is close to nature. I love rose flower more than any other flower. Rose is very useful and serves myriad purposes. Its petals are very aromatic and are also used to make many cosmetic products.

Do you use a camera?

Yes, I use camera that is in-built in my phone. These days, I don't see a lot of people using a separate camera as it requires a lot of effort to carry. So, I use camera of my phone that captures good enough pictures.

Do you like to wear perfume?

Yes, I like to collect and wear perfume on daily basis. I have a collection of 6 perfumes from all over the world. These perfumes are mostly gifted by my friends and relatives who live in foreign countries.

OR

No, I don't like to wear perfume. I am allergic to perfumes and scents.

Do you like sports?

Yes, I like sports. My favourite one is cricket and football. I like to play it on daily basis and I also watch all the live events of cricket and football.

Do you do exercise?

Yes, I do exercise occasionally. I do medium workout on weekends and holidays. I also do yoga which is another form of exercise.

OR

No, I don't do exercise as I don't get much time from my routine. I walk and do jogging sometimes which is also a helpful exercise.

Do you fast?

No, I don't fast. Fasting is a common belief in my country, but I don't believe in it. Although my mother does fast on certain occasions, but I don't do it.

OR

Yes, I keep fast quite often. There are numerous occasions in our country that requires us to do fasting. This is a tradition that is religious based. I follow religion so I do fast.

Do you get angry?

Usually I don't get angry. However, on some instances I can get angry on certain things. In most cases, I try to keep myself calm.

Do you like animals?

Yes, I like animals. My beloved one is dog and cat. Dog because it is the most loyal animal in the world. On the other hand, cats are cute, and their skin is very soft and smooth.

Do you play video games?

Yes, I play video games on the weekends with my friends and cousins. I have a Microsoft x-box console at my home. I mostly love to play car racing games.

OR

Not really, I am not at all interested in playing video games. I find it very difficult to concentrate on the screen for a long period of time. I usually prefer to play in the park.

Do you read comics?

No, I don't read comics. I used to read comics in my childhood. I can remember few of them. Robin hood, superman and batman were one of my best comics in childhood.

Do you watch cartoons?

No, I don't watch cartoons. I used to watch it when I was a kid. Pokemon, Scooby-doo, Jackson's and Tom and jerry were my preferred cartoon programs.

Do you like your job? (for general training students)

Yes, I like my job. I am working as a software engineer and I have few responsibilities on my shoulders. I like everything about my job.

Do you drive a car?

Yes, I drive a car. I have Hyundai make car. It is an SUV car. I go to my office on that car and I also take out my car on the weekends for long drives and outings.

OR

No, I don't drive a car yet. I am also learning the skill right now. I think that I will be able to learn car driving in a month's time.

Have you ever played football?

Yes, I have played football recently. It's a wonderful game and requires phenomenal strength and stamina to play that game. it's a great game which also enhances teamwork.

Have you been to a disco club?

Yes, I went to a disco club once in my life. I am not the kind of a person who likes to party a lot. I went there on my friend's birthday last month. It was a new experience for me.

Have you ever been to a foreign country?

Yes, I have been to Dubai. It's a great place for adventure and fun. It's a desert area but the infrastructure built there is fantastic. The roads are wide, and the city is neat and clean.

OR

No, I have never visited a foreign country. If given a chance, I would like to visit Canada. I have heard from my friends that it is one of the most beautiful countries in the world.

Have you seen an animated movie?

Yes, I have seen numerous animated movies over the years. The best ones were the adventures of Tintin and Avatar. These movies were hugely popular all over the world and in our country as well.

Do you enjoy your birthdays?

Yes, I enjoy my birthdays very much. I love to celebrate birthday of mine and my family members with great joy. I generally go to a decent restaurant and relish the evening.

How did you celebrate your last birthday?

Last year I remember that I went to a mall with my friends and cousins. There we did bowling for two hours and then we went to watch a movie. After the movie, we took dinner in a fancy restaurant. This is how I celebrated my last birthday.

Do you have any memory of your childhood?

I have many memories of my childhood. Most of them are wonderful and I laugh a lot when I recall them. I remember once I had gone to a doctor for vaccination and I was so scared that I started crying loudly, all the people were looking at me and I felt very embarrassed.

Did you enjoy your childhood?

I thoroughly enjoyed my childhood. I was a naughty kid and my mother tells me that I was very active and would not sit idle for even a second. I hardly remember any unhappy memory from my childhood. My childhood was wonderful and full of enjoyment.

What things did you enjoy doing in your childhood?

I enjoyed playing cards, marbles and cricket in my childhood. I used to play it on daily basis in the evening. I was also active in art, craft and music.

Do you wear traditional clothes?

Yes, I wear traditional clothes on certain occasions like Diwali and Independence Day. I think that these two days hold a great importance in the history of our country. I like to wear white coloured traditional gown and lose pants on these days.

What kind of clothes do the people of your country wear?

People in my country wear all sorts of clothes. It depends upon the individuals and age group. Older people like to wear traditional clothes whereas youngsters like to dress in western attire.

Which one do you prefer, desktops or laptops?

I prefer laptops for a few reasons. First one is that it is a portable device and easy to carry around. Moreover, laptops are easier to work on and consumes less electricity.

Do you feel that everyone should know how to use computers?

I think that basic knowledge of computers should be held by everyone. In this era, it's very difficult to survive without knowing how to operate computers. These days, I often see that even the elders are learning the computer skills.

Do you ever change your daily routine?

Yes, I like to change my daily routine on weekends. Usually I wake up early in the morning and go to study or work. But, on the weekends, I like to get up late and do things that I don't do on weekdays.

Is it vital to have a daily routine?

It's essential to have a daily routine because it makes our life manageable and planned. A fixed daily routine helps us to do more things than a person who does not have a fixed routine.

Which is your favorite room in your house?

I like my own room the most. In my room, there are all facilities like T.V, air conditioner and attached bathroom. I also have an old but beautiful study table which is kept in my room.

Describe your neighbourhood.

I live in a gated colony that consists of apartments and individual houses. There are many wonderful people in my locality of all the age groups. They are friendly and polite. There is a huge park where people come in the evening and morning for walk. I like my neighbourhood very much.

Do you generally use a dictionary?

No, I don't use dictionary regularly these days. When I was in school, I used it extensively for finding the meaning of the words that were alien to me.

What are the advantages of reading dictionaries?

There are two major advantages of reading dictionaries. Firstly, it gives you the meanings of the words that you don't know. Secondly, you can learn a great deal of synonyms for simple words.

How do you spend your evenings?

I usually spend my evening with my friends and occasionally with my family as well. I go out in the parks and play cricket and football. Or I just stroll in the neighbourhood.

Speak about your favourite friend.

My favourite friend's name is Anuj. He is older to me but he's one of those persons with whom I like to spend time. He is living in a foreign country these days, so we meet each other once in a year.

Do you like to spend time with your family or friends?
I like to spend time with both family and friends. I usually go out with my friends on the other hand I celebrate occasions and other festivals with my family members. Whenever I need some counselling regarding anything in my life then I generally prefer my family members rather than friends.

Is there any flower that has a special meaning in your country?
Lotus has a special meaning in my country. People of my country revere it to gods Vishnu and Brahma. This flower is considered as pure and beautiful.

Who likes the flowers most, men or women?
I think women are more impressed with flowers than men. They like to receive flowers on certain occasions. Flowers are more of a feminine thing than a masculine one.

Is there any food item that you don't like?
I like most of the food items. There are certain things that I don't relish like okra, some lentils and meat. Other than that, I eat every kind of food item.

Speak about a common meal in your country?
Meals differ from state to state. Rice with lentil or a green vegetable along with Indian bread would be an ideal meal in most parts of my country.

Do you sing?
I don't sing that much. I would rather say that I am a bathroom singer. I like to sing when I bath, other than that I never sing in public or in front of anyone.

If you could sing like a singer, who will it be?
If God would give me powers than I would like to steal the voice of Sonu Nigam. He is one of the most melodious singers that our country has ever produced. I have seen a lot of his musical concerts and I always dream of singing like him.

From which source do you get news?
I get my news from newspapers and internet. I read newspapers for at least thirty minutes every day. I also keep myself updated with the latest news from many applications in my phone.

Which type of news do you like to read?

I prefer sports and news from around the world. I like cricket and football, so I read latest news about these two sports and I also relish international news.

Do you have an e-book?

Yes, recently I bought a kindle edition of a book. The reason I bought the e-book was that the paper back was too costly, so I paid for the softcopy of the book.

Do you prefer e-books or paperbacks?

Honestly, I prefer reading e-books than paperbacks. The main reason is that I can carry my e-book in my phone or tablet. I can even read it when it is dark. E-books are cheap and thing of the future. E-books also saves paper.

Which transport did you use to get here today?

I reached the exam center via car. This is my dad's car and I borrowed it for today.

Do you use public transport?

Yes, I use public transport regularly. I prefer to travel by bus locally. It is a convenient and cheaper way to commute.

Is there any place to swim near your home?

There are two places where I can swim in my city. The first one is the government sports complex and the other one is a private pool where great number of people come for swimming.

Do you keep/write a diary?

No, I don't write a dairy. I usually have less time for things like this but if I will get time in the coming years then I would certainly write a daily dairy.

OR

Yes, I write dairy regularly. I have kept that diary as a secret, and I don't show it to anyone. I write the day's proceedings in that and specially on those days when some important things happen.

What are the benefits of travelling by boats or ships?

The biggest benefit of travelling by boat or ship is that it is a cheap mode of transport. Also, you can enjoy scenic views of rivers and oceans along the voyage.

Do you feel that travelling by boats will get more popular in the future?

I think that it will get a lot famous in the coming years as the road traffic is becoming a huge problem these days and I think that travelling by boats can be a wonderful alternative.

Do you carry a bag when you go out?

I usually don't carry a bag when I go out, but I carry a sling bag when I am travelling to somewhere far away from my home. In that I can carry some snacks and clothes which will be helpful for my travel.

OR

Yes, I carry a handy sling bag when I go out. I keep my purse, mobile, sanitizer and other important things that can be required when I go out of the house.

What do you carry in the bag usually?

If I am carrying a bag, then I generally carry important things in that. I carry a mobile charger, some snacks and cash.

What type of bags do you like buying?

When I plan to buy a bag then I always look for the best quality. I like Wildcraft brand which is widely known brand all over the world. I like to buy medium sized bags with a lot of pockets and zips.

Do you feel that sunny days are the best days?

If you ask me then I would say that sunny days are the best. I don't like cloudy days as it gives me feeling of boredom and it depresses my mood.

OR

No, I don't like sunny days as it can be hot in the most parts of my country. I like those days when the sun is covered with grey clouds. I like the gloomy weather.

What do you like to do when it's a sunny day?

If it's a sunny day and hot weather, then I prefer to stay indoors to avoid heat stroke as the weather in this part of the world can get hot. I also drink a lot of liquids.

In which months it rains more in your country?

July and August are the wettest months of the year. I wait for these months after the long summer as the temperatures get a bit lower and the environment gets a bit cleaner due to the rain.

What do you do in the rainy days?

I like to sip in some hot drinks along with traditional Indian snacks. On some rainy days I just sit outdoors under the shed and adore the nature.

Do you save all the photos on your computer?

I always try my best to save all the photos in my computer. I believe that rather than saving in computers, one should take out a photo print and save pictures in an album.

Do you like looking at you in the mirror?

Honestly, I don't like looking at the mirror for no reason. I only look at myself when I am getting ready and see whether my clothes are looking good or not, or do I need to do something to improve my looks. Other than that, I don't like looking in the mirror.

What are the uses of mirrors?

Mirrors are mostly used in the almirahs and dressing rooms where one gets ready. Mirrors are also an integral part of the cars. They are used for viewing the rear side of the car while driving.

Which type of shoes do you wear?

I wear all types of shoes. I like casual and sports shoes when I am at my home or I am roaming somewhere. I wear formal shoes when I go to work, college or in a party.

Do you wear comfortable or fashionable shoes?

I can never wear shoes that are not comfortable to the feet. I always prefer comfortable shoes. I like shoes that has a soft and fluffy sole.

How often do you take a taxi?

I use taxi quite often. These days, taxi has become a cheap and convenient mode of transport. More and more people are travelling in taxis these days. I regularly book taxi from my mobile phone application.

Do you feel that taxi is a convenient mode of transport?

It is very convenient to commute from one place to the other via taxi. It is luxurious and one can book a taxi within seconds using numerous mobile applications.

Are you a polite/humble person?

Generally, I am a polite person. I have always been taught by my parents to be humble. On certain instances I get a bit candid but most of the times I like to be polite.

From where did you learn to be polite?

I learned politeness from my parents and my grandparents. They always tell me the importance of being polite. I also learned politeness from my teachers at school.

Are the people in your country generally polite?

Most people in my country are polite and helpful. I have heard from some foreigners that people of India are best in their hospitality and are very polite.

What are the benefits of being polite?

I think if you are a polite person then any one can easily interact with you in less time. People will respect you more and they will take you more seriously than a rude person.

How do you react if another person is not polite with you?

I react in a polite manner and I wait till he or she gets calm. If that does not happen then I simply ignore that person. If I indulge in a banter, then I think that I will be the one who will suffer more.

Do you lose your patience?

Yes, I lose my patience sometimes. Generally, I am a patient person but in some cases I get a lot of anxiety. When I am getting late in the morning, I lose patience and try to hurry a lot.

How do you keep yourself patient?

I keep myself patient by listening to the music and by doing some work that is time consuming like making a greeting card or reading a book or a newspaper. When you do things that are slow, it increases your patience level.

What type of sounds do you like?

I like the sound of airplanes. I am fascinated by the sounds and shapes of the aero planes since my childhood. So, whenever a plane passes over, I like the sound of it.

What kind of songs you dislike?

I dislike the songs that are too fast and has loud beats. I generally don't like these types of songs as they don't have smoothness. I like songs that calm my mind.

Do you feel that environment is becoming noisy these days?

Indeed, environment is getting a lot noisier nowadays. The major reason is the growing industry and the noise from the vehicles. It is becoming one of the major reasons behind migraine problem in many people.

Is it easy to book a train in your country?

It's a piece of cake to book a train in my country. There is a government application named IRCTC from where we can book all the trains in few easy steps and pay online, and one can get the mobile ticket on the mobile application itself.

How do people travel long distances in your country?

Most of the people travel through train as India is a big country and has a wide network of railway lines. Travelling by train is very convenient, luxurious and cheap.

Do people drive to work in your country?

Yes, many people drive personal cars to work. I think that it is a common mode in some cities and in other cities like Delhi, people use more public transport.

How do people raise children in your country?

People mostly raise children with a lot of care and love in our country. They take care of all the needs of their kids and they also teach a lot of religious values to them.

Are parents too possessive about their kids in India?

In our country I have seen that people are more possessive about their kids than the other parts of the world. In this way, children can get more dependent which is not good for their growth.

Do you feel that children should be given freedom to do whatever they want?
I think they should be given freedom up to some extent. If they are given more independence, then they can get out of the hands. Parents should give liberty, but they should keep an eye on them.

Have you ever hosted a foreign visitor at your home?
Yes, I have hosted my cousins' friend at our house. My cousin lives in Canada, so when he returned last time, his friend came along. He is very interesting, and we had a great time together. He stayed at our house for two days.

How can people save money while travelling?
People can save a lot of money by sharing the cars or by using car-pooling. I think this trend is growing day by day and many people are saving a lot of money by sharing their empty seats of their cars.

Do people exchange greeting cards on festivals in your country?
I think that this fashion has become out of date these days. People generally exchange gifts and sweets in my county rather than giving cards to each other.

Have you ever given a greeting card to anyone?
Yes, I have given many cards to a lot of people. I remember once I gave a greeting card to my best teacher in my childhood. I prepared that card on my own by using a lot of creativity. I gave that card on the eve of Christmas.

Do you follow celebrities?
Yes, I follow celebrities on social networks and websites. I like to see what they are doing these days and how they are working to achieve more in life.

Do you follow any foreign celebrity?
Certainly, I follow many foreign celebrities. They are mostly actors and sportspersons. I like Lionel Messi and Christiano Ronaldo from sports and I admire Morgan Freeman and Matt Damon from Hollywood.

Do you feel that homework should be banned in schools?
No, I am against this kind of thinking. I think that homework should not be banned as it helps to keep the kids busy at home. On the other

hand, I would urge the schools to give it in a limited manner so that kids can do other activities apart from studies.

What type of homework should be given to kids?

Practical work should be given as a homework. Students do a lot of theory in schools, so it makes sense to give more practical and dynamic homework.

What kind of homework was given to you in your childhood?

I remember that we were given more theory work in our school time. It was just filling up the notebooks with useless topics. It was completely impractical work.

Do you feel that lifestyle of people has changed over the years?

Yes, lifestyle of people has changed drastically over the years. Previously people use to live a peaceful life but these days they are more anxious due to over dependence on technology.

Is the lifestyle more lethargic or active these days?

I think that lifestyle has become more lethargic in this era. Formerly people were more active and industrious. These days they are slower and more reliant on technology for even minutest of the tasks.

Speak about a famous product of your country?

There is a bundle of products that are famous in our country. India is famous for its variety of tea. Tea plantations are in abundance in the eastern part of my country. It is of supreme quality and is exported to every corner of the world.

Tell about the area of your country where you live.

I live in the northern part of my country. people here are vibrant and joyous. Northern part of our country experiences all sorts of weather from summers to winters and from monsoon to spring and autumn. There are large areas of plains and there are high ranges of mountains as well. It's a wonderful place to live.

Do you have all the amenities at the place where you live?

I live in a gated colony which is a posh area of our town. There we have all kinds of shops and facilities like a swimming pool and parks. I think that we can have access to all sort of amenities at the place where I live.

Do you want to change anything about the place where you live?
If given a chance, I would like to add cycling tracks at the side of the roads wherever possible. I think that our colony lacks this facility and if I need to do something regarding that, I will add cycling tracks everywhere.

Do you recycle rubbish?
No, I generally don't recycle rubbish myself, but I always keep the plastic waste separately in a bin outside my house so that it can be easily recycled by the authorities.

What do you do with your plastic and paper waste?
Plastic bottles are very useful for a few purposes. Sometimes I cut the big bottles into half and use them for growing plants in it. Paper waste is generally thrown into the bins.

Have you ever won a prize?
I have won a prize in my school time for participating in a sports event. I played cricket and represented my school in a local competition. We won that tournament and the team was handed over a glittering trophy.

Do you shop in street markets?
Yes, if I need something locally like fruits or vegetables then I certainly shop in the street markets. There are some products that are difficult to find in the supermarkets, so in that case I prefer local shops.

Do you share your things with others?
Yes, I always try to share my things with others. It gives me a lot of satisfaction and delight. My parents always encourage me to share things with friends and cousins.

How can we learn sharing?
The best way to learn sharing is to play in a team game or a sport. This way children can build a habit of sharing things with the teammates and other friends as well.

Do the people in your country like to drink tea or coffee?
People of my country are obsessed with tea. Myriad people also drink coffee, but tea is largely consumed in every part of my county. It is mostly taken with milk but these days green tea's popularity is also on the rise.

Do you prefer tea or coffee?

I prefer both. I feel that coffee is tastier, and it has laxative properties which helps sometimes. I like to have tea in the evening and coffee in the morning time.

What type of tea is famous in your country?

In my country, milk tea is the most common variant preferred by people. This type of tea can be found everywhere in our country. Nevertheless, green tea is slowly making a name for itself.

Is it a good idea to make friends online?

It's not a bad idea to make friends on social networking sites. I think that one can make many friends from all over the world using online services.

Do you feel that friends on social networking websites are loyal?

Not all friends are loyal on social networking. You can't judge the nature of a person on the internet. I think that making friends online is easy, but you can't trust them all.

PART TWO

Cue-card Topics with Solutions

IELTS Cue Card Topics for 2020-2021

A poisonous plant you know
Which is the plant and how do you know about it
What is the shape of that plant?
Have you ever seen that plant?
India is rich in flora and fauna. There are millions of species of plants that a person can't count in his entire life. I know about a handful of plants that are harmful or poisonous. The one which I am going to talk about today is Wild Carrot.

It is one of the most poisonous plants that are found in my country. This plant was first found in temperate regions of Europe and Southwest Asia. This plant can also be found in some areas of North America and Australia.

I came to know about this plant when I was in school. I had participated in a botanical exhibition where schools from all over my hometown had come to participate in that exhibition. Our teacher selected me and one of my friends from my class to participate in the exhibition.

Our teacher told us the details of the plant and the school administration arranged it for us. That plant doesn't look so big. It is only a foot tall over of the ground. The leaves of the wild carrot are very thin and spiky.

The leaves are of light green colour and has small flowers on it. The colour of the flowers is white and pale yellow. It has a solid but thin stem that supports hairy like leaves at the top. The leaves are very thin and curved at the edges. The leaves are in the shape of a needle. Thick at the bottom and it becomes thin at the top.

This plant blooms in summers and just before the winters start. Its leaves are also allergic and can cause irritation to the skin when held in hand. This plant is very rare, and people can also mistake it for the real carrot that we eat. The plant is similar in size, but the carrot's texture and colour are different.

I had never seen such a plant in my life before. We handled that plant with care and explained the features to everyone in the exhibition. We used surgical gloves to touch the plant as it might have caused allergy to us.
(Note: You can also search and speak about Tobacco – as the poisonous plant)

A poisonous flower you know
How do you know that flower?
How is that flower poisonous
Is that flower useful
I am not a botanist, but I know one flower that is very poisonous and can be deadly if not handled with care or misused. I am talking about the Opium flower. It is a widely known flower in the world that is used to produce drugs and medicines.

It is also known as Poppy pod or Poppy flower. The flower is of light green colour and is spherical in shape. It mostly grows in cold areas of the world. The main areas where the Opium grows is Afghanistan, Burma, Colombia, Laos, Mexico, India, Pakistan, Thailand, Turkey and China. Its origin is possibly Asia, Spain or some argue that it originated in France.

The usual Opium flower is around 100 grams in weight and of the size of a fist of an adult person. Opium flower grows on a lush green plant. The leaves are broad and curly. The stems shoot up from the middle of the plant that supports the opium flower at the top. The stem is around two centimetres thick. The top of the Opium flowers has rounded spikes that resembles a crown on the head.

The flower contains latex which is a thick white liquid. The flower is cut or slit to get the Latex. The latex is used to produce heroin chemically. It is one of the most expensive flowers in the world. The average cost of an Opium flower per kilo is US$ 20,000 approximately. It is the most smuggled flower in the world. A drug called morphine is extracted from the latex of the Opium and is converted into heroin which is a very strong drug and is banned in many countries.

People in the past have been collecting Opium. Some researchers say that people have been using it as a medicine since 3400 BCE or prehistoric times. In some societies, Opium has also religious significance. Some societies have known to worship Opium.

A poisonous fruit you know
Is that fruit common in your country?
Have you seen that fruit?
Can that fruit be used for something

I have seen many fruits on internet that are known to have poisonous properties. There are rare fruits that are poisonous and dangerous for humans to eat. I came to know about one fruit that can be poisonous and fatal for humans if they consume it.

The name of the fruit is Star fruit. The reason it is called a star fruit is that it has 5 or 6 ridges along its sides and when the fruit is cut in cross section, it resembles a star. The colour of this fruit is yellow. This fruit is consumed by many people across Southeast Asia, the south pacific, Micronesia and parts of East Asia.

Some people eat it raw and some cook it to make certain dishes. According to some people the star fruit is tasty and has few health benefits. Star fruit is low in calories, high in fibre, and loaded with vitamin C. it is sweet and sour in taste and the skin of the fruit is also edible.

However, star fruit contains high number of Oxalates that can cause poison in the body. Unfortunately, anyone with weak kidneys can die after eating this fruit. Even a healthy person can face kidney failure and death in case of excessive consumption of star fruit.

This fruit can also react with certain kinds of medicines. Despite that some people eat this fruit but it is not recommended by the experts. Apart from eating it for leisure there are no health benefits associated with this fruit.

I have never seen this fruit in my life as it is not grown in India. But I read about this fruit in a general knowledge book. Even if I get this fruit in my hand, I will never eat it.

Talk about a time when you visited somewhere and lost your important thing there

Where you went

What you lost

How did you lose that thing?

I have lost a couple of things in my life. Today I would like to tell you about a thing that was very dear to me, but I lost it in a wedding and I still regret it. I went to my cousin's wedding at Delhi last year and lost one of my most precious possessions.

I lost my smart watch and I was so upset when I was not able to find that. I will tell you the whole story that why and when I might have lost that

43

watch. That watch was given to me by my sister on my birthday. I was so attached to that watch that I would never give it to anyone.

That day I was wearing that watch on my left wrist. I wear that watch even when I sleep because it tracks my sleep as well as activities for the whole day. It also shows me that how many calories I have burnt and how many steps I have taken in a day. That watch also shows me notifications for calls and the messages.

I remember when I reached at the wedding I was sitting at a corner with my relatives. We were having some snacks and light conversation. At that time, I recall that I was still wearing the watch.

After some time, we all decided to go on the dance floor and show some moves. We started dancing and I felt a bit irritated by the watch. The watch was clinging on my jacket. So, to get rid of that I untied the watch and kept it in my jacket.

I decided to wear the watch after the wedding. To my surprise when I came back from the wedding, I couldn't find my watch. I was so worried and started searching it in my jacket and other pockets. I felt so sad when I was not able to find my watch. I called my cousins to ask them whether they have seen my watch or not. But I couldn't find it at all.

I was so angry with me and blamed myself for my loss. I wouldn't have lost it if I was still wearing it. It was an expensive watch and I had never lost something that costly before that. I felt so embarrassed that day, but my family consoled me after that incident.

Describe a person who apologized to you
How is the person related to you?
Why did he/she apologize
Did you forgive or not?

There have been few instances in my life when people have apologized to me for certain things. On some occasions people were at fault but on the other occasions their actions were unintentional. Today I would like to tell you one incident in my life when a person sought an apology from me.

The name of that person is Rajiv and he is one of my old friends. This happened when I was in my 10th standard. Me and Rajiv went along well.

We used to sit together in class and shared a lot of things and secrets with each other.

One day we both were playing a game in which we had to tell about one of our secrets. We promised each other not to reveal those secrets to other friends. While playing the game I was asked to tell one of my secrets. I told him about one of my pet names kept by my friends in my colony. The name was very funny, but I knew that Rajiv won't tell it to anyone in school as we had promised each other.

But what came to my surprise that everyone in the school was teasing me with that pet name the next morning at the school. I was very upset and angry with him. He kept on telling me that he hasn't done it, but I knew that this secret could only be leaked by Rajiv as no other student knew about it.

I changed my sitting plan with another student and stopped talking to Rajiv for what he did with me. I could see from his face that he was apologetic and feeling guilty. Afterall we were good friends before that incident.

One day he came to me quietly and said sorry for what he did. He admitted that he was the one who told my pet name to one of his friends, who spread it like a wildfire. I accepted his apology and told him to not repeat such behavior with anyone. I told him that if you keep a promise then fulfil it no matter what the situation is.

After that we became friends again but from that day onwards, I never shared any secrets of mine with him.

Talk about a time when you unexpectedly met someone

Who do you meet?

Why was it unexpected

What did you do?

There have been a lot of instances in my life when I met people unexpectedly. Once I was totally surprised after meeting one of my childhood friends after 10 years.

I was astonished because I was meeting my classmate after so many years and I could hardly recognise him from his appearance. This happened when I was travelling in a train to New Delhi. I boarded an express train which takes three hours to Delhi from Chandigarh.

I was sitting on the window side and on the next stop, one person came and quietly sat on my adjacent seat. He introduced himself as Harman. After every two minutes he was looking at me and I was doing the same. The reason I was looking at him again and again was that I thought that he and his name resembles my childhood friend from school.

After a while I asked him about his primary schooling. I was astonished to hear that he was the same person whom I was thinking about. I told him my name and after a few seconds he recognised me as well. We shook our hands tightly and laughed for a while.

I never expected to meet him in a train in India. The reason is that he studied with me till the class 4. After that he moved to United States of America with his family. I was stunned to meet him after so many years in a train journey.

I asked him about his life and shared a lot of things with him. He told me that he had come to India after 5 years and was now going back to USA. He had to catch a flight from New Delhi Airport. I really enjoyed my time with him in the train.

We chatted on length about our childhood and school. We talked a lot about our colleagues and teachers. Soon the journey was about to get over. So, he asked me to give him my contact details. We exchanged our numbers and addresses. I also connected with him on social networking sites.

In the end we said goodbye to each other at the New Delhi railway station. It was a great meeting with an old friend. Even now I am in touch with him on the internet.

Talk about a performance you gave at school or college
Did you often participate at school?
What was the performance about?
Did it go well

I was not someone who gave a lot of performances in my school time. However, I remember one that I am going to share with you today. Once I participated in a skit that was performed on the annual day function of our school.

Me and four of my other friends from my class were the part of that act. The performance included different characters of animals and sea creatures that would demonstrate the effect of plastic waste on animals. Many people are not aware about the fact that thousands of animal species die due to pollution from plastic in the ocean and on land. So, our teachers decided to do this skit with five of us. First, they took a screening test and then finalized five students from our class.

The function was held in our school's auditorium. It was a big hall with a seating capacity of over 500 people. I was feeling nervous at the start but slowly gained confidence as the skit went on. Everyone had to perform for about a minute and lecture about the cause.

We all had to dress up like different animals and mammals. One of our friends became a Penguin and told the audience about the deadly effects of plastic straws on Penguins. He told that the Penguins eat straws mistaking it for food and choke themselves to death in the ocean.

I was dressed as cow and told the spectators that throwing away plastic or polyethene bags are deadly for the cows. There are thousands of stray cows in India. They gobble plastic with their feed that can stuck in their internal organs or the throat. This cause severe problems and many cows die because of that.

One by one we came at the centre of the stage and gave our one-minute speech. The audience were looking very interested in the information and applauded loudly after our performance was over. The act went very well. We all were very happy. We also got recognition from the principal for bringing up such an awareness.

Describe an important journey that was delayed
Why that journey was important
Where were you going
Why the delay happened
In the given topic I am reminded of a situation that occurred in my life and I learned a great deal of things from that incident. I am talking about a journey that I had to make early in the morning and reach Jaipur for an important scholarship exam.

This exam was held by the Rajasthan government and students who would score good in the exams would be handed over scholarships to study in top Rajasthan universities for free of cost. I came to know about the exam through the internet.

I filled the form and took my father's consent to go there. I started preparing for the exam as it was still a month away. I was getting ready for my exam and packing for the trip a couple of days in advance. Jaipur is located 500 kilometres away from Chandigarh.

I booked a flight ticket that takes one and a half hours to reach Jaipur. I was very excited for the journey, but one silly error proved a learning curve for me. My exam was on Sunday at 10 AM and I booked the flight for Saturday. I was scheduled to reach on Saturday. For that I had also booked a hotel.

The time of my flight was 7 in the morning, but I had mistaken it for 7 in the evening. When we reached the airport, I came to know that the flight had already left in the morning. I was dejected as I had prepared for the exam so hard and I was ready to give it. I started weeping but my father quickly sorted the issue.

He booked a taxi on the phone and decided to go with me to Jaipur. It took us 10 hours to reach Jaipur and another hour to find the exam centre. I reached at the venue just in time and gave the exam. My exam didn't go well as I was so tired after the journey. But my father supported me and told me to learn a lesson from this mistake.

From that day I learned to check the departure and arrival times of the railway journeys and flights. I couldn't clear the exam but learnt a great lesson that day.

Describe your dream workplace

Why is it your ideal workplace?

Do you wish to work there one day?

Are most people able to work in their dream workplace?

My ideal working place would be working as a Travel Video logger, popularly known as Vlogger. The reason behind this is I love to travel, and I like to see new places. I get very happy when I see new people and interact with them. My ideal working place would be all over the world.

I wish to work as a travel vlogger every day of my life. I know it is not an easy job. One needs to be highly motivated if he/she wishes to work in such an industry. A Travel vlogger needs to be travel fit and should be open to any kind of challenge while travelling.

There are many famous Travel Vloggers in the world like Drew Binsky and Renata Perrera. I am a huge fan of these vloggers and I never miss a chance to see their videos. They make superb quality travel videos and engage their viewers in a very interesting manner.

I wish to work as a Travel Vlogger for my YouTube channel. I would like to travel the world and visit the most exotic and charming places. I will tell people about country, culture and region I visit. In my travel vlogs I will give information on how to travel to new places and what are the things to keep in mind while travelling there. What are the places to eat and where to do shopping?

In my travelling vlog, I will plan to visit every country in the world. It will take a lot of money and efforts, but I am making plans for that. After doing a job or business for a period of 5 years, I will work as a full-time Travel Vlogger. I will also look for sponsors for my channel.

In my opinion most people are not able to work in their dream places. I think the main reason behind that is money. People these days run after money rather than passion. I am lucky enough to have parents who support me in any decision I make.

Describe a company which employs many people in your hometown
What that company is about
Have you ever visited that company?
Tell about that company in detail

There are two or three huge companies that employ a lot of people in my hometown. There are companies like Mahindra & Mahindra and Infosys. But I would like to speak about Reliance Industries. Reliance is one of the companies that employ thousands of people across our country.

There are many subsidiaries of Reliance Industries. The company is one of the largest brands in India. The name of the owner of Reliance Industries is Mr. Mukesh Ambani. They provide hundreds of services to the people in our country.

One of the newly launched service by Reliance industries is JIO. This provides fast speed internet and satellite channels at a low cost. They have employed thousands of people in this field over the past few years. I have met a lot of people who are working with Reliance Industries in my hometown.

Apart from this, Reliance has thousands of clothing and groceries stores all over the country and my hometown. You can find their store in literally every city of India. Not only this, Reliance employs thousands of people in petroleum and yarn industries as well.

There are Reliance digital stores in my hometown that deal in electronic gadgets. There is a huge Reliance Mart near my house that sells groceries on a wholesale rate. There are many stores and offices of Reliance industries in my hometown.

I have been to most of their stores in my hometown. There is one store that opened recently by the name of Trends. It sells latest clothes and garments. I went there last week and bought a pair of jeans. Moreover, Reliance has myriad retail stores of groceries around my town.

I admire this company a lot as they have certainly employed millions of people across India and thousands in my hometown alone.

Describe a bicycle tour you took
Do you often ride bicycle?
What was the tour about?
Who were the other participants?

I don't ride a bicycle often, but I have one bicycle at my home. I go on a ride a couple of times in a month. I like riding the bike when I am free but I hardy get a chance due to my busy schedule. Recently I saw one guy who rides bicycle every day in my colony.

I connected with him and he told me about his group. He has formed a group of around 20 people who get up early in the morning every day and go for cycling. They go on different routes and do cycling for around an hour. The name of his group is cycler's corner.

I was impressed with his idea and asked if I could join the group and go on a cycle tour with them. He instantly agreed and added me to his what's app group. He introduced me to his other friends and told me about the timings and place of gathering a day before the tour. I had previously told him that I won't be a regular member but would love to go on the bicycle tours when I get time.

Next morning, I was ready to go on the tour at 5 AM. We all gathered at a nearby landmark and began our journey. Our leader led us to a garden nearby where we breath in fresh air. After that we went to the Sukhna Lake which is in the east side of my hometown.

After cycling for about half an hour, we all took water break and continued our journey. We took the best roads in the town that are integrated with a cycling track. After a few minutes we reached near our assembly point and parked our bikes there.

One of the group members then took out his phone and start clicking selfies and photos of all the riders. We talked to each other for about 5 minutes and everyone started going back to their destinations.

I thanked the leader and told him to keep me informed for the weekend tours. I thoroughly enjoyed that day and will never forget it for a long time.

Describe a popular teacher you know
Who's that teacher
Why that teacher is popular
Have you met him/her?

I know quite a few teachers from my senior secondary, but I clearly remember one of the most popular teachers in my hometown. Her name is Ms. Shanti.

The reason I know her is that she is probably the most renowned teacher in my hometown. She has taught thousands of students in the field of Mathematics. She runs a coaching centre in a prominent area in Chandigarh. She teaches about 4 or 5 batches in a day.

Her teaching methods are well known to many all over the town. Previously she was a schoolteacher in one of the biggest schools in Chandigarh. Some years ago, she left her job and started teaching at her house. Soon she became so popular that she had to setup a huge academy to cater a greater number of students.

There are many reasons that why Ms Shanti is popular. The first one is that she is very polite. You don't see many mathematicians who are so polite in their interaction. Moreover, she is very hardworking as she teaches hundreds of students every day. Also, she has won many prizes in the field of mathematics over the past few years.

She is also famous because she has made so many students believe in themselves. She has helped thousands of students clear the complex exams of mathematics. When I was in my 10th class, I was struggling with my maths.

I came to know about Ms Shanti from one of my uncles. I joined her coaching class and met her for the first time. I was feeling more interested and confident in the subject as her teaching methods were fantastic. I scored more than my expectations.

Not only me but she's been helping weak students get stronger every day. She is like a motivation for me and for many others.

Describe a night when you could not sleep at all
Why you couldn't sleep that night
Do you often feel insomnia?
Did you wake up well the next morning?

There have been few nights in my life when I was not at all able to sleep. The one that I remember the most is when I visited a foreign country for the first time.

This happened a couple of years ago. My father gave us a surprise holiday package. Me, my father, my mother and my younger brother were set to visit Dubai for the first time. This was the first foreign trip for all of us.

I remember that I started preparing for that trip a month before we had to board the flight. I was feeling very excited for the trip. A couple of days before the trip I finished my packing and was eagerly waiting for the trip to get started.

I remember that one night before the trip I couldn't stop thinking about Dubai. I couldn't sleep even for a minute. I was so curious for the tour that I had already taken out my clothes and shoes that were to be worn the next day.

I tried hard but I was feeling highly insomniac. However, I was also aware that if I couldn't sleep well tonight then I will find it difficult on the next day. So, I decided to try a method to get myself some sleep.

I tried reading some old books and listening to some old songs but that too didn't help. I also called my father to help me in sleeping. He told me to do light exercise in order to get some sleep. I did some exercise for 15 minutes but that didn't work either.

I was so frustrated with this that I decided to stay awake. Decision of staying awake was not a good one because the next day when all were fresh and ready to go, I was feeling sleepy and tired. But I had to manage as I couldn't have afforded to miss the trip.

Describe a person who likes to travel by plane

Why that person travels in plane
Does he/she travel frequently in plane
Do you like to travel by planes as well?

I know a few people who like to travel by plane. Today I would like to speak about my cousin who loves to travel by plane. His name is Ashish and he lives in New Delhi. He is working in a Multi-national organisation there.

His favourite hobby is to book a plane ticket and travel the world. He often takes breaks to go around the world. He has visited more than 30 countries over the past few years. He is a frequent traveller by plane. He journeys more than five times through plane in one year.

He says that he feels rejuvenated when he travels through plane. He has collected all the plane tickets of his past journeys as a memoire. He is so obsessed with travelling by plane that he books plane tickets to even places where it is easy to reach by train or bus.

Recently he flew to Jaipur from Delhi for leisure. He wanted to just experience a short flight. The distance from Delhi to Jaipur is only 250 kilometres that can be covered in merely four hours by car or bus. But he chose to travel by plane just to experience a short journey.

Recently he completed his 100th journey by plane. He tells about that to everyone with a sense of pride and achievement. I have never seen a person like him in my life who loves to travel by plane so much.

53

His love for planes is amazing. He has even bought a huge replica of Boeing 787 and kept it in his lobby of the house. I am not as crazy as him when it comes to travelling by plane. I don't relish the plane travel much as I feel it's quite tiring and congested.

Describe an advice you received on your subjects or work OR Describe some good advice about choosing a job or subject

What advice did you receive?

Was the advice helpful

Do you often take advice on your subjects or work?

I have had wonderful people in my life who have supported me in all aspects and have given me words of wisdom in every situation. I have received many useful and some great advices from people around me.

One advice that I remember I took from my elder sister proved to be vital in my life and career. I remember when I was studying in 10th class I never thought of choosing my subjects in senior secondary. But my sister always encouraged me to choose the subjects while studying in 10th class so that I could plan my future well in advance.

When I stepped into 10th class I was confused about choosing subjects for my further studies. I understood my sister's thoughts about choosing the subjects in advance. This allows a student to manage his/her future properly and in a better way.

I was confused between choosing medical or non-medical. I thought that I was good at medical subjects but that was not the case. To be successful in medical field one needs to be good at memorizing thousands of terms and medical substances. I thought that medical field was restricted to only biology. Moreover, I wasn't the kind of person who could sit for very long hours and study same subject repeatedly.

So, my sister came to my rescue. She explained me about the current scenario of subjects and bright future in the field of non-medical. This subject is not restricted to only one type of job like the medical field is and gives you more choices after the senior secondary level in India.

After discussions with my sister I chose the non-medical field and felt quite confident about it. After that I never looked back and worked hard on that subject. So, her advice in choosing my subjects proved fruitful.

54

An activity that you found boring

Which activity is that?

Why did you find that activity boring?

Do you often get bored from doing similar activities every day?

There are not many activities that I don't relish. I don't easily get bored from any activity. However, there is one thing that I found very boring. The activity was compulsory drawing class. I never found drawing to be interesting and attractive.

Whenever there was drawing class in the school, I felt very boring. I was never interested in this subject. There were many things about drawing that I didn't like. The first one is that I am not that patient, and I can't fill colours in designated areas. It takes a lot of toll on me. I feel that drawing required a lot of patience and precision.

I am not the kind of person who possesses a lot of concentration and patience. I was always angry when I had to draw a certain sketch or fill colours in an image. I was never a big fan of drawing from my childhood itself.

I always felt that it was just a waste of time and energy. I never felt happy in my drawing class. I always found ways to avoid the class but couldn't do it as it was a compulsory subject. I remember once I was sitting in the drawing class and was feeling very sleepy. My teacher came up to me and asked me if I had any problem. I couldn't say anything but told her that I was not well.

There were not many activities that I found boring in my school life. But drawing is such an activity that I found the most boring.

Describe an experience when you were with people and got bored

Where were you and why did you get bored

Did other people get bored as well

Did you do anything to get out of that boredom

I remember one instance in life when I was surrounded by a lot of people and got really bored. This happened a couple of years back when I was going to Mumbai to my Aunt's house for a holiday.

I had to board my flight from New Delhi and reached the airport 2 hours before the departure. I checked-in my baggage and went to the boarding gate to wait for the flight's departure. I was waiting there and was well on time. I saw a lot of people coming there one by one.

There were still 30 minutes to departure but there was no sign of flight gate opening. I asked a person at the inquiry counter about the flight departure, but he didn't give me any information regarding it. He told me to wait for another 10 minutes.

After some time, an announcement was made that the flight was delayed by 3 to 4 hours due to a technical slag. I was very disappointed for the delay as I was so excited for my trip. I went to the inquiry desk again and asked about the issue. They assured that the flight won't be cancelled but the delay will surely happen.

That wait proved to be very boring for me. There was no entertainment source at the boarding gate. There was no TV and the WIFI at the airport was also not working. I felt so jaded at that time.

I didn't have a book or a movie in my mobile to kill some time. I was looking at the faces of people around me and I could sense that everyone was feeling frustrated and bored.

There were about 300 people who were waiting for the flight to depart. I couldn't connect with anyone as they were all strangers for me. I was feeling so alone and fed up at the time that I have never been in my life. I tried many things to get out of boredom, but I couldn't do it. I can easily say that it was one of the most boring moments in my life.

Describe a time when you first met someone OR A famous personality you have met.
Who was the person?
What did you do in that meeting?
How do you react when you meet a person for the first time?
I have met many people for the first time in my life, but I can hardly remember about most of the people. However, there are some people who leave a strong impression on you. I would like to tell you about a person whom I met, and he had a great influence on me.

I am talking about Mr Sachin Tendulkar. He is a great personality in our country and around the world. He was the best Cricket player of his time. He had broken numerous records while playing the game for India.

I was very fortunate to meet him accidently in Mussoorie. Mussoorie is a quiet hill station situated in the northern part of our country in Uttaranchal Pradesh. I went there with my family and was staying there for a week.

On the second day of our trip we were roaming in the market early in the morning. There was no rush as it was an early morning of a winter day and there was a lot of snow everywhere. Suddenly I saw someone coming from the other side of the road. That man was wearing a blue woollen cap and as he came closer, I recognised him and loudly took his name.

At first, he ignored it, but I chased him and told him that I had recognised him. He was kind to me and stopped and acknowledged my greetings. I told him that I was one of his biggest fans and always dreamt of meeting him one day.

I shook his hand tightly and hugged him lightly. I asked for a selfie and he smiled to my request. I requested him to stay with me for a minute as my parents were also coming from behind. The next moment my parents were there, and they were very shocked to see Sachin Tendulkar.

They couldn't control their emotions and we again clicked a few pictures with him. After that we bade goodbye and I can never forget his smile and his humbleness while meeting his fans.

That day he inspired me a lot. Regardless of all the success and despite of having everything in life, he was so humble and down to earth.

Describe a time you were sleepy but had to stay awake
Why were you feeling sleepy?
Why you had to stay awake
How did you manage to stay awake?

There have been times in my life when I had to stay awake till early in the morning or till late night. But on those occasions, I remained awake intentionally. Either I was with my friends enjoying or I was in a party and came late. But I remember one situation when I felt the need to sleep but had to wake up the whole night.

This happened last year in summer days. There was a power cut in our area in the morning. The electricity didn't show up till afternoon and we waited till evening, but the electricity was not yet available. The invertor batteries went down, and we all were feeling very irritated as the temperatures can go up to 45 degrees in my hometown.

At night there was no electricity. Forget air conditioners, fans and lights were also not working due to the drainage of batteries. I was feeling so helpless and frustrated. I called on the electricity department phone and they told that there was a major fault in the electricity grid of our colony, and it would take another 10 or 12 hours to get the things repaired.

As the night fell, I was feeling so sleepy because my daytime was very hectic. I tried sleeping but couldn't sleep as I was choking with heat and drenched in sweat. So, I decided to sit outdoors and sleep on the chair. But after some time that didn't work as well.

I was feeling so sleepy, but I couldn't sleep as the heat was too much for me. I started getting scratches on my neck and back due to excessive sweating. Finally, I decided to go for a drive in my car with my brother.

We went on a long drive with its Air conditioner on full. We drove for three hours and came back early in the morning. To our surprise the electricity was still not there. Eventually I decided to get some rest, but I was still not able to sleep.

Luckily at 6 in the morning, the electricity was supplied, and everyone clapped with joy. But it was already time to get ready and go to work. So that was the day when I felt sleepy but couldn't sleep.

Talk about a handmade product made only in your country
What is that product
Why that product is only made in your country
Have you ever used that product?

There are some renowned products like Pashmina Shawls that are handmade in Kashmir. Or Ayurvedic medicines that are made by hands in some parts of India. But today I would like to speak about Jute Bags. These are traditional handmade bags that are also known as Gunny sacks or tow sacks in some areas of our country. These bags are made from

Indian jute and are very inexpensive and durable to use. These bags are also exported to many parts of the world as well.

These bags are biodegradable and good for the environment as they are not made from polypropylene. Instead they are made from the natural fibres of jute. These types of bags were invented in ancient India and are only made with Indian jute.

There are still traditional workers that weave the jute fibres and make ropes and sacks out of it. The sack made from jute is very strong and can bear a great amount of pressure and weight. These bags or sacks are tan or light brown in colour due to the colour of the jute.

These bags come in different shapes and sizes. The most common is the one that has two carry handles and can support weight of up to 10 kilos. People mostly use these kinds of bag to put daily items or groceries.

The other famous shape is the rectangle one that can support more than 50 kilos in it. This type of bag or sack is generally used to store rice and wheat in it. These sacks can be seen in the supermarkets where bulk material is packed.

These bags are very useful, and the biggest advantage is that these bags can be recycled. Even if the bag is not recycled, it is not dangerous for the environment. Moreover, it is very cheap to produce and buy.

Traditional weavers make the bags in villages and small industries in some towns. Traders buy directly from them in bulk and sell these bags in the market.

Talk about a person in news whom you would like to meet
Who's that person
Why do you want to meet him/her?
What will you do when you will meet that person?

There are many famous personalities these days in news who are worth meeting. However, if I intend to choose one person then it would be prime minister Narendra Modi.

He is the current prime minister of our country and is one of the boldest and dynamic leaders of our times. He is always in news as he is the prime servant of our country. He is known for his extra ordinary speeches and work since he took the office in 2014 as the Prime Minister.

I have read about him and his early day struggles. If I am given a chance to meet one person in news, then it would be Narendra Modi. He has inspired millions of people in our country and around the world as well. I want to personally meet him and learn a great deal of things from him.

I will ask him a lot of questions when I will meet him. I will learn myriad things from him. He's an experienced leader and can teach me a lot of things that are required to lead a great life. He is a fantastic leader and after meeting him I can seek some advice on leadership.

Mr Narendra Modi rose from a very humble beginning and reached the pinnacle of politics. He used to sell tea at a tea stall with his father and later with his brother at railway station. Despite being short of resources he fought his way up in politics.

I want to learn everything from him about life and how to acquire certain traits that he has. He is the person who is almost every day in news due to important decisions that he makes for our country.

So, if I am given a chance to meet someone who's in the news then it would be our prime minister Mr. Narendra Modi.

Talk about a meeting you attended at your school or workplace
What was that meeting about?
What was your contribution in the meeting?
Do you like attending meetings

I have not attended many meetings during my school time. But there was one instance when I was involved in a meeting. At that time, I was the monitor of my class and all the monitors across different sections were invited in that meeting.

The meeting was about preparing for the sports event. All the monitors from 10th class were selected as the event managers. We were five monitors in total and were given certain responsibilities. We were supported by our respective class teachers and we were also allocated some capital for the same.

The meeting was called upon by the principal of our school. Our principal Ms. Shalini is an inspiration for many. She is very dynamic and full of life.

She placed trust in us and gave us all the responsibility to manage and organise the annual sports day.

I was given the responsibility of arranging the trophies and medals for the participants and the winners. In total there were twenty events. The total number of participants were 300. In meeting, the principal gave us different responsibilities and asked us about any suggestions that we can give.

I was told about the participants and the events. I had to buy medals and trophies for all. I gave suggestion to the principal about the trophies. I told her to buy only medals instead of trophies as the medals would cost less. She was impressed with my idea and gave me a go ahead.

Yes, I like attending meetings because it gives a person many ideas for a certain thing or event. People in meetings share ideas with one another and I feel that participating in meetings enhances the maturity level of a person.

A time when you had to hide truth from your friend
Why you had to hide the truth
What was the truth
Did your friend find out the truth

I never hide truth from others. But there can be situations when hiding truth is the best thing. There are some situations when you tell lie but it's for the good of everyone.

I remember one situation when I had to hide truth from my best friend. This happened a few weeks back. I was at my friend's house and he was on his way from his tuition. My friend's name is Amit. I was waiting for him in his room. Suddenly I heard a loud sound from the adjacent room.

I rushed towards that room and saw my friend's father who had slipped and was lying on the floor. My friends' brother and mother rushed towards the scene and we all picked up his father. He was in a lot of pain. He said that his lower back is extremely sore and was not able to walk properly. They decided to take him to the hospital. My friend's mother told me that I shouldn't tell my friend about this incident as he was having an exam the next day. So, I stayed at Amit's home and waited for him to come. When he arrived, he asked me about his parents and brother as he couldn't find anybody in the house except me. I tried my best to hide the truth and told him a made-up story. I told him that his parents and brother had gone to his relatives to meet them.

I felt guilty for not telling him the truth. I was feeling very bothered about his father as well. But I felt that it was better to hide the truth than to tell him everything in that situation as he was having his exam next day. This incident could have affected his performance.

Talk about a time when you used a foreign language to communicate
Why you had to use a foreign language to communicate
Did you communicate well
Do you often use foreign language to communicate?
I generally speak decent English but when one communicates with a native speaker then it can be a bit of a challenge. I want to tell you about an instance when I had to communicate with a foreigner in English for some time.

Yes, I often use English in school and in daily life while studying. Although I have studied all my life in English medium schools but when it comes to communicating with a foreigner in a foreign language, it can get a bit difficult as their accent can be a lot different from us.

A few months ago, I was roaming in the most famous commercial area of my hometown with my friend. There, I saw some foreigners confused and finding a certain location. They hesitantly approached me and asked me about one of the café's in that area.

They were looking for the Indian coffee house. It is one of the oldest and famous cafes' in our city. They asked me about the directions for the café. They also inquired about the local transportation in the city. I was happy and eager to help them.

I gave them much needed information regarding the local transport system and how to bargain for the fares. I was roaming there in my free time, so I told them to follow me to the café. After ten minutes we reached there. They were very happy with my help.

They were four of them and invited me and my friend to join them. We agreed and I ordered some of the local delicacies. They enjoyed the food and I did all the conversation with them in English. They had come from

England for a holiday. We had a great time together and conversed with them well. I can never forget that day.

This was the first situation in my life when I had to talk with someone entirely in a foreign language.

Describe a wrong decision you once made

What was the decision?

Why that decision went wrong

Did you correct it after that?

There have been many decisions in my life that didn't go well. However, some choices have proved fruitful as well. One decision that I regret the most is deciding the dates for my holidays.

I was in my 11th class and me and my family decided to go on a vacation in winter breaks. We planned to go to Dubai and thought of celebrating Christmas and New Year there. At first, I thought it was a great decision by me, but we were not aware about the consequences of it.

Our flight was scheduled on 23rd of December in the evening. After reaching the hotel in Dubai, it took us so long to check in to the hotel room. The reason was that it is the peak season and millions of travelers had flocked to Dubai for Christmas and New Year.

Next day we were greeted in the morning by the tour company and the guide took us to the main malls and attractions on that day. Wherever we went, it took us long time to buy tickets and we had to wait in long queues to see the attractions.

We faced huge rush in every mall. People were all over the place. I felt that my decision to visit Dubai in the month of December was not good. For the simple reason that I don't like huge crowd. I like quiet places and places that have less people.

Due to the over tourism in that period everything was expensive. It was even hard to find a taxi. Even if we found one, it was expensive than normal days. All the prices of souvenirs went up due to the high season.

I will always remember from the next time to not plan a holiday in December. Although we enjoyed our trip, but it could have been better if we would have planned it in some other time of the year rather than December. So, I feel that this was the decision that went wrong for me.

Describe a method that helps you to save money

What is that method?

Does that method work every time?

How much savings do you do every month and how do you spend it?

I am the kind of a person who likes to save money. I use different methods in my life that can be helpful for me to collect money. I don't eat outside food and I also don't buy expensive clothes. I save that money and keep it for my future.

The method that I use to save money is cycling. This activity saves me a lot of money. I commute by cycle to my school and work. Cycling saves me from burning a hole in my pocket as there is not a great transportation system in my hometown.

People rely mostly on their private vehicles to travel from one place to the other. So, the private scooters and autos for mass transportation are expensive in my hometown. To save money, I use cycle and I prefer to walk to short distances.

Cycling not only saves me a lot of money but it is also time saving. I can beat the traffic at peak hours. This way of transport is also environment friendly. Moreover, it keeps me healthy. I prefer using cycle for going anywhere in my hometown.

It is safe to ride a bicycle in my hometown as there are dedicated cycle tracks all over the city. I maintain my cycle myself. I have a small kit that includes all kinds of stuff needed to maintain the bicycle.

Till date I have saved a lot of money by riding this bicycle and I hope to do the same in future as well. So, this is the best method that helps me save money.

Describe something that helps you in concentration (yoga/meditation)

What is that thing

How does it help you to make concentration?

What breaks your concentration

I know a few methods that helps me to improve my concentration. One sure shot method is doing Yoga or meditation early in the morning. This is the best activity that helps me building concentration from a lot of years.

Not only this, yoga and meditation also help me in maintaining good health and temperament. I usually do yoga in the early hours of the day. I have learnt certain postures of Yoga from my mother as well from television. I see videos of Yoga from specialists and have tried to learn the positions and exercises to improve concentration. Distorted concentration is the most common problem that people face today especially the youngsters. Even I was facing this issue in the past. But since I started the Yoga, I started improving my concentration. I do Yoga and meditation early in the morning. I usually get up at 5, then I do certain postures and take deep breath. There is one exercise that I do the most. In that exercise I sit on the floor with my legs folded. Then I keep my index finger on my forehead and rest of the fingers over my closed eyes. I use my thumb to close the ears. Then I inhale and exhale for at least four to five minutes continuously without interruption. This exercise really helps me in improving my concentration and it also reduces my stress levels.

There are certain things that breaks my concentration. While studying I need pin drop silence. Previously I was disturbed by even the slightest of disturbance, but now I have changed. Due to Yoga and meditation I can bear disturbances without breaking my concentration.

I recommend everyone to do Yoga and meditation to get rid of concentration problems.

What makes you angry
Do you often get angry?
What are the things that makes you angry?
How do you get rid of your anger?
No, I don't often get angry. But there are few things that disturbs me and can also make me angry. I don't like people telling lie and I get angry of someone who is behaving in an amateur way other than kids.

One thing that makes me angry is the wastage of valuable resources. I can't simply tolerate the wastage of natural resources. When I see someone misusing water, electricity and wood, I get very angry.

I can never see the wastage of water. I see many people washing their cars with flowing water. That makes me very angry. I have had many altercations with people who do such activities. There was one guy in our colony who used to wash his car daily and wasted hundreds of liters of water on one wash.

I explained him the importance of water, but he refused to listen. I always keep all the fans and lights switch off when not required. I get angry when any of my family member keeps the lights on when not in room.

This kind of attitude irritates me to a great extent. Sometimes I explain myself that it is not a thing to be angry. But I can't resist myself from getting angry if anyone is wasting natural resources.

I feel that these resources are very expensive to produce and if these resources are exhausted, we will not be able to get them again. Resources such as water and fuel are limited hence, we should be responsible in using them and them for the future generations.

Talk about a high paying job in your country

What are the high paying jobs in your country?

Why do you think that this job is highly paid?

What are the advantages and disadvantages of this job?

There are many jobs in my country that are well paid. Top engineers, scientists and sports people earn a great deal of money from their profession. In my opinion, doctors and surgeons get the most handsome salary in my country.

There are other fields such as IT that are also very well paid. However, most of the doctors and surgeons earn way better than most of the other professions in my country. Doctors can open clinics anywhere in our country with easy permissions from the government.

They can also earn good salary by working in hospitals. Although becoming a doctor is not an easy thing but they can earn good amount of money. Doctors earn a great respect in our society. They are given the designation of God in our country. I think this is the reason they are paid well.

A famous doctor or a surgeon earns much more money than a scientist or a businessman. No doubt that the job of a doctor is not that easy. It is one of the most stressful and hardworking jobs. This job should always be highly paid, and I think that doctors should be compensated for these efforts and struggles they make during their life.

There are many advantages of being a doctor. Doctors know the anatomy of the body well and can give advice to sick people and benefit them. It is a very satisfying job. It has another big advantage that people give a lot of respect to the doctors.

On the other hand, being a doctor is very tiring and responsible. Doctors always have a huge responsibility on them. They medicate their patients and take care of their surgeries. They have very little time for their families. They have high risk of getting infected as they are always exposed to sick people. Being a doctor is a very thankless job as well.

In the end, I would like to sum up by saying that being a doctor in my country is highly respected and a good earning profession.

Talk about a person with whom you like to spend your leisure time
Who's that person
Why do you like to spend time with him/her?
Do you often spend time with him/her?

There are many people in my life with whom I can spend my leisure time. I can spend my leisure time with any of my family members or my good friends. The one person whom I am very fond of is my elder sister.

I like to spend time with her, and I usually spend a lot of my leisure time with her at home and while touring. She is three years elder than me and we have a lot of things in common. I call her DIDI, usually a name used in India to call an elder sister with respect.

She is studying Law and is a very knowledgeable person. Whenever I spend time with her, I get to learn a great deal of things. She has similar hobbies as I have. She likes to read books, watch sports and play several computer games.

She is my senior, so I have learnt a great deal of things from her. Whenever I faced issues in any subject, I simply looked up to her. She has taught me many things related to study and life. If I am given a chance to spend my leisure time with anyone then it would be my sister.

We are generally busy in our day to day routine, but we never miss a chance to spend time together. We read together in the evening and watch TV as well. We spend more time on weekends and play a lot of games together. So, my sister is the person with whom I like to spend time.

Common dress that female in your country wear

What is the common dress for people of your country?

Is that dress comfortable

Do you feel that a person is judged on attire he/she wears?

It is very difficult to say that exactly what is the common dress code in our country. Ours is a big country and all the different states have variations in dress code for both male and female. If I talk about the general attire of female of my country, then I would say that nowadays young women like to wear jeans with top.

Some also wear formal and long dresses, but jeans and top are one of the most frequent attire of women of today's society. Previously women were more inclined to wear Salwar Suits and Sarees.

If you see in today's scenario then women mostly prefer Jeans and top. There are many reasons behind choosing this type of dress. The first one is that you don't need to iron this type of clothing. Moreover, you can wear it on most of the occasions.

Apart from this, one doesn't need to wash jeans after every wear as it doesn't get dirty easily. Jeans is durable and can be worn easily. There are many designs and styles of jeans available these days. Jeans look good on any body type.

As far as the tops are concerned, they are light, easy to wear and comfortable. In our country where most of the months in the year are hot, it is a good type of dress to wear. Tops come in different colours and styles. Tops and jeans are not that expensive as well. Most women are more relaxed in wearing this type of dress.

I feel that in today's era a person is judged from his/her dress. I don't think it is the right attitude though, but it is a bitter truth.

A female leader you would like to meet

Do you follow politics

Why would you like to meet that leader?

What will you do when you meet her?

There are quite a few female leaders that I would like to meet in my life. I like Michell Obama and Angela Markel from outside India. But if I am given a chance to meet a female leader in my life then I would love to meet Mamata Banerjee. She is the 8th Chief minister of West Bengal.

She is one of the most powerful female leaders in our country. She is currently serving as the Chief Minister of the state of West Bengal from the year 2011. She has been the most successful leader in West Bengal till now. She was the first women chief minister of West Bengal. She is popularly known as DIDI, an elder sister.

Previously she also served as the Minister of railways for two terms. She was the first women railway minister. She held several ministries and positions previously in the central government. She started her political career with congress and soon rose the ranks and became the head of youth and women congress in west Bengal.

After some controversies with the congress party she left the group and formed her own party in Bengal by the name of All India Trinamool Congress in 1997. After that she defeated her rival in 2011 and became the Chief minister of West Bengal for the first time. She continued her success and won the second term elections in 2016 and is still the chief minister in 2020.

She adorns a simple and light coloured Saree and lives a modest lifestyle. She has achieved many landmarks in life. She has reached the pinnacle of politics despite being a woman in a country like India. She is also considered as one of the most powerful women in Indian politics.

If I meet her then I would first greet her and will ask about the secret of her success. I will ask about the things from which I can learn. I admire her as a leader and will like to meet her if given a chance.

A piece of clothing you received as a gift

Do you often receive gifts?

What type of attire was gifted to you?

Did you like the gift?

Yes, I often receive gifts from my loved ones. I generally receive gifts on my birthday but a piece of clothing I got as a gift was not on my birthday. I got a dress gifted by my aunt who returned from Canada.

She lives in Canada from the past many years. She is my beloved aunt and I have a cordial relation with her. She is my mother's sister. Whenever she comes to meet us, she brings a lot of gifts from Canada.

Last time she came to India in December. She brought a beautiful jacket for me. As soon as she handed me over the gift, I quickly opened it and thanked her for that. It was a blue coloured leather jacket of xxxx brand. She has a great choice in selecting clothes for everyone. I instantly liked the jacket and tried it. It fit me properly and I was looking good in that. I stood in front of the mirror and checked my looks. I was looking more sophisticated in that.

The brand of the jacket is famous worldwide and is also expensive. There were many pockets in and out on the jacket. All the pockets were lined by a steel zip. The colour of the jacket was bright and the leather had a crumbly texture.

The texture gave it a great look. It was a full sleeves jacket with an option of removing the sleeves and converting it into a sleeveless jacket. I had never seen that before in any jacket. There was a zip on the shoulder that could be opened in order to remove the sleeves. The zip on the shoulder was nicely tucked by an overlapping seal. There was a removable hood at the back of the collar as well.

I was so impressed with that jacket that I used to wear it every second day of the winters. I flaunted that jacket to all my friends in the neighbourhood. They also liked it very much.

Your visit to a lake

I live in Mohali; it is a city adjoining Chandigarh. Chandigarh is one of the cleanest and planned cities in India. There are two lakes in Chandigarh, the first one is the New lake which was built recently and the other one is the Sukhna Lake.

The lake is located near the posh area of the city. The roads nearby are wide and clean. There is no entry fee to the lake, and anyone can visit it from 5AM to 11PM. Sukhna lake is one of the biggest man-made lakes in our country. There are two entry sides to the lake. The main entrance is the most popular amongst people and the other entry is known as the back side or the Buddha Garden entry.

In the backdrop of the lake we can see the beautiful Shivalik hills. There is a wide road along the length of the lake where people generally stroll but entry of any type of vehicle is prohibited there. There are several games and amusement corners where kids can enjoy. Near the entry of the lake, a big section includes the food court and one souvenir shop.

People from all walks of life and age groups visit the lake. Mostly, early morning is the busiest time of the day and a lot of people come in the evening as well. In winters, many people come in the afternoon to enjoy the sun light and to witness a variety of migratory birds that flock there at this time of the year.

The span of the track is around two kilometers and there is a running track which is built parallel to the main track. A lot of trees are grown there, and the greenery is well maintained in the premises. The lake water level is generally more in summers and people enjoy boating in the water.

I feel so rejuvenated whenever I visit the lake and I feel that this kind of lake should be built in every city of the country.

Visit to a mall

These days more people than ever visit malls. Local markets are losing its importance due to the advantages that the malls have. I live in Chandigarh and I am fortunate enough to have many malls in my city.

Recently I visited Elante Mall. This is my favorite mall as it is centrally located and can be accessed from any part of the city easily. This is a gigantic mall and has a great parking space. I went to the mall with my friends as I had to shop for my brother's wedding. The mall has a big grocery store in the basement section. There are so many different segments of the mall that are organized chronologically.

I generally prefer branded clothes, so I visited the mall instead of going to the local market. One of the biggest benefits of mall is that we get every brand and all our requirements at one place. There are numerous branded and local branded shops and stores. My personal favourite is lifestyle store. That store has all the different brands under one roof. I bought a couple of shirts and a trouser. After shopping for clothes, I went to the top floor of the mall to watch a latest movie. The movie was wonderful and the seats in the theater were super comfortable.

71

After watching the movie, we went to the second floor where we window shopped for electronic gadgets and latest mobile phones. This mall is huge, and one needs a lot of time to witness all the sections.

We were tired after so much of a fun day and we decided to have some rest at a cozy restaurant. So, we went to the food section at the top floor of the mall and ordered our meals. It was a great day and I came back to home in the evening.

Favorite day of the week

I think if you ask this question to anyone, I feel most of the people would say that Sunday is their favorite day. I like Sunday too, but it is not my favorite one. The day I like the most is Saturday. There are several reasons behind this.

The biggest reason is that I have two weekly offs, Saturday and Sunday. I generally take rest on Sunday or I do any household chores that are pending. But Saturday is the day when I enjoy the most. It is like a gateway to holidays. I generally wake up on Saturdays with a lot of excitement and plans.

On this day I mostly wake up early in the morning and do some yoga and exercise. After this I like to take heavy breakfast as I do a lot of activities on Saturday. I usually tell my mother to make traditional potato stuffed bread with a lot of butter and milk.

After my breakfast, I like to go to temple on this day. There I sit for at least an hour and pray for me and my family then I do a bit of voluntary work over there. I feel tranquil after visiting the temple.

Then I call my friends and make plans for excursions. Most of my friends are free on Saturday so I am never short of company. Last Saturday, we went to the Shivalik hills that is near to my hometown. It takes around 2 hours to reach the hills and the view over there is serene.

I also like to visit malls and local markets on Saturday. I have a lot of free time on this day and I can go anywhere but I don't like to stay at home. I also take out time on Saturdays to visit my relatives and cousins.

Saturday is the perfect day for night outs at friend's house and that's why I like this day very much.

Speak about a time when you felt anxious

Emotions are a wonderful thing. They reflect the state of our mind and they are also the index of our mind. Through emotions we can judge a person's thought process. There are a wide variety of emotions that people run through every day and nervousness is a very common sign that can be seen on the people's face or in their actions in daily routine.

I get nervous on several occasions but the time when I got overly nervous happened when I was waiting for my class 12th results. The thing is that I was not very well in my exam days and I thought my exams didn't go well. Although I was well prepared during the exams as I studied regularly throughout the session rather than studying more in the exam days.

I was suffering from mild fever during the last three exams of 12th class. These subjects were important, and it was necessary to score good in them as I had to apply for a student visa. One of the subjects was English. I was not very well prepared for this subject during the session and I thought that I would prepare it during the exams.

But to my bad luck I couldn't get any time and intent for studying it during the exams. I was suffering from viral fever and was unable to concentrate on my study. I hardly read about the English syllabus and on the exam day I went and gave my best in the exam.

The result was to be declared in a couple of months after the exam. On the result day, I was very nervous as I was worried about my scores in English exam. The result was scheduled to be declared in the evening. So, from morning itself, I was anxious and barely relaxed. As soon as I received the result, I was relieved, and all my nervousness was gone.

Although I didn't score high in the subject, but I was satisfied given my preparation and health. So, this is the day I remember when I was very nervous.

Visit to a marriage

Marriage is one of the most important moments in one's life. This is an occasion where all the family members come together for rituals and customs. In our country, marriage is a sacred bond between two souls, and one shall commit himself/herself to the partner loyally.

73

I live in Punjab and this is the place where the marriages are celebrated like a grand occasion. People generally spend a huge amount of money and put in a lot of efforts in the marriage celebrations. Mostly north Indians are known to celebrate marriages in majestic style. In this part of the country we generally have a lot of marriage parties and functions. It is like a four to five or even a week's duration of events and celebrations.

I have attended one such wedding recently and enjoyed a lot. I am talking about my cousin's wedding. There were quite a few functions in his wedding. The first gathering was held on the Ring ceremony in which the boy and girl exchanged the rings.

In this function, there were only close relatives and the gathering must have been around 150 people. This occasion was followed by the wedding day on which the rituals of the marriage took place. The venue for the wedding was one of the renowned resorts of the city and the venue was decorated beautifully from inside and from outside as well.

We reached the venue at 7 PM and the party began. We danced to the beats of the latest songs on loud music and enjoyed a wide variety of food as well. The gathering must have been near about 500 people so sometimes it can get a bit annoying.

Nevertheless, I enjoyed the day very much. Wedding functions are a great place to be as one gets a chance to meet all relatives and family friends. We enjoyed together and conversations went on for all night. The wedding day was followed by the reception party for the couple and with that the marriage celebrations came to an end.

Visit to a government office

I have visited many government offices in recent times. The one which I am going to talk about is the municipal cooperation office in my locality. I had to visit there as we were facing the problem of water supply and incidents of stray dogs in our local area.

From the past few days, there were some incidents of dog bite from stray dogs. Recently an 8-year kid got bitten by a stray dog and was hospitalized for a week. There was a scare of dogs in our area from the past one month and people were refraining from roaming freely in the locality.

The second problem that the people in my area were facing was the issue of water supply. The water supply was cut in the morning from the previous week and people were suffering a lot. The water supply cut was a menace as it would disturb the routine of working people because the cut was scheduled in the morning when the water supply is much needed.

We were fed up with these two problems and after a lot of complaints to the offices and no action taken, all the locality members decided to go to the municipal office to take up the matter with the concerned officer. The office is in the central part of the city and was renovated recently and looked beautiful.

The office is a huge building and there are a lot of departments in that. We had to go to the local area officer, so we asked about him at the reception. The receptionist guided us towards the room of the officer where we had to wait for 15 minutes as he was busy in a meeting.

After that, we were escorted to the concerned officer and he was humble and patient with us. He listened to all our issues and gave satisfactory reply. He also assured of solving the problems as soon as possible. It was great to visit this government office as we felt very contented.

A plant you like

India is such a big country in which we have rich variety of flora and fauna. This topic is tailor made for me as I am a plant lover. I like to do gardening in my free time, and I try to learn about new species of plants whenever I get time.

I like a lot of plants, but my favorite plant is the basil plant. It is known as Tulsi in Hindi. This plant is miraculous and serves a lot of purposes. In India, we have two varieties of Tulsi plant, the first one is known as Rama and the other one is known as Shama.

Both are not as distinctive as one would think but the person with the knowledge of plants can easily recognize the different variety of Basil. This plant can be grown in almost every type of conditions. It requires minimum sunlight and can also be grown in the places where water is scarce.

It has small leaves with a height of about three feet of a fully-grown plant. The branches are brittle and there are thousands of pollen seeds along with the leaves on the plant. You can also smell the fragrance of the plant from a distance. I have grown this plant at my house in a big earthen pot. I regularly water this plant as soon as I wake up in the morning.

The Basil plant is known to have medicinal properties. The leaves of this plant can be consumed directly to relieve sore throat, or it can also be put in tea for fever relief. Some people have this belief that high fevers and dengue can also be cured by consuming Basil leaves. Most people keep the Basil plant at the entry of the house as they believe that this plant brings good luck.

According to Hindu mythology, Tulsi plant is also worshiped as it brings in a lot of benefits to the humanity. This plant holds a significant importance in our culture. Most of the people in my country like this plant, so do I.

Your favorite item of clothing

Clothing is a basic need of human beings. But now it has become more than a basic need. It has become a style statement. Nowadays people spend more money on clothes than ever. Numerous brands and stores are in existence everywhere in the world. I like to be updated with my clothing and I am very conscious of the latest trends.

I generally like to wear informal clothing in my daily routine. A pair of jeans along with a nice shirt or a polo. I like to keep my clothing comfortable rather than body fit. I think I like every item of clothing, but I have to say that I like my jeans the most.

I have around six or seven jeans in my wardrobe. I like to buy only Wrangler and Levi's jeans. These two brands are on the top when it comes to buying jeans. I like to wear dark colored jeans as it can be worn on a stretch for many days without even washing it.

I read somewhere that Levi's was the person who invented the jeans for the construction workers as they wanted something durable and clothing that don't get dirty easily. So, Levi's came up with an idea of jeans and gave workers a new type of clothing. Today, Levi's is one of the top brands across the globe who manufacture jeans. The story is so inspiring.

There are several advantages of wearing jeans. Most of the jeans go with every kind of shirts and uppers. There is no need to wash the jeans after every use. You don't even need to iron most of the jeans. The life and durability are also the best when it comes to jeans. I mostly like to buy blue and black jeans. These colors suit me the most.

Jeans can also be worn with formal shoes and it also looks good with the casual shoes. This is the beauty of jeans, it's so versatile. I have a knack of buying jeans whenever I feel bored from the old ones. Recently I bought the most expensive jeans that I have bought till date. It cost me around 5000 rupees. Buying jeans give me immense satisfaction.

A book you have read

Book reading is one of the best activities that a person can have. I am a book lover. I have around 50 books in my personal library at home. I generally love to read all kinds of books, but I am always inclined towards the biographies and autobiographies of famous personalities. I have read the autobiography of Mahatma Gandhi, Albert Einstein, and many other great personalities but my personal favorite is the autobiography of Nelson Mandela.

The name of the book is 'Long walk to freedom'. This is an autobiography and was published after he became the President of South Africa. In this book, he gave detailed insights from when he was born till he became the President. He also included the years when he was imprisoned and wrote about his family and friends.

Nelson Mandela was a freedom fighter for more than 5 decades before he became the first black president of South Africa in 1994. He stayed in the prison for about 3 decades. He and thousands of his fellow freedom fighters were imprisoned by the white government. Many were executed and few of them were send to the jail for lifetime. Nelson Mandela was one of them.

He stayed in the jail for so many years, but the struggle continued out of the jail and as a result the white government was forced to release the political prisoners and Mandela was freed in the year 1990. He continued with his freedom struggles after his release and continuous negotiations with the government led to the first ever fair election in South Africa. This was the first time that the majority blacks could cast their votes. In 1994 the election results were declared, and Nelson Mandela won by unanimity of the people of South Africa and became the first ever black President of South Africa. I learned all this information from the book.

This book had a long-lasting impression on me, and I never knew anything about Nelson Mandela before reading this book. This inspired me to read more such books. Mostly, I read book in the morning time. I like to wake up early in the morning and read books for around 40 minutes. This is a great habit as it gives you a lot of knowledge and you can also improve your reading skills.

An occasion when you helped someone

Helping someone gives immense pleasure. It is great to have done voluntary work in life. It doesn't give you money, but it does gives you innate peace and joy. I am fortunate enough to have received help from a lot of people in my life when I needed it and I have also helped a few people when they need it.

I remember helping an old man who lost his way. This happened last year when I was waiting for my bus at the bus stop and an old person came to me and asked for help. He told me that he was going back to his hometown, but he mistakenly got off the bus at the wrong station and his belongings were left in the bus itself. He was looking worried and helpless as he had also forgot his wallet in the bus. He also told me that he was feeling very hungry and could not eat anything as he doesn't have money. I calmed him down and offered him some food at a nearby restaurant. He was very old and was using a stick to walk. So, I decided to take him to the restaurant and his home myself. I took him to a restaurant and ordered tea and some snacks. We had the food and I asked him to come with me. We waited at the bus station for about 20 minutes before the next bus came. I boarded the bus with him and paid the bus fare. Then I started asking about him and his family. He told me that he had gone to his village to attend a funeral of one of his childhood friends and now he was returning to his son's house where he originally lived.

We talked a lot on the way and soon we reached our destination. I escorted him out of the bus and said goodbye, but he convinced me to come to his home to meet his family. When we reached his home and he

78

told his story to his family members, they thanked me and give me a gift as a token of love and appreciation.

On that day, I was so happy and when I told my parents about this, they hugged me and told me to help people in future as well.

Something you planned to do but haven't done yet

Well! This is a very interesting topic because I love to do new things every now and then. There are so many things in life that I have planned to do but I am waiting for the right time and funds. The thing that I have planned to do before I die is sky diving.

It is one of the extreme sports that many people do not dare to do. There are select people who chose to do sky diving and I am one of them. I planned to do sky jump last year along with my best friend. I searched on internet about the best places from where we can perform this activity. I found that Gujrat, Thailand and Dubai are the best place for sky diving according to the reviews and suggestions from the people on the internet. So, I decided to call the one in Dubai as I also wanted to go to Dubai one day. They were very responsive and told that they have different packages with diverse tariffs. The best package that I found included the skydive with a professional and video recording was to be done by them. There was a video recorded clip of dive and the photos of the same was included in the package. The price of the package was exceeding my budget, so I decided to know about the other places.

Then I followed up in Thailand and found that the package inclusions there were like that of Dubai, but the price was almost half. I got excited to know this and decided to immediately book the package and flights. But after discussing it with my parents my dreams were shattered. My father had invested a huge sum in a property recently so I couldn't get the money for this, but they assured me that whenever they have extra money, they will surely give it to me for skydive.

This is my long-cherished dream and the day I get time and money to do it, I will go for it.

An important letter you received

These days the trend of writing letters is vanishing day by day. People nowadays are using e-mails and other electronic stuff for interaction. I used to send and receive letters from one of my pen friends in my childhood, but it's been a while since I have received a letter.

I can never forget the letter that I received last time. It was very important for me. The letter was regarding the cash prize that I won during a lucky draw. I went to a shopping mall and there was a counter at the exit of the mall where a lot of people were gathered. There was a lot of chaos, and people were looking excited.

I went there in anticipation and asked what was going on? The person at the counter told me that it was a lucky draw for the customers who shopped at the mall. I told him that I bought certain items and would like to participate in the draw. He told me to fill up the form and put it into the lucky draw box. I wrote the details like phone number, name, address and gender on the form and put it into the box and waited for the result with excitement.

There were a lot of cash prizes and numerous other items to be given away by the mall. The lucky draw scheme was to commemorate the completion of 5 years of the mall. I was excited and on the other hand I was a bit pessimistic on whether I would win it or not?

But to my surprise, one day I received a letter and before opening it I had no clue regarding the lucky draw as it was nearly a month since I had gone to the mall. The letter stated that we are happy to announce that you have won a cash prize from the lucky draw. I was astonished to see that.

The cash prize was 20000 INR which was a huge amount for me at that time. I was so happy after reading the letter. It also stated that you must collect the cash prize from the mall office. So, I went to the mall, got my cash and I was so happy.

That is the letter that I think was very important and if I hadn't received it, I would have regretted it.

A time when you teamed up with an old person

Teamwork is very important in achieving success. I have teamed up with a lot of people in my life, but I always enjoy the company of my grandfather.

I have played a lot of table tennis matches and tournaments with him over the last few years.

My grandfather is a champion player himself. He had played on national level during his young days. He is very fond of playing table tennis. We have a proper table to play table tennis at our home. I have learnt the sport from him 6 years back.

First, I wasn't interested in playing the game but one day I picked up the bat and never looked back. I learnt a lot of tricks from my grandfather and I used to beat a lot of my age group players at school and locally.

One day my grandfather told me about a table tennis competition that was to be organized in our locality. It was a doubles tournament in which you must team up with one player and play against the other two. We decided to team up and play that tournament as there was no age restrictions for participants. I knew that we had good chances of winning the tournament. There were 10 days to prepare for the competition, so we decided to practice table tennis every day for at least an hour in the night. We used to play single games, and, on some occasions, I used to call my friends so that we would have four players to practice in a team.

On the day of the final match of the tournament, my grandfather was feeling tired and some cramps were disturbing him. So, I decided to take the lead and play to my full potential.

In the end, we won the tournament and the credit goes to our teamwork. This was the time when I teamed up with an old person and enjoyed very much.

A gift that made you happy

I have received many gifts in my life. Gifts makes a person feel euphoric and excited. Last year I celebrated my birthday and received numerous gifts but the one which I like the most was the smart watch.

This gift was given by my sister. She knew that I wanted it badly, but it was too expensive for me to buy. When I unwrapped the gift, I had tears in my eyes as it was something that I desperately needed. The gift was a Samsung smart watch. I hugged my sister tightly and thanked her for the gift.

This watch was of black color with silver lining on the edges. The strap had a sporty look and felt very comfortable. The price of this watch is around 40,000 rupees in India. The watch has a lot of variants but mine was the latest.

This watch has a display screen which is primarily used to see time, but it does have a few other functions as well. I can see the notifications on the screen of the watch. If someone calls me on my mobile phone, then I don't need to take out the phone from my pocket, I can simply see on the watch screen and I can also answer or disconnect the call directly from the watch. I can set alarm and I can also get notifications for my messages. The biggest advantage of having this watch is that it also shows us the real picture of our health. I can see the number of steps that I take in a day or in each period. I can also get my heart rate on the display. I can also set reminders for my important works. I can see emails and I can also respond to the messages that I receive.

In free time, I can see videos on the watch. The screen is not that big but is big enough for entertainment. I love this gift very much and I will keep it with me as long as I can.

An achievement

I haven't been able to achieve a lot of accolades in my life but there are some achievements that I would like to share with you. The one which I am going to tell you about is when I was in school.

This happened when I was studying in 10th class. In that year there was a compulsory debate and speech competition organized by our school in which more than 200 students from our school had to participate.

I was very shy in nature but there was no escaping. Everyone in our class had to participate. It was a compulsion and no choices were given. I was very nervous when I came to know about this debate competition because I was really introvert and could hardly speak a word in front of 10 people. The debates were to be performed in front of more than 2000 students and teachers of our school.

There was only one week to prepare, and we were given three topics each. We chose one topic and start rehearsing on it. I took me around 4 days to even speak in front of 10 students while practicing. Slowly and steadily I gathered my courage and prepared the speech topic.

On the competition day I had mixed feelings. I was excited as well as timid. Once my name was announced, I rushed to the stage and took a deep breath.

I started with my speech topic and I thought I spoke very well. I had practiced hard due to the fear of failure and I think it really helped. When my topic was over, I had a huge sigh of relief. I came back to home and realized that I achieved a big thing in my life that I could now stand in a group of people and speak my mind.

However, I didn't win the competition that day but the courage I won was a big achievement for me.

Your ideal home

Having a house of own is the biggest dream of every person. I live in a medium sized house with decent construction. I would like to have a house of my dreams which would have all the amenities in it that I want.

An ideal house would be difficult to describe but I will try to describe it in my own version. An ideal house would probably be big. Its exterior will be of plain white color as this color sooths my eyes and it gives positive vibes. It should be a multi-storied house with a lot of big windows and airways for great ventilation and sunlight.

The main entry gate of the house would be huge with wooden work on it. There would be huge space for the parking of cars. At least 3 to 4 cars should easily accommodate in the house. Apart from this, there should be a minimum of 6 to 7 rooms where everyone in the family can have a private or separate bedroom.

Moreover, the house style should be duplex in which the upper floor can be accessed from the inside of the ground floor. There should be a lot of wooden work as it looks classy. A big kitchen should be there with a large dining table having at least 8 chairs.

At the entry of the house, there should be a small garden where colorful flowers will be planted. An ideal house should be in a posh locality as there will be more security and the area would be neat and clean.

I would want my ideal home to have a terrace garden or an artificial turf. Some plants on the terrace will increase its beauty. I am a sports lover so I would like to have a gymnasium room or a games room where I can spend my leisure time.

At last I feel that an ideal house is a house that has all the facilities and luxuries of life.

Your favorite sports

India is a big nation and we play most of the sports on international level. I love most of the games and sports as I am a big sports lover. Hockey is a team sport that is native to India but other sports like football are also picking up the craze.

But I would like to mention that I like cricket the most. Cricket is considered like a religion in our country. Most of the youngsters play this sport in our nation. India has won two 50 over and one T20 world cup title in the past three decades.

Over the world, cricket is played by more than 30 nations. I play this sport from my childhood. This is played between two teams having 11 players in each team. There are different formats of cricket, the longest being the test cricket and the shortest is the twenty-20 cricket match. The most prevalent is the 50 over one day match.

In the game of cricket, one team bats first and sets a target for the other team to chase. The other team must chase the target in the given 50 overs or as per the format of the game. The team that score more runs, wins the match.

Cricket is played primarily between 10 top nations and some domestic leagues are also popular across the globe. One of them is the IPL (Indian Premier League). This is held every year in the month of April. In this tournament, cricketers from over 12 prominent nations participate every year.

The one-day cricket world cup is mostly held after four years and the twenty-20 cricket world cup is held after two years. There is a huge frequency of the number of matches these days and cricketers are the highest paid athletes in our country.

I like this sport very much and I have seen numerous live cricket events and contests in my life.

A product of your country

India is such a big country and we have a lot of products that are produced and grown locally. Be it aromatic spices in the southern part of the country or the beautiful and colorful saffron in the north part of India.

India is also famous for red chilies that are grown in the west but today I would like to talk about the Assam tea which is grown in the eastern part of our country. Although tea is also grown in other states like Himachal Pradesh and Uttarakhand, but Assam tea is the finest.

This tea is grown in the state of Assam as it provides the best weather for the growth of tea buds and the landscape is suitable for tea plantation. The workers who work in the tea gardens often experience drowsiness after working in the farms as the tea leaves contains sedative compounds.

Most people of our country consume this tea. There are a lot of varieties that are grown there. Huge industries are set up there to produce huge amounts of packed tea. A large ratio of production is exported all over the world and sold as premium tea in many countries.

Assam tea is most aromatic and palatable. Most of the tea companies in our country source the finest tea from Assam. The Assam tea is pure, and it is one of the tastiest teas around the globe. Recently I read somewhere that this tea was exported to more than 80 countries across the globe.

Tourists can also take a tour of the tea gardens and can also see the production and packing of tea at the local factory. When tourists visit the factory, they are welcomed by unlimited variety of tea.

I have never been to Assam, but I have seen the pictures on the internet. It looks beautiful and serene. The tea gardens look marvelous and lush green farms are a sight to watch. If I ever get a chance, I would like to visit the Assam tea farms.

A big company/organization near you

I live in Mohali which is not famous for big organizations and industries. It is famous for its greenery, neat and clean roads. Infrastructure is fabulous and the life in Mohali is royal.

There are few medium sized organizations and industries and a couple of big ones as well. Today I would like to talk about Mahindra Swaraj Tractor division that is situated in Mohali. This is a huge industry and has its branches all over the state of Punjab and India.

The one which I am talking about is famous for producing Swaraj tractors. It is one of the most famous brands in our state. I visited this industry as my uncle works here and one day, he told me to accompany him as he wanted to show his office and factory where he was working.

I was also excited to visit as it was my first visit to such a big organization. We went there in the morning and were greeted by few security men who gave us the pass and allowed us to enter the premises.

As we entered, I saw a big assembly area. Along the path there were a lot of flowerpots that were placed in a stylish manner. Then we entered the main complex of the organization. It was a huge compound with a big screen welcoming the visitors.

Then my uncle took me to his office where I was received by his colleagues. I was offered some snacks along with a cup of tea. Then I was taken to the workshop where the tractors are manufactured. It was a humungous workshop and numerous tractors were lined one after the other.

After that I went to the testing area where the finished product was tested by the experts. After visiting all the sections of the factory, we came back, and I was feeling so tired. It is such a big organization that it took me around 3 hours to see the whole area.

It's great to visit big organizations as we come to know about the workmanship of such a great company and learn a lot from there.

A businessperson you admire

I have always dreamt of being a business tycoon in my life. If given a chance I would like to start a business rather than doing a job. There are several big shots in our country, but I am a huge fan of Mr. Mukesh Ambani.

He is one of the biggest tycoons all over the world. He is the largest shareholder of Reliance group and his company has also featured in the fortune 500 hundred companies. Once, he reached the pinnacle of the world when he became the world's richest man.

Reliance industries deals mostly in refining, petrochemicals and in the gas and oil sectors. Its other subsidiary is the reliance retail which is also the largest retail chain in India.

Mukesh Ambani was born on 19th April 1957 and has three siblings. He did his schooling in Mumbai and completed Chemical Engineering. I admire him very much as he has achieved a lot in his life.

Although he inherited everything from his father Mr. Dhiru Bhai Ambani, but he worked day and night to take his industries to the top.

Currently he lives in Mumbai. His house is Antilia which is probably the biggest and the most luxurious house in our country. Antilia house is the world's second most valuable property after the Buckingham Palace of United Kingdom.

He has also bought a cricket team by the name of Mumbai Indians in Indian premier league. He is a sports lover and can generally be seen supporting his team in the crunch matches. He has stretched out in almost every field and continue to grow.

Recently Mukesh Ambani launched a telecommunication service by the name of Jio. It has spread in every corner of our country like wildfire which provides reasonable services to its customers.

I wish I can become like him one day and rule this world.

A holiday you enjoyed

I have been to a few places and enjoyed holidays with my family in India and abroad. I would love to speak about a family vacation that I enjoyed with my family members when I passed my tenth class.

We decided to go to Dubai. Dubai is a city in the United Arab Emirates. It is one of the fastest growing cities in the world and has provided a lot of jobs and opportunities to the deserving people from all over the globe.

Dubai is such a wonderful place that you don't want to come back from there. We landed there on 24th of December, a day before Christmas. The atmosphere was amazing throughout the city. The main parts of the city were decorated with the themes of Christmas.

On Christmas day we went to Dubai mall which is the biggest mall in the world, and we spent our whole day there. This was our second day of the vacation.

On the next day we went on a city tour in which we saw the main attractions of the city. We went to see the Burj al Arab, which is a seven-star hotel. We also went to the JBR Beach and enjoyed a lot there. At night we strolled around the downtown area of the city.

The next day we were scheduled for desert safari. We were picked up from our hotel in an expensive SUV car. We were taken to a middle of a desert and did dune bashing. In this activity, the driver of the car drives and make the car jump through the desert dunes and makes the ride adventurous. At night we went to the Dubai creek cruise. We took the boat which went through the creek and we enjoyed buffet dinner on it. The next day we planned a visit to Abu Dhabi which is a city in UAE. It took us 2 hours to reach there.

In Abu Dhabi we visited the Ferrari world which is the biggest Ferrari museum in world. There are few roller coasters rides that we took. I took the world's fastest ride there.

Next day we came back from Dubai. I must say that it was a great experience and I will never forget my visit.

A person you admire from a foreign country OR A person who has inspired you from abroad

I admire several personalities from foreign countries. As I love to admire great personalities from all over the world like Barak Obama, Bill Gates, Jack Ma, Steve Jobs but the person I admire the most is Nelson Mandela. He died in December 2013. I wish I could meet him. I came to know about him through his book.

The name of the book is 'Long walk to freedom'. This is an autobiography which was published after he became the President of South Africa. In this book, he gave detailed insights from when he was born to when he became the President. He also included the years when he was imprisoned and wrote about his family and friends.

Nelson Mandela was a freedom fighter for more than 5 decades before he became the first black president of South Africa in 1994. He stayed in the prison for about 3 decades. He and thousands of his fellow freedom fighters were imprisoned by the white government. Many were executed and few of them were send to the jail for lifetime. Nelson Mandela was one of them.

He stayed in the jail for so many years, but the struggle continued out of the jail and as a result the white government was forced to release the political prisoners and Mandela was freed in the year 1990. He continued with his freedom struggles after his release and participated in the first ever fair election in South Africa as the president of the ANC. This was the first time that the majority blacks could cast their votes. In 1994 the election results were declared, and Nelson Mandela won by unanimity of the people of South Africa and became the first ever black President of South Africa.

This story had a long-lasting impression on me, and I never knew anything about Nelson Mandela before reading this book. From that day onwards I admire him as the greatest leader and symbol of peace and reconciliation.

An interesting place in your country that tourists don't know about

I live in India and everyone knows that it's a huge country. We have a lot of natural marvels and people from around the world come to see. I will not talk about famous places like Goa, Jaipur or Mumbai but I would like to share an interesting place which most people in my country are not aware of!

I am talking about Andaman and Nicobar Islands. It is an archipelago of over 300 islands famous for its palm lined white sand beaches. This is an Indian Union territory and is located in the Bay of Bengal. These islands are famous for diving and snorkeling as there are an abundance of coral reefs which supports the marine life.

The area of Andaman is far away from the mainland Indian territory. The islands are located near Thailand on the east coast. Port Blair is the capital and Havelock and Neil are the more famous islands among the few tourists who manage to go there.

In the bygone years, this island was used as a cellular jail where most of the freedom fighters were imprisoned in the British era. Havelock is the largest island and is famed for parasailing, scuba diving and other sea activities.

The bustling city of Port Blair gives you the local feel and you can also witness few historical sights, architectural monuments. You can reach this place through air. There is an airport in Port Blair that serves as the main airport for people who are travelling to these islands.

This part of our country is least explored by Indians as well as the foreigners. The cuisine here is a must try as it is entirely different from what you get on the mainland India. People generally use a lot of coconut in their dishes and the main course is usually the sea food.

I haven't been to these islands, but I have seen a lot of videos and searched a lot on internet regarding this. I would recommend anyone who wants to visit a unique place in India should go to the Andaman and Nicobar Islands.

Your visit to a library

I am a book lover and whenever I get time, I just pick up a book from my bag and start reading it. I have a collection of over 50 books that I have already read. Reading books has a lot of advantages and to read books in a library is a wonderful experience all together.

I have visited a few libraries in my life, but my personal favorite is the government library in phase-7, Mohali. This library was opened in the mid 80's and I have seen this from my childhood. The first time when I visited this library was when I was a kid. I went there with my father who had some work there. It was the first time when I saw a library.

Recently I visited the library last week. I generally go there when I am feeling anxious. Reading books in a peaceful environment gives peace to my mind and releases my stress. This library is a very big place and it has got a great collection of books.

I like it very much as it is government funded, hence the membership fee is very nominal. You just need to pay a small amount for the yearly membership and then you can take books on loan for free. There is a limit of 5 books per month and a book should not be kept for more than 15 days at a stretch.

At the right side of the entry door, there is the desk of the head librarian and they have around 10 big tables and chairs which have the capacity of over 200 people who can sit together and enjoy reading books at one time. Different sections of library are segregated beautifully and systematically. You can read all sorts of books and the collection is just phenomenal. These days computers have also been introduced in the library for storing e-books and soft copies of books that are rare and in deteriorating condition.

I regularly visit this library and I really enjoy my time there.

Visit to a museum

Museums play a vital role in preserving our culture and history. There are so many museums that I have visited in my lifetime and I liked every one of them. It is hard to describe about one. But out of the ones I have visited, I would like to speak about the Government museum which is situated in sector – 10, Chandigarh.

Its full name is Government museum and art gallery. This museum opened in 1968 and it is one of the leading museums in North India. The main contents in the museum are manuscripts, textiles, decorative art, pottery, numismatics, stone sculptures, metal sculptures, and a lot of other historical items.

I have visited this museum a couple of times, but I would like to speak on my recent visit. This museum is nicely built and has 4 floors in total. The ground floor has a big lobby and it is also the waiting area. The best thing about this museum is that the entry is free.

At the ground floor they have the history and artefacts related to our city Chandigarh. One can learn about the ancestors and what they did before this place was colonized. As we move ahead, there is a wide staircase that leads to the first floor.

At the first floor, there is a huge collection of textiles from different eras and various parts of our country. It was astonishing to see that how diverse the clothing was in the ancient times. These days the clothing styles have become common throughout the world.

When we reached the second floor, we saw tremendous assortment of art and craft. There were paintings from the past time. Some even dated back to the 14th century. I was mesmerized to see the art and craft there.

At the top floor, there were stone and metal sculptures and tools that were used by our ancestors. Tools for hunting and gathering food and tools for making wooden art. I felt so satisfied after visiting the museum.

The museum gets the full credit for maintaining and preserving such beautiful things from the past. I would love to go there again and again. I would also recommend people to visit there.

Describe a sports event you have seen

I have seen numerous sporting events in my life but those were mostly cricket matches. I have seen a couple of hockey matches as well but the event that has a long-lasting impression on my mind is the 2011 cricket world cup semi-final played between India and Pakistan.

In 2011, the world cup was co-hosted by India, Sri Lanka and Bangladesh. Everyone expected India to lift the cup as the semi-final and final were scheduled to be held in India and our players knew the conditions well. India eventually went on to win the cup, but I am going to talk about the semi-final match as I saw it live at the PCA stadium, Mohali.

I live in Mohali and we are fortunate enough to have an international cricket stadium. I have seen several live cricket tournaments at this venue. This was an important match and all the top leaders and celebrities from India and Pakistan were present at the stadium. The environment was amazing and there was a lot of buzz even before the start of the match. The match was scheduled to begin at 2 PM but people cued up outside the stadium as early as 8 AM. We reached at 10 AM and it took us around couple of hours to enter the stadium. When we entered the match, practice was going on in the ground and we got a chance to see a lot of our favourite players from close quarters.

India won the toss and decided to bat first. India put up a decent total to defend but Pakistan had a flying start to the match. They scored 70 runs in no time without losing a wicket.

Then suddenly our bowling clicked, and we start taking wickets at regular intervals. In the end, we won the match. Sachin Tendulkar scored the highest number of runs in that match.

We were so excited and stayed in the stadium till mid night and celebrated the victory with other people. On our way back we saw people dancing in the streets of the city and celebrating the victory.

This is the sporting event that I saw, and I can never forget it my whole life.

Describe a leisure activity near sea

I am an adventurous person and like to do all kinds of activities. I have been to beaches a couple of times. The last time when I went to a beach was in Goa.

It is in the western part of India. It's a beautiful place with a lot of beaches lined with lush green trees. I have been to Goa twice. When I went to Goa last time, I did a lot of sea activities.

One of the most popular activity near sea is the para sailing. It is adventurous and scary. I had never heard about this activity before visiting a beach. I saw people flying in the air with a parachute tied to their backs and connected with a boat that was floating fast in the sea.

First, I thought of skipping this activity but after some time I agreed to do it. We went to the activity corner and deposited 2000 rupees. Then I was given some instructions by them and I had to wait for some time as other people were in cue.

My turn came after 30 minutes and they tied a lot of harness and safety equipment on my waist and shoulders. The person who was assisting me wished me good luck and then I was ready to go.

When you parasail, you must run when the boat starts otherwise you could get bruised or fall on your face down. When I was pulled up in the air, I felt adrenalin rushing in my legs. The world looks so different when you fly. I was in the air and enjoyed the eagle's eye view of the ocean and beach. To my left I saw people on the beach and on the right-hand side there was the never-ending ocean. I felt on top of the world. The ride lasted for about 10 minutes and this time passed so quickly that I hardly realized.

When I landed, I thanked everyone who assisted me, and I was really impressed with their professional work. I think if anyone gets a chance they should definitely go for this activity.

Favourite newspaper

Reading newspaper is a wonderful activity. These days the technological advancements are on the rise and due to that most people now prefer to read news on the internet.

Although e-news has become a part of our lives, but I don't feel that newspapers have lost their importance. There are several newspapers in the market that comes in a variety of languages but my favourite one is the Hindustan Times. This is an English newspaper that is printed since 1924 and around one million copy is circulated everyday across the country.

I have been reading this newspaper since my childhood. It is one of the top selling newspapers in our city. It has different subscriptions along with the main paper. Every Wednesday and Saturday HT Classified is distributed for information on various platforms.

Supplements such as education and jobs are also supplied regularly or once a week. The main page of the newspaper is always full of top news from our country and around the world. The sports news is printed on the second last page of the paper. Sports columns are written by famous sports personalities of our country.

Last page of the newspaper generally consists of the international news from around the globe. There is news from the different states on the dedicated pages. There is a separate page for the latest updates in the education sector of our country.

Apart from the main paper, there is always a Chandigarh HT which is a supplement for the local news. This contains the happenings of the Tri-city which is Mohali, Chandigarh and Panchkula. This is great to read as one can know about the things happening nearby.

The print quality and the clarity of the pictures is superb. I have tried all the other newspapers, but Hindustan Times is the best.

An international leader or politician you like

I have followed a lot of local and international leaders like Barak Obama, George W Bush, Bill Clinton and many others. But my favourite one is Nelson Mandela. He was a freedom fighter who fought for the rights of the blacks against the white imperial rule.

He is considered to be one of the most iconic personalities in the entire world till now. I have read one of his books that is his auto biography, Long walk to freedom. Once I read that book, I became a fan of Nelson Mandela. Soon I did some research regarding his nature, life and struggles. I was so impressed with his achievements despite the difficulties he had to face. No one can believe that he lived in the prison for about 30 years and later became the president of the republic of South Africa.

He was followed by millions of people from all over the planet. Many organizations and people from all walks of life came to meet him when he was in prison. The white government had to release him because of the international pressure.

After his release, he became the leader of ANC, African national congress and fought the elections in 1994 and became the president. This was the first time that blacks were free to cast their votes alongside whites.

He was a true international leader who visited myriad countries and inspired millions of people through his speeches and thoughts. After becoming the president, he did his best to remove the gap between the blacks and the whites. He was instrumental in controlling crime, increasing harmony among people and promoting South Africa on a world stage. He's no more but he still inspires all of us to live peacefully. He is a great symbol of reconciliation and peace.

An English lesson

I have learned uncountable English lessons in my life as I studied in an English medium school. But the lesson that I am going to talk about is the lesson that I learned from my IELTS trainer.

I took my IELTS coaching in Mohali and I was fortunate enough to get amazing IELTS coaching from Aman ma'am. She is a wonderful teacher and a great human being. I remember when I went for the first day of my class, she taught us incredible things regarding English language.

The moment our class began, she told us to focus on the English language rather than focusing on the IELTS. She explained that IELTS is a part of English and if we are good at English then we can give answer to any question that is asked, and we can also write on any essay that we get in the exam.

When the class started, I thought that it will be regarding the module of IELTS, instead it was a pure English language class. We were around 50 students in the class, and she started with vocabulary words and its importance. She noted down more than 20 vocab words that were alien to me and most of the students. Then she told the meanings of those words and asked us to write one sentence each on it so that we can memorize those words. It was a wonderful exercise and as it allowed me to learn 20 new words that day.

Next thing that we discussed in the class was common spelling errors and common grammatical errors that happen in English. When we finished this task, I was so impressed because no teacher had told me so many things in one English class before. I learnt a lot of things that day.

This was not the end, after that she gave us few readymade introductions and templates for important essays of IELTS. I noted down all of them and I have still got those notes in my copy. Those lines were pretty useful in the exam.

I think this was a complete English lesson that I learnt recently.

Describe a piece of art (a statue or painting)
Not many people these days love art. But I am the kind of a person who relishes art in every form. I remember when I was in school, I always participated in every type of art competition. I loved doing painting and draw sketches in my free time.

The piece of art that I am going to describe today is the statue of Unity which is located in Gujrat. This statue is of great freedom fighter Sardar Vallabhbhai Patel. He was also the first ever home minister of independent India. He was hugely respected for his efforts in uniting the 562 princely states to form a single union of India.

The statue of unity is situated in a river delta in front of the Sardar Sarovar dam on river Narmada. The nearest city is Vadodara which is located at about 100 kilometers in the Northwest direction of the statue.

The construction of the statue began in the year 2013 and was inaugurated by the Honorable Prime minister of India, Narendra Modi in 2018 on the 143rd birth anniversary of Sardar Patel. This is the world's tallest statue that has a height of 182 meters.

This is a humungous piece of art that includes five zones. Three of these zones are open to public in which there is a museum that describes about Patel's contribution towards our country and about his early life.

There is a huge viewing gallery at the height of 153 meters from where people can see 360-degree view of the nearby places. The lifts are swift and smooth and can take up to 26 people at one time. The government of Gujrat also faced some criticism due to the huge expenditure spend on the statue, but the matter suppressed with time.

Describe a time when you went to a crowded place

I have been to a lot of places that are crowded. Today I would like to speak about a sports event that I have seen. I am talking about a Hockey match between India and Australia.

This is the Champion's cup match from the year 2015 that happened in India. I am a big fan of sports especially hockey. This match was scheduled to be played in the Hockey stadium, Chandigarh.

I booked the tickets for me and two of my friends online at a reasonable price. We bought the VIP tickets that had the best view according to the website. I remember the ticket price was around INR 200 for the normal and INR 500 for the VIP ticket.

The Hockey match is of 70 minutes in total with quarters of 15 minutes each divided by short breaks. The match was scheduled to start at 8 PM. So, we decided that we should reach at 7 PM to avoid any delays.

But to our surprise, the event was sold out and there were long queues even for the VIP block area. We stood in the line for at least 45 minutes before we could enter. Standing there wasn't boring as people were chanting for the support of the Indian team.

As soon as we entered in the stadium, we were filled with excitement. There were songs that were played on the loudspeaker and everyone was dancing to its beat. The match began at sharp 8 PM. In the first half Australia were leading 1-0.

The crowd was so tensed and started cheering loudly for the Indian team. The stadium was packed with supporters. In the second half the momentum shifted towards India and they scored 2 goals back to back. In the end we won the match by 2-1 margin and the crowd was so happy. In the end, we tried to escape from the stadium but were stuck in the crowd. There were around 30000 people who came to watch the match. I had never seen such huge crowd at one place before.

Favourite author

I like to read books in my leisure time. I won't say that I am a regular reader, but I have around ten books that are at my home and I pick them randomly when I have free time. I mostly like to read autobiographies and inspirational books.

A book that left a long-lasting impression on me is the 'Magic of thinking big' that is written by David J. Schwartz. He was an American motivational coach and writer. He published this book in the year 1959. Since then, millions of copies of this book have been sold in more than 150 countries across numerous languages.

He has written many other books but the magic of thinking big was his best-selling book across the globe. I admire him because he was a wonderful coach and a great motivational speaker. The way he has explained different things in his book is amazing.

He has covered all the aspects of life. He constantly motivates his readers to be positive in every situation. In one chapter he has described how we can achieve greatness by repeating positive words and concentrating on good rather than bad.

He constantly tells his readers to concentrate on the things you need rather than the things you want to avoid. He has written this book beautifully with tremendous amount of conviction to the readers. The language used in this book is simple, so I think that it is perfect for all age groups.

I believe that he is one of the best authors of all time. He has changed the lives of many people through his book. I gained a lot of things from his book and I recommend everyone to read this book at least once in their lifetime.

Something that you bought online

Shopping online is the leading trend these days. There are thousands of e-commerce websites from where people can buy anything from a needle to a car. The most prominent websites are Flipkart, Amazon and Myntra.

I usually buy a lot of things from these online platforms. I see a lot of people complaining about the quality and authenticity of the products, but I have never experienced any shortcoming from these websites.

Normally I buy clothes, shoes and electronic gadgets through online shopping. The recent product that I bought was an IPhone. I bought the latest model of the IPhone from Amazon.com. My experience was amazing while buying this product.

There was a sale on the website for selected customers. I participated in the sale in which a person needed to give answers to five questions that were related to the general knowledge. I gave all the answers correctly, so I was selected for a special discount on certain products.

I was given a list of products along with their maximum retail price and discount offered on them. Suddenly, my eyes were stuck on the column that read 25 percent discount on the IPhone. I was stunned to see this offer as this product is never on discount in India due to its heavy demand. I had long imagined of having an IPhone. So, I asked my father about it. He was reluctant at first but later on agreed to pay the amount for it. I quickly paid through my father's debit card and thanked him for the wonderful gift.

The delivery took around four days to reach our doorstep. I eagerly opened the package and switched on my brand-new phone. There was a congratulatory letter along with the delivery box on winning the discount competition. I felt lucky that day and thanked the website through an e-mail for their wonderful gesture.

An important city

Our country is a nation of diversities. All cities are full of multiple religions and cultures. I have visited many cities of my country. All of them have something special in it.

But, the one I like the most is Delhi. Delhi is the capital of India. This city is the most important city of our country because it is the capital of our country and has various historical and cultural remains. Various political and constitutional bodies are placed in this city which makes it the center of politics. All the decisions regarding the future of our country are made here.

Being, one of the oldest cities of India, it is equipped with great infrastructure and facilities for the people living there. The employment opportunities in this city are in huge numbers and people from every corner of India are living in Delhi to support their families.

Not only this, Delhi is the hub for various commercial, industrial, political and entertainment activities. There are various historical places to visit in this city such as Qutub Minar, India gate, Lotus temple, Humayun's tomb and many others.

The population of this city is more as compared to other cities and so is the source of income and employment opportunities. To set up any new business, people usually prefer Delhi because of such diversity and proximity to the biggest international airport of the country.

The transportation system of this city is very well managed as public transport is the major source of mobilization. Buses, metro and railways are the busiest means of transport in this city. Due to such large population, the traffic management is a bit difficult job, so metro and other mass transport systems were introduced in the city for the convenience of people.

Health care facilities in the city are excellent. Various foreign specialist doctors are also there in the hospitals of Delhi. Delhi being the national hub of the country holds the people of all states, religions and cultures together.

You were going on a tour and your vehicle broke down

I like to travel a lot with my family and friends. There have not been many instances where our vehicle broke down, but I remember one occasion when our car broke down partially.

Last year I remember an incident when we were going to Shimla with my friends on my father's car. We were four friends in total and one of my friends was driving the car. The highway to Shimla was under construction at that time.

There were some large potholes and diversions on the way to our destination. At one blind curve my friend slowed the car and turned it smoothly, but it bumped into a sharp piece of stone and we heard a loud bang from the bottom part of the car. It was like a small bomb blast.

I got panicked and immediately got out of the car and inspected the damage. We found that the radiator which is in the front of the car was punctured from bottom and it started leaking. I was afraid and thought that we have incurred a huge loss.

We had no clue about that place and didn't know of a workshop there or anyone who could help us in this regard. The nearest town was 10 kilometers away but there was a risk of engine getting seized if we would have driven without the coolant in the radiator.

But one of my friends had good knowledge of automobiles and told that if we keep the coolant level in the radiator up to the mark and drive slowly then there is no harm in driving the car until we find a workshop

So, we carefully drove the car and kept on refilling the water in the radiator from time to time and reached the town. There we found a workshop and got the car repaired. I was so relieved and after that we enjoyed our trip and came back.

A national building in your country

Our country has a rich history and there are numerous monuments and national buildings which are preserved over the years. The building that I am going to talk about is the Red Fort. It is situated in the capital of India. It used to serve as the main residence of the Mughal dynasty emperors for two centuries.

It is built in the center of the city and houses a bundle of museums. Apart from accommodating the emperors, it was a major political center of the Mughal rule. It was built over a period of 9 years. The exterior of the fort is made of red sandstone hence giving it the name, Red Fort. It is a massive structure with excessive tall walls just like any other Fort.

Its unique architectural design influenced other builders in the states of Punjab, Rajasthan, Delhi, Kashmir and elsewhere. When I went to the Red fort, I felt remarkable. Nowadays, there are several souvenir shops that are built inside the fort.

We also went to one of the museums inside and learnt about the history of the Red Fort. There is a massive flagpole which supports a gigantic Indian flag that is built at the front side of the Fort.

Every year on 15th August, our prime minister hoists the flag in front of thousands of people gathered for the Independence's day celebration. This program is also telecasted to the millions of watching at home and on this day, the prime minister delivers a speech on National harmony and peace. The fort looks magnificent from outside. There is a lot of security in and out of the Fort and I also saw a number of CCTV cameras installed in the premises of the Fort. Unfortunately, there was a terrorist attack on the Fort in the year 2000 that resulted in the death of two soldiers and one civilian.

When I visited the Red Fort, I learned a lot about its history and construction. I must give credit to the government for maintaining the cleanliness and I hope they continue to do the same in the future as well.

Favourite weather

In my country, there are basically four seasons throughout the year namely, spring, autumn, winter and summers. All the seasons have their own atmospheric conditions. People like weather as per their comfort and choice.

For me, winter is the best season as it stays for long time with low temperatures. I like cold weather than hot and humid summers. High temperature causes sweating and I don't like it as it causes various skin problems. Summer in our country is very hot and sometimes unbearable.

While, cold weather here is cold but not intolerable. Early mornings and late nights are probably cooler than the rest of the day but that is endurable to the body. Cold weather in our country starts from November and lasts till February while, December and January are the coldest months of the season.

The weather pattern changes every year as per the Himalayas atmospheric conditions. It's very cold only in few parts of the country during this time whereas many cities record pleasant weather. In my city, it is quite cold in the winter season.

I really like this season because one can have variety of hot food, drinks and get cozy in the blankets. One can even go out during the daytime as sunshine appears to be delight for the body. I love to wear jackets and scarves in this season, so it remains to be my favorite one.

I usually visit hill stations in this season to enjoy the falling snow. The snow fall makes me very excited and I love to play in the snow and make snow man.

The cold weather is very suitable to my skin and makes me extremely glad. Well, I am a great coffee lover so, I love to have a sip of coffee early in the morning in cold weather.

One thing which makes this weather difficult to bear is when it fogs. There is much fog and mist in the air during night which causes difficulty in driving and there are many cases of accidents every year due to it. Even then, I eagerly wait for this weather.

A tranquil place you enjoy going to

I am a peace-loving person. I like to visit peaceful places in my leisure time. One such place is Dagshai which is located in Himachal Pradesh. As I am a resident of Chandigarh, places in Himachal are never away. It takes about ninety minutes to reach Dagshai from where I live.

It is a cantonment (Army) area and is finely preserved by the government. This small town is situated in Solan district. It's very easy to reach there as the roads are well maintained. There are many attractions that can allure people to Dagshai.

First of all, it is famous for Dagshai public school. It is one of the best residential schools in the state. Dagshai is a very quiet town with lots of greenery. It is located on the peak of a hill, so the climate remains cooler even in the summers as compared to the plain areas.

Another thing that this place is famous for is the graveyard. There is an old graveyard where solders from world war 1 and world war 2 are cremated. The graveyard is located in the south side of the town and is visited by limited people. Thus, making it a very peaceful place.

Apart from this, there is a Dagshai jail that was built in the nineteenth century by the Britishers. That jail is preserved nicely and is converted into a museum for the visitors to see. That jail has been recreated in the same way it was in the bygone era.

At the corner of the town, there is a football field that is built at the top of another hill. From there one can see great views of the valley. I have met many locals and felt they were very humble in nature. I go there at least 8 or 9 times in a year, and I find eternal bliss and tranquility.

Sometimes I just go there to relax my mind and to get positive vibes. I always feel peace at body and mind when I go there.

A foreign dish you want to eat

I am not a foodie, but I like to try new dishes and cuisines whenever I get chance. I have never visited a foreign country, but I have tried a lot of foreign dishes that are available in my country. I have had a chance to eat most of the famous dishes from around the globe but there's one dish which I haven't eaten yet.

The name of the dish is Panini. I came to know about this dish from TV. I was watching a travel program and the host was praising this dish. It is one of the most common dishes in Italy. Many people eat it on daily basis.

It's an Italian dish that is primarily made of Italian bread and stuffing. I have not seen any of the restaurants in India that are offering authentic Panini dishes. It's my dream to visit Italy one day and eat a traditional Panini.

Panini in Italian means small bread or bread rolls. It is basically a sandwich that is usually served warm by grilling or toasting it. Panini is not sliced sandwich, rather it is filled with some ingredients. The filling can range from meat, beef, chicken, fish, cheese or vegetables.

I like the cheese Panini. This type of bread is generally filled with different vegetables along with mozzarella and cheddar cheese. After filling up the fresh bread with all the stuff, the bread is grilled and warmed to an optimum temperature.

Panini can be served with a lot of side dishes. I like potato fries and coleslaw with it. I have seen a couple of restaurants serving Panini, but I feel that it is nowhere near the traditional Panini that is found in Italy.

If I am given a chance to eat a foreign dish, then I would definitely go to Italy and eat cheese Panini.

Any recent change or development in your hometown

I live in Chandigarh. It is one of the most livable cities in my country. It is neat and clean. There are numerous parks and facilities that makes the life of people easy. On the other hand, there are not many public transportation facilities in our city because people like to use personal vehicles to commute from one place to the other.

There have been huge developments in every corner of my hometown in the recent years. The most commendable is the construction of cycle tracks along the roads of the city.

This has been undoubtedly the best addition to the city's list of achievement. Everyone is praising this effort from the government. Not only the main roads but all the link roads and the city roads have been added with this facility.

This is a great bonus for people who like to do cycling and for people who use cycle as their main mode of transport. I think it is now safer for those who use cycles. I see that school kids are the ones who have benefitted the most due to this wonderful step.

The cycle tracks are wide enough for more than two cyclists to pass by parallelly. The tracks have been carved alongside the roads by acquiring the open spaces on the sides of the roads. There were some places which had no room to make tracks. Instead of leaving the thought of making the tracks there, the government instead shortened the width of road a bit to accommodate cycle tracks.

Most of the tracks have been marked in blue colour and the crossings with red colour. This is done so that the car drivers can easily see the tracks and make way for cyclists when required.

This shows that how serious was government on this issue. I thank the local authority for such great step and expect same type of attitude in development in future as well.

A musical instrument you like to play

Music is one of the most beautiful things in life. It creates a wonderful feeling inside a person. People listen to music to calm their nerves. Some even say that music can heal mental issues. I like to listen to music in my free time or whenever I am feeling anxious.

I have dreamt of playing a musical instrument since my childhood, but I have not been able to achieve this dream till now. Nevertheless, I had joined guitar classes last year. For that I also bought a guitar. I enrolled in a musical institute nearby my house for a month's basic course.

During that period, I was also busy in my studies so I could not go to the class regularly. However, I learned a few tips to keep in mind while playing guitar. I learned how to hold it first and how different strings are to be treated differently.

There are many aspects that must be taken care while playing this instrument. I learned a couple of chapters and after that I did not go to the classes for a week. At the time of joining, I had bought myself a basic medium sized guitar.

This type of guitar is best suited to the people who are learning this art for the first time. Although I left the classes midway, but I kept on practicing the basics at my home. I downloaded a couple of video tutorials from a website and start spending some time in learning it.

It is difficult to learn anything on your own, but those lessons were quite helpful and simple due to which I could play the guitar. That practice helped me to learn the basics of guitar. I am not a perfectionist, but I can play a bit of it.

So, whenever I am free or I am feeling stressed, I just take out my guitar from the bag and play some songs and tunes that sooth my mind. Playing this instrument gives me immense satisfaction and it also rejuvenates my mind.

A historical building you have visited

I am very fond of visiting historical places. I have seen numerous buildings that hold great significance in our history and culture. I recently visited one building that is located in Jaipur, Rajasthan. It is a palace that was built in 1799.

The name of this historical building is Hawa Mahal. This name translates to Palace of the Breeze in English. This historical landmark was constructed primarily of red and pink sandstone. This palace is located on the edge of the City Palace.

This palace was built by Maharaja Sawai Partap Singh and was designed by Lal Chand Ustad. It has five stories that resembles a honeycomb. The windows of the palace are decorated by superb work of art. This building was designed in such a way that more air can pass through it in a way that it remains cooler than rest of the things in surrounding places even in summers.

When you enter the building, you can see fountains in the center of each chamber which further on helps in the cooling effect. The entry of the palace is from the side where City palace is located. The huge door of Hawa Mahal opens into a huge courtyard. There are doubled storied buildings on the three sides of the courtyard.

There is an archeological museum in the yard. The Hawa Mahal is built on the eastern side of the premises. This place was the favourite resort location for the previous emperors as Jaipur gets really hot during summers and this palace could provide the perfect stay.

Now this building has been turned into a historical museum that is open for the people to see. The entry ticket to this palace is of nominal cost. Hawa Mahal is one of the most interesting historical buildings that I have seen.

A speech you heard recently

There have been a lot of speeches, talks and lectures that I have heard since my childhood. Today I would like to tell you about a speech that inspired me to do well in my life. I can't forget that speech as it still echoes in my mind.

This speech was delivered by the honorable Prime minister of India, Mr. Narendra Modi. He never uses slips or premade notes in his speeches. So, I feel that the talk comes directly from his heart.

One such speech that left a long-lasting impression on me was the speech that he delivered when he became the Prime minister for the second time in 2019. Naturally he was elated by the landslide victory over his opponents, he could not hide his happiness in that speech.

He thanked everyone who voted for him and who gave him a chance to serve the nation second time in a row. He spoke about the things that he fulfilled in the first term and talked about the things that he was not able to do. He was very confident of the fact that we are in the race of becoming a country with all the facilities and safety. He also guaranteed that he will control inflation.

He promised that he will fulfill all the promises of the manifesto and will take our country to new heights by his leadership. He also assured that minorities of this county should feel safe as he will be intolerant against any kind of crime against minorities.

When he speaks, he connects with the people. He is from a humble background but has reached the pinnacle of politics. He has a wonderful way of presenting things through his speech. He has also influenced the youth of the country to do well.

What kind of job you would like to do in future?

Everyone wishes to have a dream job in their lives, some get it, and some don't. I have made a checklist of the things that my dream job would provide.

I think that there are number of things that I would want from my job. First of all, my job should be highly paid because only highly paid jobs can give satisfaction of work. I reckon that high pay will also make me feel secure in this expensive era. I would like to earn anything between 50 to 60 lacs a year.

The second thing that comes to my mind is the timings of the job. Work is only a part of life, so it should be treated like that only. Work is not life, there are several other aspects of life that needs to be addressed like family and friends. So, I guess that I should work anywhere between 7 to 8 hours, not more than that.

I am a travel freak so I think that my job should be related to that. I would love to work in tourism industry where I can get a chance to see the world. I want a job that allows me to grow as a person. Travelling is one activity that makes a person smart and sharp.

Apart from this, I want an appraisal system in which salary would increase every 6 months by at least 15 percent. The increase should depend on the quality of work I deliver. I would like to work in an environment where everyone encourages each other, and the team members respect each other's opinion.

Lastly, I would like to have a decent boss who is encouraging and polite. I will not work to impress him rather I would work for the company and betterment of the quality of whatever we deliver.

So, these are the things that I am looking for myself in a future job. I hope that I get this kind of a dream job.

A prize/award you want to win

I have dreamt of winning a number of prizes in my life but there's one that I have long tried but could not win. I would still like to win that prize if I am qualified to take part in it.

I am talking about the Cadbury Bournvita Quiz Contest that began in the year 1972 and was sponsored by Cadbury, India. This show is one of the most famous quiz TV shows in India. This show is witnessed by huge audience in our country. Through this show, one can learn numerous things about the history of our country and about the science and technology.

Previously it was conducted live in different cities across the country but later it became a radio show. Eventually in the year 1992, this show was telecasted on television for the first time on Zee TV channel. In this show, the host asks some questions regarding different fields to students one by one. Children with most correct questions are qualified for the next round. This show was last hosted on colors TV. In this, students from across the country participate in a round robin of quiz contest. Then the winners

109

move to the advanced rounds where they face other winners in knockout rounds. From there the losers are eliminated and the last standing team wins the competition.

The number of members in team are two or three, depending upon the format of the quiz and episode. Most part of the show was hosted by one of the famous personalities in India, Derek O'Brien. To be eligible to take part in this competition, the teams from the quiz show pick most awarded students in reputed schools across India.

Children who take part in the show must be able to present themselves clearly in Hindi or English. All the contestants who reach the finals on national level, are presented with an iPad along with some gifts from Cadbury.

This show is amazing as it gives you a platform on national level. I tried hard in my school time but could not get an entry in the show but if I am given a chance, I would try my best to win this prize.

What will you do if you win a huge sum of money?

I would like to thank God if I win a huge sum of money. I have a lot of dreams to full fill. First, I would like to make a written plan about spending my money.

My biggest dream in life is to travel the world so I would keep a chunk of money for that sake in a separate account. After keeping that money, I would like to offer some of the cash to my parents so that they can wave off any liabilities that they have.

After that, I will give some portion of money to my sister/brother. He/she is very fond of shopping so I think that it will be a great idea to give some money to him/her.

After distributing money to my family members, I will start spending money for my requirements. The first thing I would like to buy is a car for myself. I will buy Toyota Fortuner as it's a muscular car. I am in love with that car since I drove it for the first time.

Then, I will look to buy a new duplex house. I am very fond of this type of house. I would like to choose a house in a posh area. Next, I will I invest some money in mutual funds in which I can get good returns.

After distributing the cash and spending money on all these things, I will buy flight tickets to Singapore from there I will board the cruise ship that travels all over the world in 4 months.

This is the dream from my childhood and would like to achieve it if I get a lot of money.

An occasion where you arrived late

Generally, I am a punctual person and like to be on time for my appointments and meetings with friends and family. But I can remember an occasion when I arrived late, and I was embarrassed for that. Last year, I was scheduled to go to Goa for a destination wedding of my cousin. Me and my family members packed the bags in excitement as we received all the tickets of flight and hotel bookings sponsored by my Uncle.

There were two functions that were planned, the first one was the engagement and the second one was the main wedding function. We were supposed to reach there on 1st of December to attend both the functions on 2nd and 3rd December. Our flight was in the morning from Delhi airport as I live in Chandigarh and Delhi airport is the nearest one from where we can get a direct flight to Goa. When we got the boarding pass from the ticket counter, it was announced that the flight will be delayed due to heavy fog and extreme weather.

We were very nervous as we had to reach there on time as all our relatives had already reached there and we were still at the airport. The flight got delayed by almost 24 hours as all the flights from Delhi airport were cancelled on that day. When we reached there the functions had already begun and we were feeling guilty. We told the whole story to my uncle. He was supportive and told us to not to bother about reaching late and told us to enjoy the rest of the functions.

Speak about a time when you participated in a competition

I wasn't great at co-curricular activities in my school time, but I always participated in cricket and activities associated to it. I remember once in my tenth class I got a chance to participate in a cricket competition.

This tournament was on national level that was conducted for tenth class school students. Schools from all over India partook in that tournament. There were around 100 schools that participated in that competition.

I remember that how I was selected for this elite competition. Best cricket players from schools were told to assemble in the school ground. There we went under trials in which we were given a chance to show our skills with the bat and ball.

I was selected along with 16 other players. After a few days of practice at school, we left for Delhi to play in the tournament. There we were provided with kits and other amenities. We stayed at a hotel that was sponsored by the organizers.

This was a knockout tournament in which a team would be eliminated as soon as it loses. We had to play five matches before we could reach the finals. We won all the matches and the mood in our camp was exuberant. The final was to be played on Sunday. Due to this, there was a huge crowd that came there to cheer us and to witness that game.

The number of overs for each side was 15 in the initial stages but it was increased to 20 for the finals. However, that day, there were a bit of clouds and the field was also wet due to early morning rain showers. So, the match started late, and it was reduced to 10 overs each side.

It was not a great day as we lost the finals, but we were still contended that we won the runners-up trophy from over 100 schools. When we came back to the school next day, we were awarded some cash and all the students welcomed us with a lot of warmth and respect.

An animal you like the most

I am a huge animal lover. I like all animals and I frequently visit zoos to explore different kinds of animals and see their behavior.

I am fascinated by zebra because of its striking looks. I also like camels due to their distinctive body structure but my favourite one is cow. Its nature is not aggressive. It is a friendly animal and seldom attacks humans. They are of different varieties, sizes and colors of cows in India.

Cow is given the designation of a mother in our society. It is considered as a sacred animal. Most people in my country worship cow. People feed special food items to cows on special occasions and festivals.

The reason it is given the designation of a mother is that it gives us milk. Its milk is digestive and is full of calcium and essential nutrients. There is a yellow tinge in the color of the cow's milk.

Most farmers in our country keep cows for milk and other purposes. Cow's dung is another useful product that is used as a fuel. People burn traditional clay style ovens by using cow dung. You will be surprised to know that after cow's death, it is left for the hungry birds to be eaten up and decay. After that the skeleton is bought by pharmaceutical industries as they use it to make some of the medical products.

There are many cow shelters around our country where cows are taken care of and they are fed with proper food. Government has taken a lot of initiatives to protect cows as cow killing in our county is illegal.

Some people also drink cow urine as they believe it cures a lot of diseases and keeps a person fit. Cow is a tremendously useful and loving animal. So, I like it very much.

A bird you like

I am a nature lover. I like to go out in the woods and witness flora and fauna. I have seen so many different species of animals and birds there. I like birds for their ability to fly. I always wanted to be like birds, I desire to fly like them.

I like pigeon the most. They are firm-bodied birds with dwarf neck. Their main source of food is seeds, fruits and plants. Pigeons and doves come from the family Columbidae. They are the most common birds in the world. They are found in all the continents and possibly in all the countries of the world.

Dove is generally referred to pigeon that is white or nearly white. In scientific world, dove is used for the smaller species and pigeon for the larger one. Pigeon is a French word and dove is a Germanic word. Pigeons build relatively fragile nests, often using twigs and other wreckage.

Unlike other birds, both sexes of pigeons produce milk that is fed to the young ones. They have short legs, small heads on large and firm body. The wings are large in size and has eleven main feathers. The muscle of the wings is also strong that comprises of 35 to 45 percent of their total body weight.

Body feathers are very dense and with large wings they can maneuver themselves easily in the flight. They can launch quickly and have the ability to escape from predators. Pigeons have a knack of remembering the paths of flight.

For this reason, they were used by the Australian, French, German, American and UK forces at the time of world war 1 and 2 to deliver sensitive messages and vital plans to Allied forces on the borders of Germany.

All the information that I have told you has been learned by me from a book that I read about the pigeons.

A language you would like to learn (apart from English)

Language is a way to communicate our feelings with others through words, certain noises and pauses. There are thousands of languages that are spoken across the globe.

Some are prominent like Chinese, French and Portuguese. There are some languages that which are spoken by old tribes or by a handful of people and are not known to general public.

If given a chance or if I have enough time, then I am prepared to learn Spanish. I am inclined towards that language since I saw one of the most prominent sitcoms, Narcos.

This series was about the drug menace in Columbia and this series was made in Spanish with English subtitles. I watched the first episode and after that I could not stop myself. After I completed watching the series, I promised myself that one day I will learn this language fluently.

That day, I logged into my you tube account and downloaded a couple of Spanish lessons by Spanish teachers with English explanations. I learned it for three or four days but could not learn further because of my daily routine and busy schedule.

Although I learned some common phrases and some greeting words in Spanish. For example, Hola is hello and adios is bye. I also learnt that gracias is thank you.

I am still in a mood to learn this language as it really excites me. The tone and words allure me instantly. I regularly watch movies made in Spanish and some Spanish sitcoms as well in order to learn the language.

I have also downloaded a mobile application by the name of duo lingo which helps to learn any language on the go, without any books or notes. So, I can easily say that whenever I get a chance, I would like to learn Spanish from an adroit.

A game you played in your childhood

Childhood is a great time in which most of the kids are involved in playing hundreds of games. I was no different. I played all the games that were popular at that time.

The one which I played regularly with my friends was Mario. It is a video game which is produced by Nintendo and was invented in the 80s. This game took over the world by storm as everyone was indulged in playing it. I remember when I cleared my fourth standard exams, I demanded a video game console and Mario game cassette from my parents. My father was kind enough to fulfil my demand and I remember that we bought it on my birthday which falls in April.

I was so excited as I unwrapped the box of the game. My father helped me in installing the game and taught me to do that. Once it was installed, I played it for more than six hours that day.

I played this game mostly in the summer holidays and not on the normal days. I was not allowed by my father to play this game on daily basis. Games can be very addictive, and I remember that three of my other friends use to come to my house in the morning and leave in the evening after playing the game.

Mario is made in such a way that you must clear all the stages in order to win and complete the game. In this game there are several stages that you need to clear and reach the last stage where you save the princess from the evil dragon.

Every day we played that game for more than six hours. We played in a team and helped each other to clear the levels. Playing this game also created a special bond between us.

Exercise people do in your locality

Exercise is an essential part of our life. People do exercise in order to keep themselves fit. There are various exercises that people do according to

115

their choice and age. I have seen a lot of people of all age groups do exercise in my area.

I usually get up early in the morning and like to go out for a short walk. I always see people do different exercises in the morning. The most common is yoga. I live in a society that has a big park and it is well utilized by the people of my area.

Every day in the morning, generally people of middle and older age gather in one corner of the park and do yoga. Yoga is one of the most common type of early morning activity that people of my country do.

I also see many people running and jogging. I think this is the best exercise to keep yourself fit. There is a running track in the park which people like to use for running. I see people wearing sports shoes and fitness watch when they do exercise.

People also like to do cycling as a part of their exercise. Myriad people burn their calories through cycling. This type of activities is generally preferred by the youngsters.

On the other hand, some old people do only walk and light exercises. They also participate in laughing exercise. In this, a group of people gather, and they laugh out loud for around 10 minutes. It is said that this activity increases the flow of blood through the body.

I think exercise should be a mandatory part of a person's life and I also reckon that people have become more aware about their health these days, that's why they do exercise.

Anything you would like to buy from foreign country

I am the kind of a person who likes to shop a lot. I like to buy unique things that gives me satisfaction. If I am given a chance to buy something from a foreign country, then it would be white coffee from Malaysia.

The first time when I tasted this coffee was last year when one of my aunts brought it from Malaysia. I fell in love with this coffee when I drank it for the first time. It was so delicious that I instantly asked for more of it.

She said that all her coffee was now finished, and this was the last sachet that she had given me. I was so disappointed and asked whether she can arrange more in the future. She assured me that she would try her best.

My aunt's sister lives in Malaysia, so she called her to ask about that coffee. Her sister told her that she would send it next week through courier. She kept her promise and I received that coffee in a couple of weeks.

I am addicted to this coffee and I drink it every day. The coffee brand is OLD TOWN and the type is white coffee. The price is also not that high, but the thing is that it is only available in Malaysia and a couple of other countries. If I go to Malaysia one day, then I will bring tons of this coffee with me.

This coffee is so simple to make. You just need to boil water and empty the sachet into it. The premixed powder contains coffee, sugar and powdered milk. Just stir it well and enjoy your coffee.

If I have to buy something from a foreign country, then it would definitely be white coffee from Malaysia.

A season you like the most

I live in the northern part of India and I am lucky to experience most kinds of seasons that the Earth has to offer. Winter, summer, autumn, spring and monsoon. I enjoy all the seasons, but the most favorites ones are when the main seasons are in transition.

I like autumn the most. India is located in the Northern hemisphere, so this season starts in September and ends in December. The reason I like this time of the year is that it is neither too cold nor so hot. It is a part of temperate season.

This season is also known as fall in some parts of the world. Autumn marks the progression from summers to winter. At this time, the length of day starts to decrease, and the temperature starts to fall as compared to the summer season.

I feel very happy in the autumn season as summers can be really hot and winters restricts some outdoor activities. In summers, people generally don't roam in the day as its too hot. But in the autumn season, there's no such problem. Another advantage of autumn season is that there is reduced amount of energy utilized for heating and air conditioning.

I prefer spending more time outdoors in this season as there is perfect amount of sunlight along with moderate temperature. I can also have my favourite cold drinks as the weather is neither too cold nor too hot. This is the best time to do exercise in the morning as well as in the evening as there is always some cool breeze.

The day temperature is not that cold but it's not as hot as summers. On the other hand, nights are cooler with a bit of gust. I don't like hot weather or too cold days. So, if I am asked about a wish to be fulfilled, then I would like to have autumn weather all year round.

How's the climate of your country

India is a huge country and the climate varies from place to place. I am fortunate enough to have travelled in my county a bit and experience different climates.

The southern and western side of my county doesn't have a winter climate. The climate generally there is hot and humid. The southern part of India is mostly coastal area which has similar kind of a climate all year round.

Although there is more rain in the month of July and August. The rainfall drops from December to April. The central part of south is a bit cooler than the east and west. Bengaluru is a perfect example of that. Temperatures are very much bearable in Bengaluru all year round.

If we go to the eastern side, the winters are cold, and some parts also experience snow fall. Far east has a great climate all year round. The temperature there doesn't go beyond 30 degrees. Eastern part of India is also very green and clean. There is a huge amount of rainfall throughout the year in the eastern part of India.

The hottest climate is on the western side of the country. States such as Rajasthan experiences extreme hot climates during most part of the year. It is mainly a desert area with very low amount of rainfall.

If I talk about the northern side, I have to say that it experiences every kind of climate. December to February is very cold with temperatures getting as low as 0 degrees in winters. Summers can be as hot as any place in the world. The extreme temperatures of June can reach up to 47-48 degrees. July and August are the monsoon seasons in which there is a relief from the scorching heat.

I believe that India experiences all sorts of climates that are known to be present and I think that one can visit different places in India to experience different weathers.

A time when someone helped you

There have been many situations in my life when I was helped by other people. One such instance happened in my life when I passed 12th class. I did my senior secondary in medical / non-medical / commerce ....
After I gave the final exams of 12th class I was waiting for the results. I expected to score around 80 percent aggregate in that. After the result was declared, I got 77 percent. I was disappointed as I predicted a better score.

After I got my result, I was in a dilemma weather to choose a degree program or to go for a more practical kind of a course. I believe that passing the secondary and choosing the right course after that is one of the most important tasks in one's career. I was so bamboozled that I could not make my mind whether to go for Indian college or to study in a foreign university.

If you go for the wrong course or the college, it can have a detrimental effect on your future. I believe it is good to take some advice from a senior teacher, friend or a relative to get some information regarding suitable course.

I did not go to any educational counsellor or free-lance advisor. I told my plight to my cousin and sought out advice on my career options. I went to my cousin for advice because she is very successful in her field. So, I thought that she would be the person to get guidance on my forthcoming development.

She explained me to study in a foreign university or college. She cited the reason that Canadian education is much better than most countries in the world. She also emphasized the fact that I will get more exposure while living in a foreign environment. She continued and said studying in an international environment would get the best out of me.

After the meeting, I was so determined that I went to an educational consultant to decide the course and college for Canada. They suggested me to take the IELTS exam and score 6.5 Band overall. I feel that she helped me in a great way as I was not able to decide about my future and I was also getting frustrated day by day. She came to my rescue and steered me towards a goal.

So, this was the time when I was helped by someone and I will always be grateful to her for this help.

A quality that you appreciate about your friend

I don't have a lot of friends but there are a few whom I love very much. I would like to speak about a friend who has tremendous qualities. His name is Amit and he lives in the United Kingdom these days.

I remember when we became friends in our school time. We were studying together since childhood but became good friends in the 10th standard. We used to sit on the same bench, and we shared a lot of things in common.

If I talk about his qualities, then I would have to write a big essay on that. The quality that I admired in him the most is his patience. He is a very patient person and remains cool in all the situations. He's never too excited about anything nor he is nervous in troubling situations.

He is a great friend and keeps his calm in every aspect of life. I will give you an example of his patience. Once our school bus was struck in a traffic jam and everyone was getting annoyed by that. We were having an exam on that day and everyone was praying for the jam to get cleared.

On the other hand, Amit was as cool as ice and was studying a book rather than worrying like others. I asked him that why he's not getting annoyed. He replied that I never worry about the things that are beyond my control.

I was taken aback by his patience and learned something very interesting from him. From that day onwards I try to inculcate this quality in me as I feel that a calm person can win in every situation. We all were worried that day, but my dear friend utilized that time to study. He converted that worry time into study time.

So, this is the quality that my friend possesses, and I feel that this makes him stand out from others.

Describe a time when you complained about something

I am the kind of a person who doesn't complain much until the water goes over the nose. There have been some occasions when I complained about certain things in my life. The one which I remember vividly happened recently. I went to a restaurant and was highly unsatisfied.

Last month, me and my family members went to a restaurant on Sunday. The restaurant is nearby and the quality of food they serve is generally great. This restaurant is one of the most renowned restaurants in the city. It is a buffet style restaurant with a wide variety of options in cuisines. That day was a holiday and the restaurant was packed with people. The moment we reached there, the staff was bamboozled and took a long time to even prepare our tables. The preparation was so wicked that they did not even provided all the cutlery on the table.

Then the snacks were served in a haste. All the snacks were cold, and the taste was not up to the mark. After the snacks were over, we went on to take the main course. There were no plates on the station to take food. I was so frustrated with this thing and called a waiter and complained about the situation.

He replied in a rude manner, so I decided to complain to the manager of the restaurant. The manager was kind enough to note down my complaint and give me assurance that this kind of situation will not arise in the future.

He also waived off the food bill as we were not served with all the food items in the main course and the snacks as well. So, this was the time when I complained about something and I felt that my grievance was taken seriously and worked upon immediately.

Describe a skill that takes a long time to learn

There are many things that are difficult to learn in life for most of the folks. I have tried my hands on a number of things, but I failed or quit doing it. Once, I took up guitar classes but after a while I thought that it's too difficult to learn. Similarly, there are many skills that most individuals find hard to acquire.

In my perception, the most problematic skill to learn is the art of public speaking. I reckon that this skill requires great practice and discipline to master. I have seen most of the students these days find it difficult to speak in front of a group of people.

There are many reasons behind that. The first one is that the group speaking requires a lot of confidence and courage. To be able to speak in front of more than ten or twenty people is not a cakewalk for the majority of public these days.

This skill can't be learned in a day or two. There's no book that you can cram to become a good speaker. It requires hours and hours of practice every day. One needs to be determined to learn the art of public speaking. I have seen a lot of people standing in front of a mirror and practicing their speaking skills.

This skill is the most urgent requirement for the youngsters of today. I think that this skill can take a person to great heights. You can see everywhere in the world that most of the celebrities and famous personalities will inevitably be good speakers.

So, I ponder that learning the skill of public speaking is one of the most difficult skills to learn for anyone.

Special date in your country's history / describe a significant historical event in your country

There have been hundreds of historical events and special dates that have taken place in the past in our country. We have learned a lot of things from these events and noteworthy dates.

One of the special dates for all the people in our country is 15th August 1947. On this day, our country was freed from the Britishers after they ruled this country for more than 150 years. This event of independence brought smiles to all the people of India. This event made every Indian proud and filled their hearts with joy.

Indians over the years suffered many obstacles under the imperial rule of the Britishers. Many historical movements started and ended in tragedy. Numerous freedom fighters were martyred and killed in abundance. There were huge and regular protests that were held against the British rule for many years. Most of the freedom fighters were imprisoned and killed. People feared speaking against the government.

But persistent protests and certain policies by the Indian political parties and efforts of freedom fighters led to the independence of India and forced the British rulers to leave the country. This news of independence spread like a wildfire and people felt that they now have the freedom to live and work in their own country.

One unfortunate thing happened in the process. Our country was divided, and a new nation Pakistan was born. It led to numerous riots and killing on both sides. An estimated a million people lost their lives in India as well as in Pakistan.

Today, this day is celebrated with great joy all over India. Parades take place in the capital of India. Prime minister of our country delivers speech on this day mainly highlighting the achievements of the past year.

I think that this event and date is carved in our hearts forever. This is simply the most unforgettable date of our country.

Remote place you wish to visit in the future

There are many places that I want to visit in my lifetime. I love to travel to new destinations and I always prefer to travel to faraway places with a lot of peace and silence.

A remote place that I would like to visit is Chail. It is located in Himachal Pradesh and is one of the greener and cleanest places in that state. I have heard from many people that Chail is very remote and the town is located in the middle of a wildlife sanctuary.

I have searched on the internet about the things to see in Chail. There is a King's palace which is now an expensive hotel and a site for the visitors. It was home to Maharaja of Patiala in the past. The entry fee to the palace is only 100 rupees per person. The palace is made in Imperial style with a huge lawn in front of it.

The main city of Chail doesn't have all the amenities but is one of the most peaceful places. Not a lot of tourists go there even in the peak season. I guess everyone these days like hustle and bustle. But I am not one of them, I like tranquil places like Chail.

Chail is located at a height of 2300 meters which is good enough to keep the weather cool even in the harshest of summers. It is away from the chaos of big cities. One can hardly hear any horns blown or vehicular noise. There is no pollution at that place. I have been to Chail once in my life and I plan to visit in future as well. When I went there for the first time, I hiked the mountains and felt very close to the nature. I recommend everyone to visit this place at least once in life.

Describe a shop that recently opened in your locality/city

I live in Chandigarh and I see a lot of shops that are opening nowadays. There are many local markets near the place where I live. Mostly there are grocery shops and some for clothes, electronic gadgets, etc.

Lately, a new shop was inaugurated in the main area of the city. The shop's name is Weekend Mart. It's a grocery shop that has its chain all over the country. It is one of the renowned grocery stores across India. This shop is a great place for daily needs shopping.

This store is located very near, and I came to know about its existence from a leaflet that I found at the entrance door of my house. One evening I got out of my house and found that leaflet lying near the door. It was a flashy page giving details about the shop opening and discount offers that will be available on certain products.

The opening date was 1st January 2020. I told my mother about this and we decided to go there in the evening. When we reached there, I saw huge number of people in that store as if the grocery store was distributing free food, but this was not the case.

There were huge discounts on most of the items. So, we bought many things that day. It took us around two hours to collect the items and one hour for the billing itself. That day we got massive concessions on the items that are otherwise expensive.

The store was very well organized, and one could actually witness the great variety that they had. The store size is very big, and the staff is amazing. From the past few months, this store has become the landmark of that area.

Describe an invention that has changed the life of people

There are numerous inventions that has changed people's life for betterment. Discoveries such as mobiles and computers have changed the way people live their lives. I reckon that mobile phone is the biggest invention by mankind.

Mobile phones have brought a revolution in the whole world. Mobile phones of this generation can do multiple tasks at one time. Smart phones have taken over a lot of other gadgets.

People used to carry a camera with them on the excursions but with the advent of mobile phones, there is no need to carry an extra device. Smart phones can click wonderful pictures with great clarity as equivalent to the professional cameras.

One can also tune into radio with the help of mobiles. A mobile of this era can be used as a recorder. One can send an email, or you can also download a song from the internet. Mobiles can also be used as a hot spot to run internet on other devices.

Certain mobile phones can also be used as universal remotes for a lot of other electronic devices. People also use it to play games. There is no need to have a separate music system when you have a mobile phone. A mobile phone can store thousands of songs and hundreds of movies.

People can also watch movies and any sort of videos on mobile phones. There are certain applications that help people to run live channels and live stream videos on mobile phones. I think that mobiles have taken over a lot of other things and in future there will be more functions in it that are still unimaginable.

There are unlimited purposes of mobile phone that makes it a unique device that has changed the world in a better way.

Describe a nation (not your own) that you know well

I like to surf the internet a lot and I usually search different cities and places around the world. I have a knack of learning about the places that I would like to visit in my future.

One such country is Malaysia. I love this country very much. I have searched about the culture of that place and I find it really alluring. It is a country in the south-eastern side of the globe. It borders with Singapore and Thailand.

People of that country speaks Malay which is their mother tongue. They also speak good English as it is a compulsion in their primary and secondary education. The capital of Malaysia is Kuala Lumpur. It is a metropolitan city with different cultures and people from all over the globe living together.

Kuala Lumpur is also known by the name KL. People of Malaysia are very humble and helpful. One of my relatives is also living in KL. I have heard a lot of things from them. Kuala Lumpur is known for Petronas twin towers which are the tallest twin towers in the world.

There are many other cities that are famous for its culture and heritage. George Town and Melaka are well-known for its preserved heritage and culture. Both the cities are declared as the UNESCO world heritage sites. Malaysia has many towns that are located in the highlands and many other that are on the seashore. Rice is the staple food in Malaysia and Nasi Lemak is the most common meal there. Nasi Lemak is basically rice cooked in coconut milk with spicy curry.

Malaysia is also famous for its rubber production. The quality of Malaysian rubber is the finest. Malaysia also deals in the trade of timber. Malaysian wood is one of the best in the world and is found in abundance in the southern part of the country. Other famous product of this country is Batik silk. Moreover, some parts are famous for its tea and coffee plantation.

I have read a lot about Malaysia and if I am given a chance, I would definitely like to visit it as soon as possible.

Describe an outdoor activity that you did for the first time

There are many activities that a person does for the first time. One activity that was outdoor and I did it for the first time was snorkeling. It is an activity in which one goes to a shallow water body, mostly a sea or a lagoon to explore the marine life.

I did this activity in Andaman and Nicobar Islands. I went there with my family members. We stayed in the capital city of port Blair. From there we went to Havelock island. This island is surrounded by the Bay of Bengal and the Indian ocean. There are many beaches around this island.

We came to know about this activity from one of our guides. He told us that Havelock islands is famous for Snorkeling and Scuba diving. I opted for snorkeling as I have a fear of water and in scuba you have to go deep into the water using oxygen cylinders and a lot of other equipment.

In snorkeling you just need to put a face mask having a pipe on it for breathing through mouth. All my family members got ready to do this activity. I was very excited for that, but I was a bit nervous as well. You can also do this activity even if you don't know swimming. This activity is done in the presence of experts and safety jackets are also provided during snorkeling.

This activity lasted for one full hour. We saw coral reefs around the island and a lot of other marine species that I could never imagine seeing in my life. We covered a lot of area while snorkeling. The sea water was crystal clear which allowed us to see many things underneath. The total experience was unique and exciting.

I was so happy after doing that activity as it gave me a lot of relief and mental satisfaction.

A time you had to search for information

I like to search for any kind of information from the internet. I think internet has been a revolution in the past few years and has enable people to learn about anything in this world. whenever I get some free time, I like to browse for information.

Last time when I had to turn up to internet for info was previous month. Actually, I had to plan a holiday destination for me and my family. I know about certain places in our country that are amazing, but I wanted to go to a new place this time.

I have been to Goa and Jaipur before and I did not want to repeat those locations for holidays. I started searching for some new destinations that are untouched and remote. So, I just opened my laptop and clicked on to the google browser. I typed tourist destinations in India. It showed a list of the prominent and common places, but I wanted something different. Thus, I added uncommon places to my search.

I got a list of so many places that I had never even heard of before. I was shocked to see some places that were totally unexplored. I browsed all the destinations in detail and chose five of them. I showed those places to my family members and we chose one unanimously.

The location was Palampur. It is situated in the northern part of our county in the state of Himachal Pradesh. It is a quiet place with a lot of Tea farms.

Palampur is known for its world-famous tea plantation. I also came to know from the internet that it one of the wettest areas in our country. It receives highest amount of rainfall throughout the state of Himachal Pradesh.

It is a great place to relax. I read a lot of articles about Palampur and came to know that this place is one of the greenest and cleanest places in our country. I also inquired about the temperatures throughout the year in Palampur from the internet. In extreme summers, the temperature doesn't go beyond 30 degrees.

I also came to know from the internet that there is a huge tea producing factory that lies in the middle of the town. There, one can find huge variety of tea and can also buy it at a reasonable price.

After getting so much of information about this place on the internet, I quickly booked the rooms in a hotel for four people and stayed there for 3 days. It was a great visit and the information that I searched on the internet helped me a lot.

Describe a building /structure in your city

I live in Chandigarh which is located in the northern part of the country. It is one of the greenest cities across India. More than 9 percent of the city area is covered in forest. Not only this, Chandigarh is a fast-developing city in our country with growing infrastructure and ever-increasing modern facilities.

The building that I want to talk about is the Secretariat building which is located in sector 1. It was designed by the famous French architect Le Corbusier. It is a government premises that includes three buildings and three monuments.

The buildings are secretariat building, Legislative assembly building and the High court building. The monuments are open hand monument, geometric hill and the tower of shadows. This is a huge complex and probably the biggest in city. It was built in the year 1953. In July 2016, this building was inscribed as UNESCO world heritage site.

This complex has the courts, offices and assemblies of both Punjab and Haryana. This building is very well maintained and has unending sections. I remember when I visited this building with my uncle. One of his friends was working over there and he invited us to see the building on my request.

When we entered the building, just outside the entrance there were hundreds of security personnel and policemen who were patrolling the area. We were checked with metal detectors and other equipment for any objectionable material with us. The high security is there because a lot of ministers and VIP's are always present there.

There is a huge canteen in the middle of the complex and there are more than twelve floors that are packed with different departments and offices. My uncle's friend works in the courts and he took us to a small tour. I was so impressed with the security and the system that government has maintained there.

The structure of that building from outside is huge. This building looks majestic in style. It is very unique in architecture as I have never seen a similar sort of building. The colour of the building from outside is light tan. I felt so tired after we finished our tour of the building.

It was a tremendous visit and I feel that Secretariat is one of the most iconic buildings in my city.

Describe a water sport/activity that you want to try

There are many activities that I have still not tried in my life. One of them is Scuba diving. It is a water sport that I want to try at least once in my lifetime. Scuba diving is an activity that is not common in the place where I live.

This kind of activity is most famous in the coastal area as it is done in the sea. This activity includes going deep in the sea waters and exploring the marine world. Generally, people discover the corals on the seabed. This sport gives amazing adrenaline rush. This sport is performed under the guidance of experts. A huge number of equipment is put up and some lessons are also taught before a beginner can start this activity.

The first time I came to know about this activity was when I watched a Hollywood movie in my childhood. Since then I became fascinated about this sport and wanted to try my hands on it. To participate in scuba diving, I have to either go to Goa or Andaman and Nicobar Islands. These two places offer professional experience of this sport.

129

I have seen a lot of videos on internet about the scuba diving. A lot of people even make video of their expedition. The world under water looks so amazing and different from our world. Whenever I see those videos, I imagine myself swimming in the water along with fish and other species. I have also searched on the internet regarding the best companies that offer this activity. There is one in Goa that is licensed through the government and take care of every safety concerns. They also provide the best equipment for a smooth experience. I have decided that I am going to pursue this sport through this company soon.

So, this is the activity that I desperately want to try in the coming year.

An advertisement you watched on TV recently

I am not a big fan of watching advertisements as it annoys me very much. Whenever I am watching TV and suddenly an advertisement pop's up, I just switch off the TV or mute the channel. But sometimes willingly or unwillingly we see certain things that can attract us.

One such advertisement came across me while watching a cricket match. The advertisement was regarding a mobile application that you can install on your phone in which you can earn money while viewing cricket matches. The advertisement is performed by popular cricketer MS Dhoni. He is the former captain of the Indian cricket team and in this advert, he tells people to use their knowledge of cricket and apply in the application to earn money. In this advert, he explains how one can simply download the application and start playing a simple game to earn money. The name of the application is Dream 11.

In this application, a person must pick 11 players from two teams. This can be played among two or even more friends. The winning amount can be set by the players of the game and it's very easy to play.

This advertisement is very attractive as it uses mesmerizing background music with attractive themes. The designer of the advertisement should get a lot of credit as they have created such a wonderful advert. The people who are acting in this advert are also famous personalities from different backgrounds. There are many versions of this advertisement. This advert is quite frequent on every channel and one cannot ignore it easily. The moment there's a break from any show, this advert pop's up from nowhere. This advert had a great influence on me, and I could not stop myself from downloading the application and start playing the game. I think that the company should lower down the frequency of their advertisement as people can sometimes get bored and irritated from it. But I still feel that this is one of the best advertisements that I have seen in a long time.

Describe a thing that has become a fashion or a matter of status nowadays

People take pride in certain things and I believe that it changes with time. In 13th century, clothes were a symbol of status and over the centuries, this has changed.

There are numerous things that people of today's era like to own as a status symbol. Some of them are cars, sports bikes, watches, expensive mobile phones and so on. However, I reckon that keeping a dog as a pet has certainly become a status symbol these days.

I see myriad people keeping dogs as pets unnecessarily. Some breeds of dogs are so expensive that the same amount could buy you a decent car. Those rare species need special care and attention from the master. Not only this, they require substantial diets and regulated temperatures.

I would like to share an example with you, one of my friends bought a foreign breed of dog. The dog eats extensively and needs a cooler temperature than 20 degrees. We live in a country where most part of the year is more than 30 degrees. So, there's no point of keeping a dog that is not suited to our environment. It is just like keeping a showpiece at home that is of no use.

This trend is very dangerous as there can be some negative effects on the animals. They become lethargic and their mental state can get disturbed when they are not exposed to the outer environment. Moreover, it can lead to serious illness to the dog and may lead to fatal end.

I am totally against keeping dogs as a status symbol. As their job is not intended to just live in an air-conditioned room and eating loads of stuff. Instead they are one of the friendliest species who like to spend time with the owner, and they are meant to be loyal and vigil.

131

So, this is the thing that people these days keep as a mere symbol of status.

Describe certain laws of your country

laws are the rules and regulations made by the government of any country and it is the duty of its citizens to follow it. There are many laws that are fabricated in my society for the betterment of people. I would like to share some of those laws with you.

The law I like the most is the child labor law. This law suggests that no one can employ a child in a paid work who is under the age of fourteen years. I like this law as I feel that every child has the right to study and play in free time. By this law, parents of children can never force them to do paid work under the age of fourteen.

The second law that I like in my country is the ban of smoking at public places. I have always felt that people get too annoyed by the smoke from the cigarettes. It is very harmful if children inhale this smoke. In this law, if a person is found smoking in a public area then there can be imprisonment or a fine of 5000 rupees on the spot.

Another law that I admire is the law of drink and drive. There is a huge fine for drink and drive in my county. I regularly see the barricades and policemen patrolling the signals and stopping random cars to check whether the driver is drunk or not. If found guilty, there is a on the spot ticket of 20000 rupees.

Apart from the laws, there are several rights that are written in the constitution of our county which allows every citizen of India to practice whatever they want. There are six fundamental rights in total. The rights are as follows, right to equality, right to freedom, right to religion, culture and education, and right to constitutional remedies.

Describe a historical event that you find interesting

There were many historical events in the past that shaped our society in a better way. They were so interesting that those events are taught worldwide in history books. One such event is Apollo 11 which I find most interesting.

132

I came to know about this when I was 8 years old. We had a chapter in our school history book regarding the first moon landing. This mission was named Apollo 11. In this mission, three astronauts, Neil Armstrong, Buzz Aldrin and Michael Collins, achieved the feat of landing a manned aircraft on the moon.

Two of the three astronauts landed on the moon. First man in the history of world to land on moon was Neil Armstrong and after a few minutes, Buzz Aldrin landed. As soon as Neil landed on the moon, he quoted the famous lines 'It's one small step for man and giant leap for mankind.' The live telecast was aired to over 150 countries across the globe and estimated two billion people watched it live on their TV sets. I have seen some of the videos of this mission on the internet, I find it very interesting and unbelievable as it happened in 1969. It is hard to believe that scientist had this technology and they could accomplish such a complicated task back then.

This mission was achieved by NASA, an American space research organization. The whole world was in awe of this fantastic event. When the astronauts returned to the Earth safely, they were honored in every corner of the world.

They were welcomed as heroes and their names were written in golden letters in history. Neil Armstrong continued as a university professor after the mission and lead a low-profile life. He never liked to give TV interviews. Neil Armstrong died in 2012 but other astronauts, Buzz Aldrin and Michael Collins are still alive.

All three astronauts have written several books about their unique experience and shared the untold details about their life and Apollo 11 mission. I believe that till date, this is the most interesting event that has taken place.

An intelligent person you know

I have come across many people in my life who are full of qualities and unique talent. I would like to talk about one of the most intelligent individuals that I have come across in my life till now. Arti is someone whom I admire from my school days. She is one of my best friends and we studied together at school.

She was not in my class as she was 7 years elder than me. She lives near my house and we share a great mutual understanding and relation. She has sharp features and fair color. She is tall and can be easily recognized in the crowd.

She is a bit introvert, but she gets along really well with anyone she knows. I remember that how she used to teach me in my younger days when I struggled in mathematics. As she was my neighbor, and everyone was aware about her intelligence, so one day my mother asked her whether she would give me some tuitions or not.

She agreed, and I found her to be one of my best teachers as well. In her school time, she used to top all the classes and was very well known in the school. She never bothered about her fame and continued to study hard. She scored highest percentage in the matric exams in our city and was awarded with a prize money from the mayor. She prepared hard in the university exams and now she has passed her masters from IIT, which is one of the best institutions in our country.

After that she applied for a job in google and she got it. I have never seen such an intelligent person in my life. She never flaunted her intelligence and helped the weaker ones when required. She solves all the issues in a blink of an eye, whether it is work related or any problem in life.

Describe a hotel you stayed at

I have stayed in some hotels in my life but there's one that I will never forget. The name of the hotel is Taj Palace. It is situated in Dubai. It is a 5-star hotel and my father took our family to a long-awaited vacation last year.

We booked the hotel online after an extensive research by me and my father on the internet. After short listing three hotels, we finally booked Taj Palace. Its price was in our range and it is a 5-star property located in Deira, Dubai.

When we arrived at the hotel at about 6 in the evening, we all were awestruck by its façade and decoration. As soon as we entered the reception, we were welcomed by the hotel staff and were served a traditional complimentary drink.

We were then asked for our passports for identification and soon we were handed over the key to our room. They gave us electronic keys that opened the door of our room. We had booked a suite for four persons. Our suite was loaded with all the modern amenities and the rooms were attached to a common lobby and a kitchenette.

We were surprised by the looks of our room. It was like a palace. There was a king size bed in one room and other room had two single beds. The lobby was quite big and had a couple of sofas in it. The kitchen was huge and was equipped with a refrigerator and other useful utensils.

There was free wi-fi in the room. We also discovered that on the 15th floor, there was a swimming pool along with a jacuzzi and gym. The hotel lobby was humungous with great amount of sitting capacity. The next morning, we took buffet breakfast at the hotel's restaurant.

The breakfast spread was amazing and had variety of cuisines as expected from a five-star hotel. There were some Indian dishes that brought a smile on our faces. Our stay at Taj Palace hotel was memorable and I enjoyed every bit of it. I recommend anyone visiting Dubai to stay in this hotel for an unforgettable experience.

Describe a pet that you have or once had

I am a pet lover and I had a beautiful pet last year. But I had to donate the pet in a kennel as I could not give it much time due to my studies and none of my family members had time to look after it. So, I thought that it was a good decision.

I had a great relation with my pet, and I kept his name Brownie. The reason I gave him this name was that his color is dark brown like a chocolate brownie. I miss it very much and I still meet Brownie in the kennel whenever I get time.

I remember when I bought Brownie from a renowned pet shop in my city. Brownie was only a month old when we took him to our house. The breed is male Labrador. He was only a little dog and would roam in the house without any restrictions. He would get really scared when any stranger came to our house, but this changed when he grew up.

The first thing I used to do when I wake up in the morning was to feed him with his favorite biscuits. He loved them so much that he used to dance and run around me while eating it. Then I would get ready for my school and take him to a short outing.

When I would return from school, he would always greet me with warmth. He would jump onto me and lick my face in excitement. We used to have food together. I would eat mine and he would eat his dog food.

Then the best time was in the evening when I would take him to a nearby park and every day, we played with a ball. I used to throw the ball and he would bring back it to me. But when I was growing up, I couldn't give him much time. So, my parents decided to send him to a kennel. I can never forget the day when he was 5 years old and we had to bade him goodbye. I was so emotional, and I could get same vibes from him. This is the love that one gets from a pet. That day was one of the most depressing days of my life. I feel that everyone should keep a pet at least once in his or her lifetime.

A part of your rituals or customs that you don't like

India is a land of religions, customs and traditional rituals. There are so many different cultures that exist in our society. Every culture has its own rituals and traditions. Some of them are interesting and some are unacceptable, but people still follow them blindly.

A ritual that I hate is Dowry. It is a valuable security, money, gifts such as furniture or a vehicle given by the bride's parents to the groom on the day of wedding or before that. Giving or taking dowry these days is an offence according to the Indian laws.

Dowry is such an evil that it has taken lives of many brides in the past due to the lust and pressure imposed by the groom's side on the bride, but people are still continuing this tradition which is beyond my weirdest of imaginations.

I think that government should actively make some rules and regulations to control this ritual otherwise the situation can go out of hand. I reckon that this ritual should be banned completely and should not be taken forward to our next generations.

Even the educated breed of people is following this culture and giving gifts to the groom in shape of expensive cars, property and other things. This practice influences next generation in a negative manner.

136

Some people have realized this over time and have stopped this ritual with mutual understanding between grooms and bride's family. I think that this is a good step, and everyone should follow it and learn from them. I ponder that we should all come forward and neglect this evil act.

Any souvenir that you bought during your holidays

I like to collect souvenirs for the decoration of my house. I have bought numerous decorative items from many tourist places. An item that I bought during my holidays is a replica of the building Burj Khalifa.

The souvenir is made from acrylic glass and is about the height of 1 foot. It has some LED lights at the bottom that shines through the model when switched on. It looks even more attractive with the lights on. It is the exact imitation of Burj Khalifa. It is the tallest building in the world till date. It stands around 850 meters above ground. I bought this souvenir from the building itself.

Burj Khalifa is located in the heart of Dubai. I went there last year with my family on a holiday. I bought this souvenir when we went to the top of the tower. There is an observation deck that is meant for people to observe surroundings from 128th floor of the iconic building.

After we finished the tour, we headed towards the souvenir shop located on the same floor. There I saw many souvenirs that I thought were worth buying. I was flattered by the variety of items they had over there.

I went past one replica and my eyes were stuck on it. I quickly made my mind to purchase that item. I asked the shop attendant about the price of that. He quoted 200 Dirhams which was about 3500 Indian rupees at that time.

I knew that it was a bit expensive, but I pursued my father to buy it. He liked the souvenir as soon as he held it in his hand. He was kind enough to give me money to buy it. I thanked him and took it home happily.

I have kept this in the living room of my house and whenever someone looks at the souvenir, they can't take their eyes off it.

Describe a thing for which you saved money from a long time

There are many things for which I save money. I am a student, so I don't have a lot of money with me. I often save a part of my pocket money to buy expensive things or the things I like.

I remember once I saved some money to buy a laptop. The laptop was really expensive, and I wanted to buy it as I like electronic gadgets. It was not my professional or educational need, but I just wanted to buy it for my leisure use.

So, I was promised by my father that he will contribute 50% of the money for my laptop but I have to collect rest of the money. The cost of the laptop was 40 thousand rupees. So, that meant I had to collect 20 thousand.

Then I planned to accumulate the sum of money in six months. I made a blueprint and started working on it. I cut down any unnecessary expenses off my pocket money. I remember that I like chocolates very much and would buy one every second day. However, I had to sacrifice it for some months.

I also gave up eating outside food with friends as it would cost me a lot. I started walking more and avoiding public transport to save some more money. By the end of six months I wasn't able to save 20 thousand, but I managed to save 15000.

My father was impressed with my savings so he told me not to sacrifice anything more as he would lend me rest of the money. I was so glad and felt that how difficult it is to save money. It felt so good after buying laptop from the money I saved with so much of struggle.

I bought latest laptop with top configuration as it would help run every type of software and games. So, this is one occasion on which I saved money for a long time to buy something.

A comic that you read in childhood

My childhood was full of comics and its characters. I feel that these days children are more inclined towards internet, cartoons and electronic material. There is no room for comics in this advanced era.

I used to read a lot of comics in Hindi and English. There were some famous characters like Batman, Spiderman, Superman and Chacha

138

Chodhry in Hindi comics. I loved all the characters and would keep my favourite comics under my pillow when I slept at night.

My most favourite character was Shaktiman. He is an Indian comic character that resembles other superheroes around the world. He has the superpowers that all the other superheroes have. He can fly and he can swim under the water without an oxygen cylinder.

He can get from one place to the other in a blink of an eye. He is one of the most loved comic characters in India. Originally, he was not a comic character. Shaktiman initially featured as a one-hour show on TV. The show was an instant success and soon merchandise came into the market and a comic was also made on it.

I bought that comic from a bookstore when I was ten years old. I was a huge fan of this character. He was my childhood hero and I used to mimic him in my free time. The comic's size was relatively bigger and thicker than the other comic books.

All the pages were colored and contained amazing animations that allured everyone. The dialogues were written in both Hindi and English. I used to read this comic for almost two hours in a day. I have read this comic at least seven or eight times since then.

You will not believe me, but I have still kept that comic in my study desk. Although I don't read it now, but I will never give it to anyone.

Speak about an interesting tour guide

I have been to a few tourist places in my life and the role of tour guides is impeccable there. I have come across some characters in my life, but I certainly feel that I can't forget one tour guide whom I met in Dubai.

I think it is great way to travel when you are in company of a tour guide. I went to Dubai last year with my family and we hired a tour guide from a travelling agency. They gave us his phone number and told us to contact him in the morning as he will come to our hotel to pick us up.

We called in the morning and to our surprise he could speak Hindi. I was curious to meet him. He arrived at the hotel at sharp 10 and greeted us with a broad smile and handshakes. He introduced himself as Akram.

He escorted us to a van in which we were meant to go on a full day city tour with him. He took us to every important attraction of the city and told us about the history of Dubai. He told us about the past and present of the wonderful city. He was quite knowledgeable and humorous.

He instantly became friendly with us and treated us like we know him from a long time. He told us that he was an Iranian resident and was working in Dubai from the past 10 years. He also mentioned that he watches Indian movies and relish it very much.

He took us to all the main attractions and landmarks of the city. We stopped at a local restaurant for lunch. He ordered some local food for us. We savored the food and went back to the van to continue the tour.

Then he took us to the beach where we spend about an hour. He was taking care of us in a great manner and would crack jokes every now and then. We all became very friendly with him in a matter of few hours.

I think that he was the most interesting tour guide that I have ever came across.

Speak about a family that resemble yours

I have not come across many families that resembles mine. But we were all surprised when our neighbors shifted to our colony last year.

I am talking about my neighbors who live across the street. I live in a joint family of 9 members and surprisingly they are 9 members themselves. They shifted in our colony last year and we quickly bonded well on every facet.

I am the second child of my parents. I have an elder brother and a younger one as well. The same goes with them. DK Sharma, my uncle has three sons. My aunt is around 58 years old and her name is Laxmi. Their eldest son is eight years older than me and is married since 2012. He has a son who is 6 years old. It goes same in my family where my elder brother is seven years old than me and has a daughter who is 5 years old.

Their second son is a year older than me. I like his company as we share similar interests and nature. I really get along with him well. We like to study together as he is a bit older than me so if I have any problem in studies, I like to discuss with him.

My younger brother and their youngest son are of the same age. They share a good bond with each other. Their nature is strikingly same, and we all get surprised by this.

140

My father and mother are almost similar in age and nature as compared to my uncle and aunt. We all celebrate festivals together and like to dine together occasionally. They are a family that resembles ours and we all enjoy each other's company very much.

Speak about an aquatic animal

Our world is full of animals and birds. One cannot even count the number of different species that lives on the earth. There are some aquatic mammals that are famous throughout the world like Dolphins but here I would like to talk about Walrus.

It is a huge marine mammal which is mostly found in the regions near Arctic ocean and North pole. It is one of the unique and rare species of mammals on Earth. This species is further separated into two subspecies. One is Atlantic Walrus and the other one is Pacific Walrus. The Atlantic species is found in the Atlantic Ocean and the other one is common in the Pacific Ocean.

The striking feature of Walrus is the long elephant like tusks. They were hunted in the past by the indigenous arctic people for its meat and tusks. Male Walrus found in the Pacific can weigh more than two thousand kilos. Males are bulkier than the females. They generally dwell in shallow waters. They are more social than other species found around them. Walrus mostly consumes fish.

There has been a rapid decline in the population of Walrus from the last few years. It is also believed that ancient Alaskans wore dress made of Walrus skin. Some even say that these mammals were worshiped by the ancient people near the north pole as they thought that this creature was a monster. I have seen on the internet that there are a couple of conservation centers for Walrus in Canada. I think it is a good step towards the preservation of this unique species.

(You can also speak about Dolphin in this topic)

Speak about a time when you admired the sky

Do you often see the sky?

What did you admire about the sky that day?

Is it a wasteful activity?

In this fast-growing world, technology has taken over everything and everyone so much that we hardly get time to appreciate the natural beauty around us. One of the most beautiful things in this universe according to me is the endless sky above us, but unfortunately, I do not get time to look up and admire the sky often.

Today I would like to share a recent experience of mine when I was awestruck while looking at the sky. We travelled to the hills last week to celebrate my brother's first wedding anniversary. We went to Kunihar which is a small town in Himachal Pradesh. This place is surrounded by beautiful valleys and mountains and has an amazing vibe. The atmosphere is very neat and clean, and air is extremely fresh because of the high volume of trees in that area.

At the hotel, there was a big lawn, so we decided to spend most of our time there only. At night when me and my family were enjoying ourselves in the lawn, I looked up at sky and realized how enchanting it was. The bright twinkling stars seemed to be magical and the moon was clearly visible. I loved the different patterns that stars made. I was trying to figure out the different shapes that was made by the constellation of stars. Because of the clear sky, that night the moon appeared to be very close to us and I kept on looking at the sky for a long time. Here in the big cities, it is very hard to find clear sky because of the tall buildings and a lot of pollution. But that night I realized the real beauty of nature. In my opinion, one should takeout time from their busy schedule to admire the sky as it provides immense peace to a person and makes us believe in the power of God.

Describe a handcrafted item which you made yourself.
When you made the item?
Why you had to make that item?
Were you pleased by your work?

From the very beginning I was fond of art and craft and used to participate enthusiastically in the art and craft class at my school. I studied in one of the best schools in our city, where they paid a lot of attention towards the non-academic fields as well.

To polish the creativity of students we were taught a lot of handicraft stuff like paper bags, envelops, artificial flowers, jewellery box, photo frames, etcetera. But here I would like to talk about a very unique thing which I made myself, that is a tea tray using newspaper rolls. I made this item for our school exhibition when I was twelve years old, in grade 7. Our teacher taught us a new technique of hardening a newspaper by tightly rolling it on a table, several times and pasting the ends with glue.

By doing so, the newspaper turned very stiff like a wooden stick. Me and my classmates made hundreds of such sticks at first as we had to make 6-7 trays. It was a lot of fun rolling those and as kids it fascinated us how strong the newspaper got by that method. After making the sticks and letting them dry completely, I joined the sticks together to form a firm base and then stacked them on all the four sides, giving it the shape of a tea tray.

Once all the trays were ready, it was time to beautify them by painting the trays and pasting some glitters or stickers on them. Our teacher was very impressed with our job and congratulated us for our efforts.

Even I was impressed with our efforts. We made these trays as we had to exhibit something in the school's annual exhibition. We displayed our product and gave description to the audience. Everyone appreciated our work that day.

Describe a dish you like the most which is served during the festivals.
Is it a sweet or savory dish?
Is it served only during festivals?
Explain the dish and how it is made.
I live in a diverse country where multiple festivals are celebrated at a large scale and each has its own importance and value for the people of different religions and cultures. Every festival has a specific dish associated with it like Ghevar is prepared during Teej festival in Punjab and parts of Rajasthan as well, Biryani is famous during EID and Modak is another popular dish which is specifically made during Ganesh Chaturthi.
But the dish I like the most is Gujia which can be found in almost every sweet shop near the Holi festival. Holi is a famous festival in India, also popular by the name of 'festival of colors'. During this festival, the friends

and relatives' gift each other a box of Gujia as a symbol of affection. Gujia is a sweet dumpling made of flour, stuffed with a mixture of dry fruit and khoya. It is deep fried in ghee and then dipped in a sugary syrup. Mostly it is eaten cold or at room temperature. I love the texture of this dish; it is crunchy from outside and soft from inside.

The filling melts in your mouth with the first bite itself. Also, the filling is not that sweet, this balances the overall flavor of the dish perfectly as the outer coating is glazed with caramelized sugar. The good thing about Gujia is that it is also available on normal days at the sweet shops. Gujia is not only eaten on Holi but on most of the other festivals as well like Diwali, the biggest Indian festival.

Gujia originally is an authentic dish of Madhya Pradesh which is known as the heart of India. Some parts of Uttar Pradesh and Bihar are also famous for this dish, but now it is prepared and enjoyed all over the country.

Describe a place full of colors
Do you like colorful places?
Speak about that place
Will you go there again?
I am a very positive person and always get attracted by colorful things, be it beautiful flowers, a house, or a garden. Today I would like to talk about a place full of colors and that is the Diwali carnival which is held every year in my city Chandigarh.

Not only the Diwali carnival but in general any kind of a carnival is extremely colorful with beautiful lights all around. So, I went to this Diwali carnival last month. They always have a different theme for the entrance door and this year the theme was Disney Land which made it even more colorful and fascinating. The carnival is beautifully lit up by different colored bright lights so that one can know from a distance about it. Secondly the entrance gate was of bright purple and golden color according to the Disney theme. They had a huge red color carpet which covered the entire ground and gave the people a smooth surface to walk on. At the Diwali carnival there were multiple games to attract the children out of which my personal favorite was the "shoot the balloon".

144

The place was so full of colours that I could see so many different colours wherever I looked. There was one wall that was completely decorated with numerous varieties of colourful flowers. Also, there was a complete street market at the carnival that had everything to shop there from clothes, jewelry, kitchen appliances, home decor, artificial flowers to lights etcetera.

Not only this, there was a huge variety of food to choose from different stalls. There were some vendors who were selling traditional sweets that were so vibrant in appearance. I had never visited such colourful place before in my life. This fare occurs every year in my hometown and I eagerly wait for this even to happen.

Describe a product or application which is based on Artificial Intelligence

Speak about the product or the application

Have you ever benefited from it?

Is artificial intelligence a boon or bane for the humans

Humans have seen massive developments in the field of technology in the past 100 years. The major development in the field of technology is the Artificial. The AI is developing day by day and is becoming more faster, smarter and human-like.

There are many products in the market these days that are based on artificial intelligence. I am using an iPhone so I would like to describe about SIRI. It is an Apple's personal assistant that is in built in the phone and other products of Apple.

I interact with the friendly voice-activated computer on daily basis. SIRI helps me to discover a lot of information. In my phone I can simply ask her to give me directions of a particular place. I don't need to type anything. I just speak hello SIRI on my phone and give a command. Her job is to answer me anything I ask.

I can add events to my calendar by simply speaking to her. Even if I have to make a call, I can simply tell SIRI to dial that number for me. This has surely made life easier, but some people don't consider it to be a helpful thing. Instead they think that Artificial Intelligence is interfering in the life of people and can be a threat in the future.

145

SIRI uses machine learning technology to become smarter and better equipped to predict and understand our natural accents and requests. It is like a magic that people would have only dreamt of in the past. It was unimaginable to think of such discovery a few years back.

I think the artificial intelligence has surely benefitted the businesses, but it has also invaded the privacy of people in a lot of ways. I think that there should be some limits set by the government regarding the use of artificial intelligence.

A software that you often use

What is the software about?

Why do you use it?

Do you feel that the introduction of software use has eased our life?

I am not a person who use a lot of software on computer. But there is one software that is very common, and a lot of people use it. The name of the software is Microsoft office. It is one of the most common software that can be found in everyone's computer.

Microsoft office is a software that includes many other subcategories of software that are used to make official work easy. Not only this, Microsoft office is also used by students around the world to make presentations on computer. They also make a lot of projects that are given in the schools.

The most common type of software in Microsoft office is the Word. In this you can write whatever you want in different formats and languages. You can save the file on it and you can edit that file whenever you want. The file can also be printed by giving a print command from the software. The word file can also be transferred to anyone through an email.

Other software in Microsoft office is the Powerpoint. I had used this software extensively in the past for making presentations on our school projects. I have made a lot of animations and slides in my school time. In Powerpoint one can add images and symbols to depict whatever they want. Then the slides can be run in the Powerpoint mode in which we can see the slides one after one automatically.

I also use Microsoft excel in which I logged in important data such as phone numbers and addresses of my near and dear ones. I also used this software once to make a project report for the class attendance in my school.

In my opinion, using these types of software has made our lives better. In the past people used to maintain a lot of bookish records but now computers have taken their place. One can store millions of soft copies of files in a single computer.

Something kind that someone did for you
Who was the person?
What did he/she do for you?
How did you feel after that?

I have been fortunate enough to receive help from many people in my life. On one occasion I received a kind gesture from one of my friends in my school time.

He was my best friend and he helped in a situation when I needed the most. Not many people help others in this era. My friend studied in the same class as mine. His name is Ishwar and he maintains a quiet nature. He is very sober and cool minded.

An incident happened with me when we were in school. I used to go back from school on my cycle. Ishwar accompanied me most of the times as he lived near my house back then. One day we were going back to house and suddenly a speeding motor bike passed besides me and due to that I lost my balance and fell on the side.

I sustained some injuries on my elbow and knees. But the most painful one was on the head. Ishwar quickly left his bike and held me in his arms. He asked repeatedly whether I was fine or not. I told him that I have a lot of pain in my head. Suddenly I felt blood oozing out of my head. Ishwar quickly took out his handkerchief and pressed it firmly on my head.

He called people around us and asked for help. One passerby stopped and laid me in his car. Ishwar left his cycle, bag and other things at the scene. They took me to a nearby clinic. There the doctor examined me and gave me some pills to eat. Then he stitched the wound and put a bandage on it. The doctor advised me to go home as there was no serious injury. In the meanwhile, Ishwar had already informed my parents about the incident and soon my parents arrived there. It brought a smile to my face. My mother hugged me, and I told her about how Ishwar took care of me and helped me reach the clinic.

My parents thanked him, and we escorted him to his home. I can never forget that day and the kindness of Ishwar towards me. I am still in touch with him and I often smile with him when we talk about that incident.

Describe a time when you taught something new to an older person
Is it easy to teach the elderly?
What did you teach?
Was that helpful to him/her

Believe me it is not an easy task to teach anything to elders. I live with my grandfather and we share a great relation with each other. He is 80 years old but is very active in day to day chores. Despite his age, he is always keen on learning new things that he encounters in his daily routine.

I have learned a great deal of things from him over the past few years. He has also asked me about things that he can't do. I recently taught him a number of things like using a smart phone and operating emails by using internet.

But there was one thing that made him struggle a lot and he couldn't learn it by himself. I am talking about a mobile app that helps you to book a taxi. The name of the app is Taxi. One day I promised my grandfather that I will teach him this skill on a Sunday.

First, I taught him to download apps on the mobile phone. Then I registered details in the application by using his phone number. I trained him to fill in the details in that app and then started it.

After that I showed him how to select the location where he wants to travel. Then I explained him the process of booking and choosing a taxi. I gave him some tips on booking cheap taxis. He was so keen on learning this application that he understood everything at once. He also booked a taxi to test whether he learned it or not. It took him some time, but he was able to make the correct booking.

This happens many times when he wants to go somewhere but he doesn't want to be dependent on anyone. That's why it was very important for me to teach him this app. He thanked me for teaching him the skill of using this mobile application.

Describe an instance when you solved a problem using the internet

Do you often look for solutions on the internet?

What was the problem and how did you solve it?

Was internet helpful in solving that issue

Yes, I look for solutions for most of the problems on the internet. Internet is so easy to access, and I always find it a great place to look for answers to my problems. Internet has never ending content and one can use it to solve most issues in day to day life.

The problem I was facing was in my laptop. I generally use my laptop to make presentations and projects. The major problem in my laptop was that it would restart itself anytime. Whenever I was doing something important, this issue would erase everything that I did in that time period. I searched on the internet about this problem and found a website where I shared my issue. They gave me an email id where I could tell about my problem and get it solved. I emailed about the worries and they replied me swiftly.

They said that it is an internal issue and can be cured by self. They send me a series of steps that I needed to perform in order to get the problem eradicated. I followed those steps one by one and it took me half an hour to resolve my issue. I was relived and happy as I got rid of my problem as well as saved money.

The main problem was a virus in the software of my laptop. So, they instructed me to kill that virus by recovering the windows. It was very complicated, and I would have never been able to do it on my own. Or I had to get it checked from the market and it would have costed me a lot. I am thankful to that website that helped me in solving that impediment. The internet was really helpful this time in curing my issue.

A happily married couple

What is your relationship with the couple?

How they remain happy?

What do you like in them?

I have seen lots of couples in my life who are living happily in their married life. But today, I would like to talk about my sister and brother-in-law. Well, they are my favorite married couple not because she is my sister, but for the immense bonding and love they share with each other. They have a brilliant mutual understanding.

My sister got married three years back and since then I have never seen them arguing for any matter. No doubt, they sometimes disagree with each other on certain viewpoints, but they conclude and clear their differences quickly. Both have a mature and patient nature.

My brother-in-law is the best man for my sister. My sister always desired for such a partner in her life who could love her unconditionally and take care of her small and big needs. And undoubtedly, she got the right person in her life who never disappoints her for her expectations. And the same goes for my sister too. She understands all his needs and precisely does all the things that could impress him in every possible way.

Whenever they go for any party, they are the apple of everyone's eyes as their internal love can be realized by everyone. People adore their bonding and cherish their togetherness.

I still remember when my brother-in-law faced terrible loss in his business, that time my sister supported him through the tough times. She is always with him in thick and thin. They support each other in every situation.

I would also like to have someone special like this in my life. Life becomes more beautiful when you have such a partner in your life. They always remain happy in every situation and they are the most happily married couple that I have seen in my life.

A seminar or lecture you attended
Where did you attend the seminar?
What was it about?
What did you learn there?
Last week, I attended a seminar on personality development in my hometown. Usually, I don't like to attend lectures and seminars but, my cousin wanted to attend this one as she likes to attend such events. So, I joined her and honestly, I really enjoyed it. The seminar was on such an interesting topic that I thought of giving it a try and finally, I attended it. After that experience, my viewpoint about the seminars changed drastically.

The team who gave seminar was having knowledgeable orators. They gave such wonderful tips to enhance your personality and how to impress people around you. Their experience could be judged from their lectures. They exhibited several videos and PowerPoint slides that made us learn about our postures, our body language and the way to address people. Those videos were very influential for the audience.

It was a very interesting seminar for me as they not only gave motivating lectures but also invited some volunteers on stage for making the concept clearer to the audience. My cousin participated in that activity so, I was very actively heeding to all the points they were discussing.

I think there is a need to attend these kinds of seminars on a regular basis as it gives an insight into the practical aspect of life. The things that I learned there are generally not taught in the schools and colleges. So, it was a new experience for me.

Not only this, in the end, lunch was served to all the guests and believe me, it was very delicious. They also gave a small booklet which included all the points they discussed in the seminar. Overall, I really enjoyed the event and will always remember those tips in my life. Well, I am grateful to my cousin who convinced me for this seminar and made me learn such good things in life.

Something you got for free
What did you get?
How did you feel when you got that thing for free?
How do you use it?

I have got many things in my life for free. The one thing that I relish the most is the gift that I got from the restaurant owner. In this topic I will discuss the story about the thing that I got for free.

I am a big foodie and I love to visit different restaurants and taste variety of cuisines. Last week, I visited a newly opened Chinese restaurant nearby my place. I heard a lot about its upgraded food quality and decided to pay a visit to that restaurant. Thus, along with my brother I went for lunch at the weekend to the same food eatery.

As we were having our lunch, the owner of the restaurant came and greeted us. He asked for the feedback regarding the taste and quality of the food served to us. As the food was very delicious, I gave them positive comment and wished them good luck for the future of their restaurant. I also filled the feedback form of the restaurant and appreciated the things I liked.

The owner was really impressed with my reviews and to our surprise he gave us free discount coupons of 50 percent each for our future visit to the restaurant. In total he gave us five discount coupons. This was like a lottery for me as he presented us such a wonderful gift in return of a good review. These discount coupons can be cashed once at a time. I have already redeemed two of my 5 discount coupons as I visit that restaurant quite frequently. I love eating out, so these coupons save me a lot of money. These coupons are one of my favourite possessions these days. Recently, my cousin demanded one coupon from me, and I didn't hesitate to give it to him. So, this is the free gift that I cherish.

An occasion when you received a lot of guests at your home
What was the occasion?
How did you feel about that?
How many guests did you receive?

Well, I am a jovial person, so I love to attend parties and likewise, I love to throw parties for my friends and family as well. Last year, there was a huge party at my house celebrating the 25th anniversary of my parents.

It was a great event for them and for all the family members as they have happily completed 25 years with each other. We all were so excited about that occasion. It was a great day for us, so we invited all our friends and relatives.

We organized a dinner party for everyone along with music and dance. It was such a fun time. Whenever I look at the photographs of the event, I feel nostalgic. The occasion was a great success. All our guests were welcomed with the shower of flowers and attention was given to every guest so that no one could feel isolated. All the guests were quite impressed with our arrangements.

All the things were planned by my mother so systemically that there was no confusion in any of the ceremony. There were dance performances, couple dance, rituals and much more in that occasion. Everything was just fantastic.

We hired the decoration team and best caterers for this occasion as many respected personalities were also invited to the party. Everyone appreciated our preparations and congratulated us for the huge success of the party. We received so many gifts as there were a great number of people in the event.

It was a tough task to unwrap all the gifts as it took us three hours to do that. I had never experienced such an occasion in my life before this party where we received more than three hundred guests at our home.

A conversation with stranger
Where did you meet him/her?
What was the conversation
Are you still in touch with him/her?
There are many strangers whom I have come across and made them friends. There is one such person who met me in a journey and we became good friends after that. I am talking about Amit. I met him in a train journey from Chandigarh to New Delhi.

I was going to my aunt's house to spend my holidays and on my way, I met this stranger. I had booked Shatabadi Express which takes about four hours to reach Delhi. He was sitting on seat number 10 and mine was 11. I had the window seat, so I asked him politely to make way for me as I had to take the window seat.

At the first glance he looked a very humble kind of a person. He greeted me with a smile and soon the journey began. I am a very talkative person, so I was the one who started conversation with him. First, I asked him about his hometown and to my surprise, he was living in the same colony In which I put up.

I was shocked as I had never seen him there. But he told me that he shifted recently from Delhi and was going there for the same purpose. He was going to Delhi to clear his dues and to bring anything that was left there. When I asked him the reason of his shifting, he stated that he originally belongs to Chandigarh, but he was living in Delhi for the past five years as his father was posted there in a government department.

After that I told him about my background and family. We conversed a lot about our hobbies and other things. Our tuning was there from the first conversation as he was also the same age as mine. Our hobbies and interests were also very similar.

We exchanged our numbers and remained in contact with each other after that day. These days he is a good friend of mine and we share a decent relationship. He was a stranger to me when we met first time in the train but now, we are good friends.

A city or town you visited

What is special about that town or city?

What did you do there?

How did you feel after visiting that town or city?

I have visited many places in my life. My father loves to explore new places, due to that we get lots of opportunities to travel along with him. The town I visited recently is Manali, which is a hill station. We went there to visit a famous temple which was nearby Manali.

Well, the beauty of the city is breathtaking. Throughout our journey, I was constantly gazing outside the window and admiring the beauty of the nature. The lush green mountains and the fresh air was what impressed me the most about the city.

Manali is a beautiful hill station which has a small local population. Ample of tourists come to Manali to enjoy nature every year. The fresh air and mesmerizing views we got in Manali are impossible to find anywhere in other parts of our country. The people of the city are very friendly and polite. Since it was a new place for us to explore, we were not aware about the routes of the city, but the local inhabitants guided us humbly.

I believe that if the locals of any tourist destination are helpful to you, it becomes easy to travel around the place. With the support of locals and using the limited signboards, we were able to roam around the hills comfortably.

The city holds multiple markets that are embedded with different types of fashion outlets, souvenirs shops, and many other commodities.

We moved from one place to another through public transport and we were really satisfied with the taxi services there. All the tourist attractions

154

in the city were spectacular. You can enjoy the snowy mountains and do various activities like bungy jumping, ice skating and many more. It was a full adventurous trip for us.

If I get a chance, I would love to travel again to Manali as my experience was quite fantastic.

A website that is useful

For what purpose do you use that website?

Did you learn anything from this website?

At what time of the day do you use website?

I usually browse many websites on my mobile phone or sometimes on my laptop. I spend at least a couple of hours searching on the internet for new things. Since I am a social person, I love to spend hours on various social sites. But of all, Facebook is a useful website that I like to browse on a regular basis.

It is my favorite one because you get to interact with so many people through this platform. This website is so useful in establishing contact with my school friends. This site has really shortened the distance between the people, which is the most enticing feature of it. Also, we can share our photographs, videos and many other thoughts that come to our mind. It is a very engaging site. I have liked several pages on this site which are very useful to me in my personal life. I can watch the videos and latest updates posted by those famous pages.

In fact, I am also the manager of one Facebook page which has around a thousand likes and followers. This page is about the youth of our country. I post latest content every day on my page and in return I get likes and some people also share the post with others.

Not only this, I have made several new friends on this site who belong to other countries and cultures. This website is very useful in making friends from all over the world. In fact, one of my Facebook friends from another city has visited my home last year and it was a great experience living with him.

Apart from making friends, people can also do great business over this website. I have seen many companies advertising their products on

Facebook. They can reach millions of people through this website as people from all over the world are connected through it.

So, I feel that Facebook is one of the most useful websites around the globe.

A place to listen to music

Where do you listen to music?

What device do you use for listening to music?

How do you feel when you listen to music?

Music is one of the most essential part of everyone's life nowadays because it takes us away from the stress and depressing situations for some time. Listening to music is my favorite leisure activity. I love to listen to the music of various genres. I have one typical playlist of my favorite songs that I like to repeat again and again. I can listen to music anywhere, anytime. But my favorite place to listen to music is in my bedroom.

My bedroom is the place where I can make myself most comfortable on my couch and feel the spirit of the songs. No one usually disturbs me in my room. My room is located at the back end of our house so there is no disturbance from any external sound.

Whenever I get bored, I listen to music. It helps me to get into a particular mood even if I feel low on that day. In my childhood days, I was fond of listening to songs, but I would listen to any song played on the TV. These days I have become very particular about my choices and I listen to the songs listed in my playlist only.

Sometimes, I love to clean all the mess in my room while listening to music. This completes all my work without making me realize the time taken to complete that work. Music not only helps me to do all my tasks comfortably, but it also helps me in rejuvenating my mood.

Since I am fond of music, I have connected high-quality speakers in my room with my mobile phone through Bluetooth, and I love to listen to my favorite records. I can also connect them with my mobile phone through the cable to the speakers and then just play the music. Whenever I am listening to music in my room, I love to gaze at the beautiful garden near my house that is completely visible from the windowpane of my room. The mesmerizing view and the serene music make a perfect environment for my relaxation.

I listen to songs at numerous places, but my bedroom is the apt place for me to listen to my favorite songs.

A happy memory from childhood

What was the memory

When did it happened?

Did you learn something from that memory?

My childhood was a memorable one as I enjoyed a lot in my school life with my friends. Even my parents were so encouraging to me that they supported me for every activity in my school time. There are numerous memories of my childhood that I still remember and cherish them. But the happiest memory from my childhood is from my school race competition. I was in class 5th when this competition was being held. It was conducted on the state level and few students were selected from the top schools of my city. I was one of the students from my school selected for that competition

The competition was held at Tagore Academy in my city. There were around 10 schools that participated in the competition. There were three rounds based on which finalists were to be chosen. In each round, the winning candidates were to be taken to the next round and the last ones were to be eliminated. Till the last round, all the students from my school were eliminated and I was the only hope left for my school. Every year, my school wins the competition. So, there were huge expectations on my shoulders.

Finally, the last round started, and I was running like a professional athlete in the race and suddenly I felt a massive pain in my ankle. It felt like my ankle has been damaged severely. My foot twisted due to the unevenness of the track. For a second, I was very slow in the race but then the encouraging words of my coach stuck my mind and I forgot everything and stayed focused on the finish line. Finally, I came second in the race. I didn't expect such a huge success from myself as my foot was in severe pain. I was not even able to walk after the race. It was unbelievable for me to secure second position in the competition with such discomfort. If I would have not stopped for those few seconds in the midway, maybe I would have won the race.

I was awarded prize money as a reward for scoring 2nd position in the competition. I didn't win the race, but it was one of the happiest moments from my childhood.

A time you moved home

Was it easy or difficult?

Did you lose anything in the process?

How did you do it?

Shifting is undoubtedly a daunting task as it involves so much work and time to do all the packing and then unpacking things. Adjusting to a new place is not so easy as it seems to be. Two years ago, we had shifted our home to a new place as the last one was not so spacious. The process of shifting was so tiring.

Instead of hiring a movers and packers, we did all the packing and shifting of the household things on our own. The reason we didn't hire a professional is that we were living in a rented accommodation and we didn't have much things to move.

But I still remember I used to pack all the household stuff and carry it along every day till late nights. We packed all the things safely in different packaging boxes and sealed them properly so that no item would get damaged or get lost. At the time of packing we did not realize that it is so difficult to move all the items of a house.

Apart from this, leaving the place where you have lived for so long is also very difficult. We were so attached to our neighbors that it was such an emotional moment for all of us. After shifting to the new place, we recalled our old house many times in the day. But as we were so busy in setting the new house that we forgot everything in a few days and got settled at our new place. We were too excited to get into a newer spacious house where all of us were having our own rooms.

Even here the neighbors are so good and there are much better facilities than we had in our locality earlier. We all were really satisfied after moving to the new place. I have a faded memory of our old home but very soon

158

that will also be gone with the time. The new place where we moved is much more comfortable and livelier.

A time you moved school
When did that happened?
Did you like the new school?
Were there any problems at the start?
I have studied in two different schools. I left my first school at the age of eleven. I remember that I was in fifth standard when my parents decided to shift me to a bigger and better school.
I used to study in a decent school, but the infrastructure lacked a bit. Although all my teachers were amazing, but there was lack of facilities that led to this decision. My mother always wanted me to study in a big school. So, they bought admission forms and applied for the enrolment.
I had to clear five exams and based on the result; I would be admitted by the authorities. I was shifting to one of the best schools in our city. The name of the school is Shivalik public school. I was quite nervous on the first day as I knew none of my classmates.
when I reached the school on the first day, I was welcomed by everyone and my class teacher helped me a lot in adjusting to the new environment. I had never seen such a huge school premises in my life. I was helped by my classmates to a great extent. They took me to the canteen in the lunch time and showed me every nook and corner of the school.
There were so many new things that I saw for the first time in a school. This new school had auditoriums, football ground, basketball courts, gymnasium hall and many more facilities.
After that, my classmates also took my introduction. I felt so contented with the treatment of the school staff and classmates. I had so many confusions and questions in my mind before entering the gate of the school. But after the completion of the first day, I thought that my parents made a great choice and I moved to the new school smoothly.

A car journey you remember
Where did you go?
Who accompanied you?

What was special about that journey?

I have journeyed in a car many times. The one that I remember the most is when I went to Jaipur, Rajasthan with my family last year. This was my longest trip by car ever. My elder brother drove the car along with my father. And my mother was the fourth member. We were travelling by an SUV car so there was no problem of extra room. We had three full sized luggage bags as we were planning to live in Jaipur for a week.

Jaipur is around five hundred kilometers from where I live. It took us ten hours to reach there. We had a couple of rest stops during the journey. We left for Jaipur early in the morning at about 5 AM. On our way we didn't see much traffic as we departed quite early.

There was a bit of fog on the way as the highway to Delhi is surrounded by farmland. The reason we were taking a stop at Delhi was to rest for a bit. Delhi is located on the halfway to Jaipur. We reached Delhi in only three hours. We parked our cars in a restaurant and did breakfast. We chose traditional breakfast that includes stuffed bread and butter. It was so delicious that all of us couldn't restrict ourselves to overeat. After some time, we decided to continue the journey.

The highway to Jaipur is wide with neat and clean roads. We were cruising to our destination, but we had to take another stop as my brother was feeling sleepy. So, we decided to have a cup of tea. We stopped at a kiosk on the roadside and enjoyed our tea.

After that it took us only one hour to reach Jaipur. All of us enjoyed the journey to the fullest. We had so many conversations during that journey that we generally don't have at home. So, this is the car journey that I can never forget.

Your favorite TV program you watch

What is the format of the program?

How often do you watch it?

At what time the show is run on TV

Whenever I am free, I love to watch TV as there is a wide variety of choice in terms of channels nowadays. The options are abundant so people of every age group and interest can find something of their interest. I usually spend 1-2 hours watching TV daily. There are many programs that I like to watch but my favorite program is "Kaun Banega Crorepati" on Sony TV. This program is the Hindi version of the show, "who wants to be a Millionaire".

It is my best pick because it is a very knowledgeable quiz show. The best part of the show is that the host of the show is my favorite personality, Amitabh Bachan, one of the finest actors of Bollywood. His voice and personality say it all. Many people view this show just because they want to see more of Amitabh Bachan. There are several contestants who take part in a group round. They must answer a question and the person who takes the least time to answer that question, wins that round.

The winner of the first round is selected to play this game and gets a chance to become a millionaire. This show involves a huge amount of prize money on each question you answer correctly. This show is my favorite one not because it gives me ample of knowledge for various questions asked in each round but also it is a good source of entertainment. In between the question rounds, there are few humorous chats between the host and the candidate.

Not only this, from the past few episodes of the show, there is an opportunity for the TV viewers to participate in the competition from their homes to win the prize money. In every episode, one question is asked to the TV viewers and the answers are to be sent through a message. The one selected with right answer wins 2 lakh rupees. So, one can win money while watching the show.

The show is telecasted on every Saturday and Sunday in the evening time, so I get glued to my TV screen every weekend for this show.

Visit to a relative

What is your relation to that relative?

Where did you go

What was your purpose of visit?

My maternal and paternal family tree is quite big. All family members are very loving and caring. I visit them occasionally but there are few relatives whom I love to visit quite often. In this topic, I am going to talk about my visit to aunt (mother's sister). I love to visit my aunt every now and then. All her family members are affectionate and welcoming.

There are six members in my aunt's family i.e. my aunt, her husband, her two kids (both sons), her father-in-law and mother-in-law. My uncle has a very cheerful nature. He always cracks jokes regardless of the situation. My cousins are of my age group, so we love to spend time together.

The reason I visited my aunt's house was that I had winter holidays from the school. So, me and my cousins decided that we will stay together at their place for a week. We all had planned this visit from a long time. My aunt's sons are of my age, so we get along well.

They live in Delhi, so it took me four hours to reach by train. I was a bit tired as I reached late in the evening. After resting at night, we were ready to explore Delhi on the next day. We went to myriad places and came back in the evening. Then we got together for long talks and played numerous indoor games.

For the next five days, we enjoyed so much that one couldn't imagine. We used to wake up till late night and talk about each other's life. It's always a great time visiting a relative.

I was so emotional on my way back. I missed all the things that I did on my visit to aunt's house. So, this is the visit to a relative that I remember the most.

A time when you felt embarrassed

When did this happen?

what happened?

How did you feel?

There are numerous moments in life that leaves a long-lasting impression on us. There have been some embarrassing moments in my life but the one which I am going to tell you about is the most embarrassing moment of my life.

This happened quite a few years back when I was in 10th class. I had invited a few friends for my birthday party. I told everyone to come at NCA mall in the food court area. When we assembled at the restaurant, we ordered plentiful cuisines.

We had a great time together. I cut the cake in the end and asked for the bill from the hotel staff. When I was about to pay the bill, I realized that I had no wallet in my pocket. I searched it thoroughly in all my pockets but could not find it.

I felt so embarrassed at that time. I was in a shock for a few seconds. My friends were concerned and asked me about the issue. I told them that I was not able to find my wallet. I told them that I must have either left it at home or lost it on the way.

My friends consoled me and told me not to worry. One of my friends told everyone about the situation. So, everyone unanimously decided to pay the bill by splitting the amount among everyone.

I was so glad at that time and felt lucky that I have such great friends. I thanked everyone and assured them to return their money the next day. I kept my promise and retuned the money to each friend and thanked them personally.

Fortunately, I searched my room and found my wallet. I was so happy to find my wallet as I had a more money in that than usual days. Despite the help by my friends, I felt very embarrassed. From that day onwards I always check my pockets for purse before leaving the home.

A gift you gave to someone
What was the gift?
Why did you give it?
How did he/she feel after receiving the gift?
Exchanging gifts on special occasions is the celebrated culture of our society. We love to exchange gifts with our loved ones to express our joy and happiness. The gift is a token of love given to your loved ones on the special days of their lives. Even, I love to present gifts to my special persons.

Recently, I gave a gift to my mother on her birthday. It was her 50th birthday and I gifted her a new smartphone. Earlier, she was using the keypad phone which does not comprise of any latest feature that a smartphone has. She was very fond of looking for new recipes on YouTube and other applications that could make her busy in free time. Every time, she wanted to look for something on the internet, she used to ask for dad's phone or use a laptop to do so. One day I felt that my mother needs a smartphone desperately.

She never demanded this phone, but I knew that she strongly needed it, so I amassed all my savings and bought a smartphone for her. She was very happy and surprised to see the gift I bought for her. She never expected it from me as I didn't give her any hint regarding the gift.

She thanked me many times for this gift as she liked the color, built and everything of the phone pretty much. Everyone appreciated my choice of mobile phone. She uses it for myriad purposes. She listens to music and click pictures on it. She is very fond of watching videos on phone. Now, she doesn't have to ask anyone for that.

She was on cloud nine after receiving such a costly gift from me. Whenever she wants to search for anything, she googles it on her smartphone. She deserved this gift and it was a token of love from my side to my mom.

Your favorite fruit

How often do you eat fruits?

How do you eat it?

What are the benefits of eating it?

Fruits play an important role in keeping us healthy. They keep our bodies fresh and active. Fruits contain fiber and various other nutrients that are required to maintain a healthy body. There are various fruits that I like to eat but the one I love the most is the apple.

Apple is my favorite fruit because it is very sweet in taste and additionally it is full of nutrients that are very good for our body. We all know the proverb "An apple a day keeps the doctor away". I will say that this proverb is pretty much true because it contains many types of antioxidants that help us in fighting various bacteria in our body. It helps in preventing major diseases like cancer, asthma, and some skin disorders. Antioxidants present in the fruits helps to keep our skin perfect.

I like this fruit very much as nowadays it is available throughout the year in my country. Gone are those days when apple was available during winter season only. Now, there are different varieties of cold stored apples that are available in the market all year round.

This fruit is suitable for people of all age groups. From kids to the old age persons, doctors suggest everyone to eat apples for at least once in a day. This fruit also helps in the process of weight loss and many dieticians advise their patients to include this fruit in their regular diet. The nutritional value of an apple is undoubtedly very high.

Apart from eating it raw, apple is used to make several other dishes as well. I love to eat apple pudding and apple pie. The sweet and savory taste of apple pudding is all I need when I crave for a quick snack. Moreover, apple juice is also a common drink all over the world.

Recently, I was suffering from stomach infection and I was unable to digest anything and was entirely on liquids. But this fruit really helped me in my survival as I was not able to eat any solid food for three to four days. So, without a doubt apple is my favourite fruit.

A time when you had to wait for someone
Where did you wait
Why did you wait
How did you feel

I love to meet all my friends and relatives quite often as it uplifts my mood and makes me feel elated. Whenever I am stressed out, I call one of my good friends and arrange a meet with him/her so that I can have some fun time and forget all my worries and tensions of my life.

Last week I was very fed up with my hectic schedule of work and study so, I called one of my friends named Shikha. She is a very good friend of mine and she's very jovial in nature. So, whenever I am feeling dejected, I call her to relax my mind and get some positive energy in my life. But she has a very bad habit of coming late no matter what the situation is.

We planned to meet at a local restaurant in our city. We decided to have lunch at 1:00 pm. As I very well know about her habits, I reached the restaurant by 1:30 pm but still she was not there.

After waiting outside for 5 minutes, I got seated inside the restaurant and waited for her. After a few minutes, I called on her mobile, but it was switched off which disappointed me a bit. After waiting for another thirty minutes, I had to order a soup so that I could kill the time further. But it was an awkward situation for me to wait for so long sitting alone in a restaurant.

Finally, after waiting for around 40 minutes she came and started apologizing to me. I was very upset with her and I criticized her for coming so late and making me wait like this. I told her if she would have not come for another 2 minutes, I would have left. She was continuously trying to feel sorry for coming late, but I was not listening to any of her excuses. Then she told me that her car got punctured on the way and she got it repaired from the mechanic first and that's why she got late.

I felt sorry for her as she was in such a problem and I was arguing with her like she has committed a big crime. At last, I apologized, and we had our lunch and spent a very good time together.

Your favorite cousin

Tell about your cousin's nature

Speak about the things that make him/her you favourite cousin

Do you spend time together?

Cousins are just like your friends if they are of the same age group as you. Since I am blessed with many cousins in my family, I don't feel the need of having more friends in my life. Whenever I need to go somewhere or need any kind of help, I call one of my cousins to accompany me. And they too willingly join me wherever I ask them.

My favorite cousin is my uncle's (my mother's brother) son named Amit. Amit is a very kindhearted person. He lives near my place, so we visit each other quite frequently. Moreover, we are of the same age, so we used to study in the same class. We spent a lot of time together in school time. He is very close to my heart. Whenever I need to discuss anything important, I always go to him. He's like a true friend and always give me right suggestions. He is the only person with whom I can discuss my personal problems. There are some things I cannot share with my parents; I can share with him. We are quite famous in our family for the bonding we share.

I spend a lot of time with him as we live nearby. We have gone to uncountable night outs together. Since, our families are also very close to each other, we usually go out for family trips together. Last month, we both went on a trip to a hill station outside our city for a few days. It was one of the best trips of my life.

These days, he is planning to go abroad to pursue his further studies. Thus, I am very sad that we will be away from each other. But I am glad that he is excelling in his career. I am also planning to move abroad in the same country, so most likely we will be together again.

A time when you felt nervous or anxious or frightened

What happened

How did you tackle the situation?

Was it the first time when you got nervous?

There are several moments in our lives when we get nervous or anxious. But we learn something from every moment or situation that we encounter in our life. But what matters the most is how we tackle with such circumstances and what action we take at that critical time.

I would like to discuss a recent situation when I was very frightened.

Couple of months back I was travelling in a bus. I was going to my friend's house who lives in Shimla. I had planned this visit as I was having a long weekend due to a local festival.

My friend called me and invited to his house for a couple of days. I was very excited about my trip as I was about to meet my old school friend after two years. I booked the bus from an online website and departed at 6 AM. The bus takes around four hours to reach Shimla. The highway to Shimla is under construction and drivers was very cautious of the obstacles on the road.

I went in the rainy season and I saw lots of small pieces of rocks lying on the road. These rocks had been disintegrated from the hills due to heavy downpour from last week's rain. The frightening moment came when our bus suddenly stopped and skid sideways due to the heavy brakes applied by the driver. Many passengers fell in the bus as they were standing. On the other hand, my head hit the seat in front of me and I got a slight bruise.

Everyone in the bus was stunned and asked the driver about the situation. The driver asked everyone to leave the bus immediately and take a safe cover. There was a huge landslide that had happened just in front of our bus. A huge part of the mountain fell on the buses and cars that were moving ahead of us.

We were so lucky that we hadn't been the victim of that. Despite this, I was so nervous and frightened that I couldn't continue the journey. This happened at the halfway of our destination.

I called my parents and they tried to calm me down and told me not to worry. My father came there along with my brother and took me back to home. Although we were saved by the driver's presence of mind, but I felt frightened for the whole week due to this incident.

Describe a person you think is a good parent

What is your relationship with that person?

How do you think he/she is a good parent?

What sort of relationship this person has with his/her kids?

Parents are always their child's best well-wisher. They can never think of anything that can harm their children. Even my parents are very caring and helpful to me in every situation. They are always ready to sacrifice their desires to fulfill my needs.

But today I would like to discuss a parent who I think is the best example of a great parent, my elder sister. She is undoubtedly the best mother and a great woman too. She is very supportive of her kids. She has sacrificed a lot of things while raising her children.

She was working in a reputed management company at a high post. But her husband got transferred to a different state because of professional work, so she realized that her kids are not getting proper attention and they miss their father too much. She made her mind and decided to resign from her job and give her kids more time. And it was very fruitful, her extra care and involvement with kids made them quite happy.

Not only this, she has given great upbringing to her kids. My niece and nephew are very intelligent kids. They have learned many good lessons from their mother and know well how to behave with elders, their friends and relatives. She gives them space in their lives too but punishes them for their mistakes too. She has maintained a very good balance in her kids' life and allowed them to do every activity in their daily lives.

She has a huge influence on her kids as she has given them education about their culture, rituals and religion. Many parents are not able to teach their kids about their customs these days. But she has provided her kids with every possible knowledge and views.

In the end, I will say the kids are blessed to have such a mother in their life who is so caring, generous and the best person they can ever think of in their life. I hope in future her kids will also treat her with so much generosity and love as she treats them now.

Describe a piece of furniture at your home

For what purpose do you use it?

When did you buy it?

Describe that piece of furniture in detail

All the furniture placed at my home is bought with great sentiments by my family. Every piece of furniture in our house has a special purpose. But, the one I love the most is the study table of my room. It is made from top quality wood.

This furniture is very special to me because of many reasons. Firstly, I bought this from my own pocket money. Whatever money I used to get on my birthday's or any other occasion from my parents, I collected it in a savings account. When I had enough amount, I bought the study table of my room. This is not just a mere study table but a beautiful piece of art that has been carved by the expert artists. I bought the study table when I was in my school.

The table is of ideal height and width. It has two drawers on the left side and big rack on the other side, where I keep all my books and reference papers securely. There is one slider beneath the table that helps in keeping some useful papers.

The study table is entirely made up of wood. It is polished in the walnut color and has a natural wooden finish. I bought this table around five years back and it is still in excellent condition and looks like it has been bought recently. I feel very comfortable whenever I use this table to study or do any other activity in my daily life. I also love to read books on this study table. In fact, it provides a great storage capacity to keep all my books and stationery in it.

Also, it is very portable, so I can shift it to any room in the future. There is an LED bulb that is attached to the top of the table. It is very useful as it gives proper lighting whenever I am studying without affecting my eyes in any way. Hence, this is the piece of furniture that I like the most.

Describe a way to stay healthy

What is the importance of health?

What is the best way to stay healthy?

How do you keep yourself healthy?

Staying healthy is the most significant thing in our life. If one is not healthy, he or she will not be able to accomplish the dreams of their lives. Good health can make you rejoice your success in life. Not only this, it also helps you to live more happily and keeps you fresh and active in your day to day activities.

For me, eating home cooked food is the best way to stay healthy. What matters the most to our health is what we eat throughout the day. Most of the times, I eat homemade food. That really helps me to stay healthy and save a decent amount of money.

Today, most people prefer to eat junk food, which has multiple side-effects on our body. Junk food increases the amount of extra fat in the body that can also lead to obesity in some cases.

Moreover, outside food contains a lot of oil and gluten, which can be detrimental for our health. Many problems like heart disease, diabetes, back pain, knee joints pain and many more are caused by eating an excess of junk food.

Whereas, home-cooked food is very nutritious and helps in maintaining body balance. It keeps you fit and active. The oil and spices we use at our home are not harmful to our body while in outside food, various artificial preservatives, colors and other spices are used that affects our body in a negative way. It also disturbs our digestive system thus producing ulcers in the stomach, which can even lead to stomach cancer in some cases.

Most people in my country like to carry their tiffin along with them which is packed with healthy home-cooked food. They do this, because they know the importance of this healthy and hygienic home-cooked food. Having junk food occasionally will certainly not harm your body but eating it quite often will make you inch towards major health issues in the future. I can say in the end that eating homemade food is the best way to keep yourself healthy.

Describe your biggest fear

What is the fear

How did it get to your mind?

Have you done something to get rid of that fear?

Every person has some fear and anxieties in their life which they find very difficult to deal with. These phobias can be small as well as of intense level. I also have a fear in my life and that is fear of height. I can't look down if I am standing at an extreme height.

This phobia in my mind is from my childhood. My mother tells me that I fear height because of one incident that happened with me in my childhood. She told me that this happened when I was very young and I and was playing with my elder brother on the balcony of our house and sustained multiple injuries. At that time, my elder brother fell from the second floor as his foot slipped. I was terrorized at that time and after that, I got the fear of elevations. Till now, I don't prefer such activities that involve altitudes in it.

Whenever I go to a hill station, I don't prefer to look down in the gorge as I feel so scared. I also have a feeling of nausea while standing at an elevated platform. I always try to look straight throughout the way and avoid such situations that could make me feel sick. All my friends are very adventurous, and they like to do audacious activities such as sky diving, bungy jumping but I can't even think of doing those activities as they involve such great heights.

Some of my friends make fun of my fear and bully me for this, but I am helpless, and I can't overcome this fear in my life. I have tried many times to overcome my fear of height, but I was unsuccessful, and all my efforts went in vain. My brother who fell from such great heights is not at all scared of height, but that incident left a mark on my mind and memory. I hope in future I will one day overcome my phobia and will be able to have all such adventurous fun that my friends do.

Describe a task you did well

What was the task

How did you do it

Do you feel that it was your best task till now?

I am the kind of person who loves to take challenges in my work. I feel there is no fun in doing easy tasks as anything achieved easily is not valued much while achieving something in our life with difficulty is valued more. I have done many difficult tasks in my life, but the one I did very well according to me, is the decoration of the house for my cousin's wedding. All my relatives and friends really liked my decoration ideas and appreciated me for doing such wonderful work.

Two years back, it was my cousin's wedding. My cousin and her family were looking for the decorators to decorate their home for the sangeet function and other rituals to be performed at their place. It was a big opportunity for me to showcase my skills.

They initiated me for this work and gave me such a big responsibility as marriage is such an important event in one's life. If one is giving you such big liability, that means they really trust your work. And I had to get par with all their expectations.

Firstly, I made a list of the things that they wanted at their place for the decoration and made a budget for the work. With the help of two of my friends, I bought everything and did all the decorations with lights and flowers all over their house. Their house was renovated recently so when I decorated it with fragrant flowers and lights, it blossomed like a new bride. On the day of the event, everyone was elated with the beautification of the party venue. One and all appreciated my work a lot. My cousin thanked me personally and gave me a special return gift. I also took help from my cousins for this task. I can say without any doubt that I had never completed such a task before in my life and I think this was the task that I did well.

A task you completed on time

What was the task about?

How much time did you take to complete it?

Did you take help of someone to complete the project?

Completing tasks in time surely makes you a successful person in life. I am a very punctual kind of a person, so I like to do all my tasks on time if everything goes right. The task that I remember the most is when I had to complete a huge project in a limited time period.

I remember in my college days when I was given a project regarding my field to be submitted within 15 days. All students were given a different task in the class. The task that was given to me was very time consuming and difficult. So, finishing it in such a short span of time was backbreaking. There was some fieldwork involved in my project, so I used to travel quite frequently to different places to get the information and most of my day's time was consumed in travelling. So, I had to work till late night to complete my assignment on time.

This project involved a survey about an environment issue prevailing these days. In the assignment I had to collect all the information regarding the project from different parts of the city. Furthermore, I had to take survey of at least two hundred people. The survey involved questions regarding the issue and the answers were to be given in two to three lines.

No doubt, my project was a very stimulating one, but if more days would be permitted for this work, it would have been a bit easy for me to complete this. I took this project as a challenge to test my capability. So, I got motivation each day to complete it on time.

Finally, the day came when I had to submit my project. I was glad that I had completed my project on time. When I gave my paperwork to my professor, she was very happy and a bit shocked that I have completed such a complicated project on the official submission day without any discrepancy.

She told me that in her entire teaching experience, she has not seen a single student who has completed this project in the given time. She was very proud of me and gave me extra marks for completing my task in such a short time.

A child you know well

What is your relationship with that kid?

How do you know him/her well?

What sort of bond do you share with him/her?

Children are the most innocent souls in this universe. I really love kids. I love to spend time with them by playing different games. They have a pure intent and are selfless. They will learn whatever you teach them. They are far away from the materialistic things and only want love in life.

There are many children in my acquaintances but one child I know well lives in my neighborhood. She is a girl named "Pihu". She is five years old now. She is the cutest girl I have ever seen in my life. Whatever she does and speaks really makes me love her more and more.

She is a very innocent and pure soul. Her mother is a good friend of my mother and both our families are very close to each other. Pihu also loves me a lot and always tells her mom to take her to my house so that she can play with me.

Whenever she is sad, she shares all her feelings with me. Even if she has some good news to tell, she rushes to my home immediately to declare the news and share her happiness and joy.

Not only this, she loves to complete her school homework with me as I make her understand all the things very politely and in a very logical way. I integrate all her subjects with real-life activities which helps her to complete her work with great interest.

I don't have any younger sibling, so I find my younger sister in her. I share a sweet bond with her. Even her family trusts me for her safety. Next week, her birthday is coming, and I am planning to gift her a cute soft toy as she loves those a lot.

She is a very intelligent girl. She plays a couple of musical instruments very well as she is getting training for the same at her school. She is also doing very well in her studies. Her observation power is very strong, and she grasps all the things very easily.

So, Pihu is the kid that I know very well.

An expensive thing you want to buy in future

What will you buy?

Have you saved money for it?

When will you buy it?

Dreaming is everyone's birthright. We can dream of buying everything and anything in our life. There are many expensive things that I am not able to buy right now but will surely buy them in the future when I will be earning enough on my own to buy them.

Well, I am very fond of watches. I would like to buy a Rolex watch in my life whenever I get a chance. Having a Rolex watch is like a dream for me. As they are very expensive, and they are not so easily available in every store. The Rolex brand is the most valuable watch brand in the world. The cost of this watch is super expensive throughout the world. The built quality of these watches is commendable. Rolex makes hundreds of different style watches, but I would like to buy the one in black and silver. It is an evergreen design and goes with all kinds of occasions.

It is quite a prestigious watch because of the high-quality material with which it is being made. It is made up of 904L steel which is the highest-grade steel in the world. The company owns its in-house science lab that works day and night to produce fantastic watches.

Every minor aspect is checked in the labs and error free watches are being manufactured by the company. One of the best things about these watches is that they are not made by robotic technology. Even now, the machines are managed by humans which involves supervision at each step of the manufacturing.

Wearing this watch is itself a very prestigious and worthy experience. I know that this watch is very expensive, but I am in love with this brand. So, whenever I get a chance to buy something expensive, I will buy a Rolex watch.

Visit to a swimming pool

Why did you visit

What did you do there?

Do you know swimming

Swimming is a great activity that actively involves all the body parts of a person. It is known to be the best exercise. It requires great skills to learn swimming in an effective manner. I can't swim but would like to learn this skill if given chance and time.

Last week, I went to a swimming pool. I accompanied my friend to the pool because he was learning swimming from a private instructor in a club near his house. As he was taking training, I was sitting in the waiting area from where the whole view was very clear.

I could see some kids were swimming in the kid's pool area. It was a hot summer day and they were enjoying to the fullest. They were being instructed continuously by the trainer. My friend was in the adult pool and there were hardly three persons in the pool area at that time.

I was admiring the moment and was passing my free time by observing people in the pool. I saw there was a kid in the kid's pool who was very reluctant to swim freely in the water. He might be a newcomer, but the trainer was very patient and supportive. He slowly made him swim and soon I could see some confidence on the face of that kid.

I got very excited sitting there and made my mind to learn swimming. I am a bit hydrophobic, but I was now getting motivation to learn this skill. I went to the trainer and asked him about the admissions. He told me to fill the form and submit the fee before the date mentioned.

After coming back, I was again consumed by my hectic schedule. So, I couldn't learn swimming. If given a chance, I would surely love to learn swimming in my life and swim smoothly like a fish.

A time when you gave suggestion in a survey
Where did you participate in the survey?
What suggestion did you give?
Did you like participating in the survey

Nowadays, people like to get feedback from the masses so that they can get a review. The reaction from the public makes them generate a better and enhanced productivity of their product. We can see many surveys on the internet nowadays as we scroll through various sites.

There are different methods to conduct surveys. Some companies do it on the internet and some like to take the feedback from people in person. The survey in which I participated was held in a mall. Recently I went to a renowned mall in my city and I saw few officials were asking questions from random people wandering in the mall. They had all the questions written in a form and were asking people to fill it.

One of those officials asked me to partake in that survey. They told me that the 10 best feedback forms will be given assured prizes. I had a lot of time with me on that day, so I decided to give answers in the survey.

The form had questions about the mall's services and security. The hygiene in the washrooms and many other things were being asked in the feedback form. I gave all the answers as per my opinion with honesty. I go to that mall frequently, so I knew about the different aspects of the mall very well. The form was a review-based survey in which we had to give 0-10 points on the different facets of the mall. At the end of the form, I was asked to write at least five lines about the mall or any suggestion that I had which was not covered in the previous questions. So, I wrote a suggestion to reduce the car parking fee of the mall as it was too high.

At the end, they asked me to fill in my details such as name, age, sex and phone number so that they could contact me in case I win the prize. However, I did not get any call regarding the prize, but I honestly filled the survey form and gave my suggestion in that. I really enjoyed participating in that survey.

Your favorite singer
Why do you like him/her?
What are his/her favourite songs
How his music has influenced people
Listening to songs is my favorite part-time activity as this not only makes me feel good but also makes me stress-free from my daily hectic schedule. Whenever I get time, I love to listen to songs of various singers.

But my top favorite singer is Michael Jackson. The songs sung by him are very different and no one else can sing and dance like him. All his moves and vocals are just incomparable. He was a real legend.

He was a very known international American pop singer. He was known as the "KING OF POP". His music records are just brilliant and no one till date has been able to break his sales records.

177

When this legendary singer took his last breath in 2009, everyone in the world was in mourn. He was not only known for his singing style and stardom but also for the lifestyle he was living. It was just so different and odd for some people.

The most famous blockbuster album of Michael Jackson is Thriller which got sales of around 33 million worldwide. No one has been able to break such record till date for such a famous streak in the music industry.

He was famous for his various moves but the one which was a delight to everyone, named by him as Moonwalk, which I personally like very much. His other albums like *Off the Wall, Bad, Dangerous* and lastly *The Invincible.* All his songs are my favorite and make me come out of my thoughts and dance to the tunes of his songs.

He was always in news for one or the other reasons and many people criticized him for his surgeries and other facial changes. Due to his ill health and aftereffects from many surgeries, he died at a young age of 50 years, but he is still there in the hearts of his devoted fans and he will hold a special place in their hearts forever.

Visit to a strange (unexplored) place
Where it is located
Why is it strange
How often do you visit that place?

I am the kind of person who loves to travel a lot. I have seen a lot of strange places in my life but the one which I would like to tell you is located in Dubai.

Last year, I went to Dubai with my family. There are many places in Dubai that are worth to visit like Burj khalifa, museums, beaches and many more. One of the strange places that I visited there is the Dubai Mall. It is a well-known mall in that country.

Well, this mall is the biggest mall in the world, and it is like a maze for some people. I went there with my parents and brother. We were all wandering in different directions and decided to meet at a certain point after two hours. When the time passed, I started looking for that place where we had decided to meet. It was located on the first floor, but the mall is so big that it has so many different sections and buildings at a single floor. It took me more than 30 mins to reach the meeting point.

There are multiple exits and entries of the mall that one cannot identify at a single gaze. For the first time visitors, the mall is like a puzzle that is very difficult to solve.

But the mall was really pleasing to our eyes as it was decorated so nicely for one of their local festivals and there were many offers and discounts on all the brands. You can find any local or international brand in this mall but tracing any location in the mall was like the most complicated task.

Practically, it takes around three days for a person to stroll through the whole mall. I find that mall really strange as it is such a humungous place that one can't imagine.

Describe a piece of good news that you heard from someone

When did you receive the news?

What was it about?

How did you react to the news?

I have received several good news from people over the past few years. The one that comes to my mind right now is when I was selected for a quiz competition to represent my school at a national level.

That time I was studying in my 10th class and a team from a renowned quiz contest came to our school to select few students that will represent our school in the competition. This contest is telecasted on the national television and participating in it was a great deal for me.

There was a team of three people who were carrying a lot of documents with them. Our teachers introduced them to us and told us to follow whatever they had to say. Then, the team started distributing those papers to us.

All the students were asked to fill in the answers to the given questions on the paper. Those papers contained general knowledge related questions in objective type pattern. We had to just tick the right answer on the sheet. There were 100 questions in total and we were given two hours to solve the paper. On the basis of the results, five contestants from each school were to be selected. I finished the paper in the given time, and I was very confident for a good result.

179

I knew answers to most of the questions and I was hoping that I would be selected for the live quiz contest. The result was to be declared after a week, so I was very excited for that. I couldn't sleep for six days as I was expecting a good result.

The result didn't disappoint me. My class teacher broke this great news to me in the morning that I was selected along with four other students to participate in the quiz show. I was on cloud nine when I heard this news. I was congratulated by our principal and she told me to prepare hard for the competition.

So, this is the news that I heard from my class teacher and it made me happy.

Your favorite magazine

What is the name of the magazine?

How has it helped you?

Do you read it every day?

I read somewhere on the internet that there are more than 5000 magazines that are published in 26 different languages across India. I can easily say that people in my country like to read magazines. I am no different as I love to explore magazines that are related to travel and cars. Autocar and Lonely Planet are the two magazines that I read vividly. However, I would like to speak on lonely Planet today. This magazine is published and distributed all over the world. It originated in Australia when a married couple decided to write about their travel in a book.

Soon they became famous and their work was liked by people from every corner of our globe. This magazine is published monthly and is distributed in more than 100 countries. It is a wonderful piece of travel guide that people follow before they can decide their holiday destination.

The magazine has around 120-150 pages in each subscription. The pages are bright in color and the print quality is fantastic. They print images of the world's best places to travel. With that, they also give detailed information about that place like what to eat, where to stay and how to reach there.

They have different sections that are associated with different regions. I like to read all the parts from Asia to Europe. This magazine is a wonderful guide for people like me. I am addicted to travelling so I like this magazine very much.

This is a marvelous magazine for people who like to travel and explore new places. I read this magazine almost every day for 20-30 minutes. It gives me so much of knowledge about this wonderful planet.

I have taken an annual membership in which I get 12 editions in one year. Every edition has something special to offer. The magazine reaches me by post and doesn't cost a lot as well. I recommend this magazine to anyone who is looking for the best travel magazine.

A club that you have joined

How often do you go to that club?

What activities do you do there?

What is included in the club area?

There are many clubs near my place, but the one I have joined is the PCA club. This is the most famous club in my city as various international cricket matches are held in the stadium every season. Very few people are having the opportunity to join this club and I am one of them.

The club is very well maintained by the management. I usually go there to learn swimming and to play table tennis. They ponder highly upon the hygiene of the activity areas. They have a gym area, a sports area that includes various sports infrastructure such as table tennis, badminton, football, basketball and many more.

They have a very well-organized swimming pool area too that also has expert trainers from whom you can take training for swimming classes. Last year, my younger brother took swimming classes at our club and now he is a good swimmer.

There are various parties and events in the club that are organized on various occasions like New year, Christmas, Diwali. I always participate in all the parties and activities as it gives me a chance to meet new people. The security of the club is very efficient as no one can enter the club without a membership card. Non-members are not allowed to use the facilities of the club. There is a big restaurant area in the club where we usually party at any special occasion in our family. The food served at their restaurant is very delicious and of very good quality.

181

Since, it has an international stadium in it, during match days we can commonly get a sight of players in the restaurant or other club areas. I have met many cricket players at that time and taken their autographs. I got the membership because of my father. He is the main member and we are the dependent members. So, we have our own card which we can use to enter the club and avail the activities. I go to that club at least once a week.

An accident that you have seen
Where did this happen
What was the cause
What did you feel?
I have seen numerous accidents in my life that were not fatal. But the one I am going to tell you today is one of the most dangerous accidents that I have seen in my life.
It happened a few years back when we were travelling to Delhi by bus. Our bus stopped for a break and we took a bit of refreshment in the restaurant. We were having tea when we heard a loud bang from the highway side. we rushed outside and saw a passenger bus had collided with a huge truck. We hurried to the accident site and what we saw was nothing short of a nightmare. It was terrifying to see blood on the road and people lying near the bus. It was a fatal accident that had taken lives of many people.
I was in a state of shock as I had never seen such an accident in my whole life. Hundreds of people from nearby places gathered in a blink of an eye to rescue people. Both the bus and truck collided head on and both the vehicles fell sideways.
Me and my father started to help people by offering them water to drink and soon the police and rescue team arrived on the spot. They took 10 minutes to clear the way as the highway was blocked due to the accident. Onlookers told that the accident happened due to the overspeed of the bus and the truck was also going in the wrong lane. This led to a head on collision of both the vehicles.
Ambulances arrived and took the victims to hospitals. We couldn't help much as our bus was about to leave. But it was a terrifying moment for me as I had never seen such an accident in my life.

Next day we read about this incident in the newspaper and came to know that only two people died. We were relieved as we thought that the number of fatalities would be much higher due to the magnitude of the accident.

Favorite subject in your school
Why did you like this subject?
What fascinates you the most about this subject?
Do you still study this subject?
My school life has been my favorite period of life till now. It was such a great fun to be at school with friends. Those activity classes and other break sessions were the most amazing times of the school day.
I was a very disciplined and obedient student in my class. I used to study all the subjects with thorough concentration, but the one I liked the most was Mathematics. I also loved science and geography, but math's is the subject that allured me the most.
From my childhood till now, mathematics has been the subject of my interest. Since it involves logic in it, it has always attracted me. In fact, I used to get the highest marks in this subject as I used to practice math's in my free time at home.
Well, my math's teacher was also my favorite teacher because she made us learn all the logics of the subject in a very interesting way. She gave stimulating math's exercises and taught in a very professional way.
The thing that fascinates me the most about this subject is that we often use these math's logics in our day to day lives. Various topics of distance, measurement, temperature and other reasoning questions are of great use to us in our everyday routine.
I always participated in the Math's competitions in my school time. I remember once I participated in an inter school competition and I secured the first position in that competition. I was awarded with an expensive pen and a trophy. I liked this subject so much that I would only practice mathematics rather than any other subject in my study time.
I am good at this subject, so I have made my mind to continue with this subject for my higher studies as well. I want to succeed in mathematics and want to make a name in this field.

Tell about a subject you disliked in school

Which subjects do you disliked?

Why did you dislike this subject?

What type of subjects are interesting?

You will not believe me that I hated most of the subjects in my school time. I only liked math's, physics, geography and biology. On the other hand, I never liked history, chemistry and social sciences.

The one that I disliked the most is history subject. I found it very boring to study in my school time. I thought that it is one of the most useless subjects that are taught in the society. I am not a big admirer of studying past dates and events. I believe that what has happened has happened. There's no point of remembering the dates and events as we have storage devices for that. We can save all the data in computers.

Instead, kids should be taught more aesthetic and dynamic subjects like math's and geography. They can learn more in these subjects and they can also utilize these subject's knowledge in their day to day life. In the life of a common man, historical dates don't have much importance.

In our country's text books, the history subject contains the same information that was taught fifty years back. Nothing has changed and I think that information in the history textbooks is completely out of date and there are number of changes that are needed to be made to raise the standard of this subject.

According to my notion, present history is more interesting and important to tell. So instead of having historical dates from hundreds of years back, the textbooks should include history from the past ten years only. This kind of history is more interesting to read and memorize.

I remember that I used to find history subject so boring that I could not study it more than fifteen minutes. I disliked it so much that I never opened history books in my study time at home.

I couldn't learn all the dates and names of the prominent personalities from the past. I was not able to cram all the events and happenings. So, history was the subject that I disliked the most in my school time.

How do you utilize your free time?

What activity do you do?

How often do you do it?

Do you still do the same activity

Nowadays, I am quite busy in my classes. So, I hardly get any free time for myself. Nevertheless, I get some time on weekends to do the things that I cannot do otherwise. Going to the classes and coming back to the home without any fun is quite a monotonous routine and I feel very fed up sometimes with this routine.

Whenever I get some free time on the weekends, I like to go for a long walk. The walk helps me to get desired physical activity and fresh air that is difficult to get in cities. I generally go to big parks and woods so that I can cut myself from the outer world for some time. I usually carry my phone and a pair of headphones as I listen to my favourite tracks while I walk. There is a big park in my city where I usually go for a walk. I see numerous people who run and do jogging there. Many kids come there to play certain games. I feel rejuvenated during my walk. I have been following this activity from the past three years. I feel incomplete if I miss this activity on weekends.

This park is not like the usual parks. This park is humungous and has a thick covering of trees and other plants. There are separate tracks for running and walking. There is uncountable variety of flowers that are grown on the edges of the walking tracks. It is a public park so there is no entry fee to it. Although the park closes at 10 in the evening.

This habit has been one of the most productive activities that I do. I have lost a few kilos from the past few weeks. I feel more energetic and industrious throughout my day due to walking. I have limited amount of free time mostly on weekends. Hence, this is how I utilize my leisure time.

An interesting old person you know well

How do you know him/her?

What is interesting in him/her

Is there any interesting thing that you can learn?

I am the kind of person who loves to know different people. I know a lot of young as well as old people. If I could make a list, then I think that I certainly know a lot of old people in my life. In this topic, I would like to speak about my Grandfather as he's an old person I know the best.

He is the most interesting and intelligent person I have ever known. One can judge his knowledge and experience by just having a conversation with him. Since my childhood, I have idolized him as the person I want to become. His story is very interesting as he has earned a niche for himself. He was brought up in a poor family but with his dedication towards work and honesty helped him to reach the pinnacle of success. He is a retired chief executive engineer from Delhi. He reached the top position in his department in a mere ten-year period. He achieved a lot of accolades during his service life.

His age is currently more than 80 years, but still he is so active and energetic in whatever he does. He wakes up early in the morning and does his routine exercise. He is very fit and good at health as he is very diet conscious and exercises regularly for an hour every day. He is fond of watching movies and using modern electronic gadgets. He is very interesting as despite his age he is so modern and adaptable.

I am highly inspired by him in my life and I follow him wholeheartedly in my personal as well as professional life. There is so much that I can learn from him. Whatever he teaches me on a general basis is of great help to me in my daily life and I implement them everywhere to achieve success. One interesting thing that I would like to learn from him is that how he wakes up early in the morning every day and follows his routine on a daily basis.

He is the old person who is very interesting, and I know him very well.

A movie you watched recently

What genre of movies do you watch?

How often do you watch movies?

How this movie has inspired you

Watching movies is one of my favorite leisure time activities. It is a great source of entertainment. I like to watch movies on weekends as I have ample of free time. I like to watch movies based on real events or people. one such movie that I watched recently was MS DHONI – The untold story.

This movie is about my favorite sports star i.e. M.S Dhoni. He is one of the finest cricketers in our country. He is acknowledged worldwide for his playing skills and management skills too as a captain of the team.

This movie captures various moments from his personal as well as professional life. I came to know about a lot of things from his personal life that I didn't know earlier. The role of the lead character was played by one of the finest actors, Shashank Singh Rajput. His acting was praised by one and all.

The movie depicts the struggles of MSD in his initial days. The movie shows all the aspects of his life, his career defining moments, his best playing days, his achievements, his marriage, his earlier jobs, friends and family. This movie reveals a lot of things about the character of MSD. He has millions of fans all over the world who wanted to know everything about this champion. So, he decided to make a movie on him that was also a block buster.

The movie also includes some of the shots captured from his real life. This movie has left a long and lasting impact on me as we can learn so much from it. I have seen this movie many times as every time I watch this movie, I get engulfed in the storyline and brilliant acting of all the actors. I learned a huge life lesson from this movie that anyone can make his dream come true if there is right intent and hard work.

Lastly, the songs played in the movie are also composed by top musicians and singers. This is the movie that I saw recently, and it is one of my favourite movies as well.

A time when you felt angry

Do you often get angry?

What was the incident

What did you do when you got angry?

Emotions are part of one's life. Different types of emotions come out in different situations of life. Sometimes, conditions are so compelling that it becomes impossible to control our emotions and temperament.

Anger is also such an emotion that is ousted in most of the people with a very short temperament. Sometimes, even calm and patient people lose their cool in certain situations of their lives. I am such a person who does not get angry very often, but there can be some circumstances that can make me angry.

I still remember the incident that happened with me a few weeks back. I was driving back to my home late at night from my friend's birthday party. Since it was quite late, I was driving slowly.

I was on the highway and suddenly a child came in front of my car from nowhere. I quickly steered the car to the left and applied the brakes to the fullest. I received a great jerk and my car was about to hit the pavement. But thankfully that didn't happen. But I went in a state of slight tremor. After a few seconds, when I revived to my senses I got out of the car. I scolded the child and inquired about her parents. Then I saw her mother was coming across the road busy on her mobile phone talking with someone.

I got so angry looking at her mom as she was not at all concerned for her child and was busy on her phone. I really don't understand how parents could do this to their child. It was such a careless act that is intolerable for anyone.

The young kid was very scared and crying badly, so I didn't say anything to her. But I really screamed at her mother and asked about her whereabouts.

She was guilty for the mistake of not taking care of her child and leaving her alone on the road, especially on the highway.

I am so grateful to God that I was very tired, so I was driving slowly which saved the child. I hope people of our country will understand the value of using these gadgets at the right time, but not at the stake of life of their kids.

Talk about an important photograph
On what occasion the photograph was taken
Who is there in the photo?
Why is it important
Photographs are such an important part of our lives. Good cameras capture beautiful moments of our lives in a single click. Whenever we look at our old photographs, we revive various memories made with several people and places in our lives.

188

I am having a huge collection of photographs with me since my childhood days. But the one that is my favorite is the family photograph of me with all my family members taken 5 years back. The photograph was taken at my cousin's wedding.

That photograph includes all my uncles, aunts and cousins from both my maternal and paternal side of relatives. The photograph was taken at the end of the wedding party when everyone one was called upon by my grandfather for a family photo session.

The reason that this photo is very important is that this photo can never be taken again. Because two of the eldest members have passed away and some of my cousins are now settled abroad. Some are married now and some of them have now kids as well.

I remember that this photo was taken near the entry gate of the venue. As there were around forty people in the photo, it took a lot of clicks to get a perfect shot. The photographer was patient enough to deal with all of us. I was a young kid back then, so I sat in the front row with all my cousins and all the other members were arranged according to their seniority.

It is impossible for us to get clicked for such photograph again. So, it increases its importance. I approached the photographer and ordered him to make a framed portrait of four feet wide and three feet tall. It is a massive photo that hangs majestically on the wall of our living room. That photo attracts every visitor's eyes.

I love all my family members and whenever I miss them, I simply gaze at the photograph.

Describe an old thing
What is the importance of old things?
Is it important to you?
Have you kept that thing with you?

I like to collect things especially when they are given by a loved one. I have set aside a lot of old things with me that reminds me of my past. I think that old things hold a great importance in our life as we can learn from them.

I have kept few of my childhood toys and games with me. The old thing that I want to describe in this topic is a retro watch that was gifted to me by my grandfather.

My grandfather is no more with me, so I always keep his token of love with me as his remembrance. Whenever I look at this watch, I recall those moments spent with him and how he used to play with me in my childhood. I remember he used to over pamper me and always saved from my parent's scolding.

The watch that I have is of gold color with a leather strap. The strap is of brown colour that compliments beautifully with the watch. The watch is 24 carat gold plated. It is of Titan brand, which is one of the renowned brands of watches worldwide. The best part is that the watch is still in working condition. However, I had to get its battery changed last year. I have kept that watch in a watch box and kept it in my almirah safely. I specially ordered this elegant watch box from the internet.

My grandfather gave me this watch when he realized that his end was near. I was around 7 years old and he called me to his room and told me to always value the time and made me understand the importance of time in our life by gifting this watch. His words still echo in my mind. Whatever I am today is just because of his lessons and teachings.

I always keep that watch in my almirah and never allow anyone to wear it as it is so dearer to me.

First day at school/college/university
What happened that day
How did you feel
Did you find it interesting or boring?
I have studied in a couple of different schools. I would like to describe about my first day at higher secondary school. I read in a different school till my class tenth, but I changed my school after that. I don't remember anything about my first day at school in kindergarten that's why I will explain the first day at my senior secondary school.

I was new to the school like most of my other classmates. Students from different schools enrolled in this school for their higher education. I found this school to be very different form my previous one.

The new school was enormous with a lot of facilities in it. The first day when I entered the school, I was surprised as I had never seen such a huge premise of a school before. We were told to gather in the assembly area where the morning prayers took place. I felt very positive after reciting those prayers.

Then we were introduced to the principal of the school. He gave us a motivating lecture and told us about the legacy of the institute. We all were amazed to know about the facts related to the school. Then our class teacher took charge and gave us a small tour of the school.

She showed us the different parts of the building and the play area and canteen. Then we were taken to the auditorium of the school where we were shown the accolades achieved by the schools. Then we were explained the rules and regulations that we need to follow in the school. There was not a much of study that day as it was purely an orientation day. That day I was really impressed by the school's infrastructure and staff. I remember each moment of the first day at this school.

Birthday celebration you remember
When did this happen?
What gift did you get?
Tell about the most memorable moment from that birthday
My birthday has always been a memorable event for me as it comes in June when there is a vacation in my school or college. So, every time on my birthday I used to go somewhere out to celebrate it in a more dynamic way.

From my childhood, my birthday is celebrated at a grand level as in this month my parents are a bit less occupied, so they always make time for my birthday celebrations.

I still remember my 10th birthday. My father was not in the city due to his work commitments and I was really shattered. I was missing him badly as he used to surprise me on my birthday every time with one or the other exciting gifts.

But this time he was not there, so I wasn't expecting a gift from him on that day. All my friends were gathered at my place and were having fun. But I was a bit upset as my father was not there with me. My mother tried all her efforts to make me happy on my special day. She even made my favorite cake to uplift my mood.

I was about to cut the cake when I suddenly saw my father standing in front of me. I was shocked to see him and then I ran towards him and hugged him tightly. That was the best gift for me on my birthday that I never expected as he was likely to come after two days from his work, but he came on that day to surprise me.

I really enjoyed that moment with my father and cut my birthday cake with him. I enjoyed the rest of the party with more zest and energy.

It was also a special birthday for me as my father gifted me a bicycle on that day. My birthday became more special as I was demanding that bicycle from the past few months. At last, he gifted me my favorite bicycle on my birthday and made it more special with his presence.

I wish to spend such wonderful moments with my family in the future too.

An activity you find interesting

Do you do that activity

How has that activity helped you or someone?

Why do you find this activity interesting?

There are many activities that I find interesting. The one that I will discuss with you today is yoga. Yoga is basically an array of physical, mental and spiritual disciplines which initiated in ancient India. I find yoga very interesting due to several reasons.

Several diseases can be cured through yoga exercises. People can remain fit physically and mentally with regular practice of yoga. Yoga contains hundreds of body postures that are involved to align the body with the nature.

This type of exercise developed around sixth century BCE. Nowadays most of the people in our country follow this practice every day. I am not a regular practitioner of yoga but whenever I get time, I do it in the morning time.

Every year on 21st June, Yoga day is celebrated all over the world and especially in India with a lot of excitement. I always participate in celebrating yoga day as our colony organizes a mass yoga gathering every

192

year. In this assembly, a trained yoga teacher is hired who teaches different exercises and postures for maintaining good health.

I didn't believe in yoga earlier, but I saw some amazing results in front of my eyes and started believing in it. I would like to share an example with you. From the past few years, my mother was suffering from heavy breathing and uneasiness in lifting weights. She was told by her friend to do yoga on a regular basis to get rid of this problem. She started practicing yoga for an hour every day and soon she got rid of all her issues. It hardly took her a month to get relief from her problems.

I find this activity very interesting as you don't need to lift a lot of weights or need to run for kilometers. Yoga is all about making right body postures and inhaling and exhaling in a particular manner. This is not as simple as it looks. But once a person is trained, then it becomes easy to perform.

In my perception, I find yoga to be one of the most interesting activities.

An activity you do to maintain good health

How often do you do that activity?

What other activities you do to keep yourself fit

How much time do you spend on this activity?

Maintaining good health is the most important task these days. If one is not good at health, he or she cannot enjoy life to the fullest. There are numerous activities that most of the people follow in order to maintain good health.

On a personal level, I prefer dieting and light exercise to keep myself fit. The activity that I am going to explain you today is exercise. There are variety of exercises that I do to remain fit. For a start, I warm up by stretching my limbs. Then I do exercise like lifting light weights and cycling. I do this for at least fifteen minutes.

This kind of activity helps to generate adrenalin in the body which further helps to strengthen the muscles to lift heavy weights. Then I do weightlift which involves the development of the muscles of chest, thighs and biceps. I usually do all this stuff in a gym that is in my town. It is one of the best gyms and they have also provided me with a personal trainer and nutritionist. This gym is very hygienic and the equipment they have are of the best quality.

I spend around an hour every day in the gym. I like this time very much as it takes me away from my hectic schedule and helps me to keep my body in a good shape. I love to do exercise as it not only makes me physically fit but also gives me mental strength.

I love going to the gym and do exercise. I think that exercise is the best activity to keep yourself fit. I do some dieting, but exercise is something that keeps me going and maintains my health.

OR

*There are plentiful activities that I do in my daily life. The one that I do to maintain good health is to do yoga. (then you can speak about the topic **an activity you find interesting - Yoga**)*

Speak about a room in which you spent a lot of time

Why do you spend so much time there?

Do you like being indoors

How do you spend your time there?

I am such a person that I like to spend most of my time indoors as the weather in my city is hot for most part of the year. I live in a joint family. We dwell in a big house which has more than ten rooms. I am fortunate to have a personal room at the second floor of my house.

I spend most of my time in my bedroom. I go for my classes in the morning and come back by afternoon. After that I am pretty much in my room for the whole day. Sometimes I go out in the evening but for majority of days I like to be in my room.

My room is 10x15 foot in size and is equipped with all the latest amenities in it. An air conditioner is fit to keep my room cool and my room is painted in light blue color. I like this color very much so that's why I got it painted in blue color.

I have a double bed in my room. Moreover, a study table is placed against the front wall across the bed where I keep all my books. I love to use my study table for writing and reading. My study table is quite big and can hold a great number of books and other items.

The front wall is painted in a dark blue color and rest of the three walls are in light blue. The dark wall has a few things on it. There is a painting that is hanged on that wall. I bought that painting from an exhibition.

There is also a music system in my room which I play in my leisure time. I like to dance on loud music when I feel bored. I also spend time with my friends in my room. I remember when I used to study along with a couple of my friends in the exam days.

At the back side of the room, there is a huge window that can be opened easily when required. In the evenings when I feel that I am being too much indoors, then I just open the window to get fresh air in the room.

Sometimes I also like to gaze at the park that is right behind my house from that window.

My room is very special to me and I spend most of the time in my room.

A toy with which you played in your childhood
What was the toy like?
How did you play with it?
Do you still have it with you?

I am the youngest kid of my parents, so I used to get a lot of love and affection from them. I remember that they bought me most of the things I demanded. My father gifted me a wonderful toy with which I played for so many years without getting bored.

On one of my birthdays, my father gifted me plastic blocks. It is the same game that most of the people must surely have played in their childhood. It was so interested to play that I could spend hours and hours on playing with blocks

In this game, you can construct anything from your imagination. I remember that I used to make different styles of buildings and houses. It used to take so much time in constructing a shape then I would intentionally break it down to construct a new one. This game not only improves the thinking ability of the child but also helps them in building analytical skills.

I learned about most of the colors from this game only as there were blocks of multiple colors. My mother used to teach me to pick different colours and make something. This activity helped me in recognizing different colors. Moreover, the blocks were mostly in rectangular and square shape. I learned to pile up the toys to make tall structures and how to make a stable foundation.

This toy is very special to me as this was given to me by my father on my third birthday. At that time, I was excited about this toy as it was a new kind of toy for me. I played with this toy for the whole day tirelessly. You will not believe me, but I have kept some of those blocks with me as a memento from my childhood.

Speak about an adventurous person you know
How do you know that person?
Why do you think he/she is adventurous?
Do you like adventure

I am more of a peace-loving person. I am not at all an adventurous person, but I know quite a few of them. I have a big friend circle and I know some people who are very adventurous. An adventurous person whom I know well is one of my best friends, Amit.

He lives near my home and we are friends since 2012. He is of same age as mine and we share a lot of interests but an unusual hobby that he follows is doing adventurous activities. I don't like to participate in such activities, but Amit is one of those who never backs off from adventurous activities. He is a very cool minded person and he is always ready to do anything. He is very energetic and enthusiastic. He loves to travel to new places and do uncommon activities. In his everyday life, he is always making plans to do one or the other adventurous activity.

I remember that last year we went to Manali in the summer holidays. He was very excited about the white river rafting that is famous there. When we reached Manali, the first thing he did was the river rafting. He didn't waste any time and straightaway went to the bank of the river and asked the operators about getting on to the raft.

I decided to not go for rafting and rather wait for him. When he came back after an hour, he was so glad that he did that activity. He said that he did it with ease and enjoyed it to the fullest.

When we became friends a few years back, he told me that he has a long bucket list of doing adventurous activities like bungee jumping and sky diving. Today, he has done all the activities and seeks for more every now and then.

He is a real adventurous person and loves to do adventure whenever he gets time. This habit of his has a positive effect on his nature. I have seen that he is very fearless kind of a person. I think this attitude comes from doing adventurous activities that requires taking risks.

Talk about your favorite restaurant
Where it is located
What do you like the most about that restaurant?
How often do you go to that restaurant?
Usually, I prefer to eat home-cooked food as it is not only good for our health but is also very hygienic. Although it doesn't mean that I don't like eating out. I love to go to new restaurants at least once in a week.
The restaurant I like the most is the Taj Restaurant. This restaurant is located in Chandigarh. This is a buffet style restaurant and does not cater for a la carte customers. This restaurant is in the heart of the city and huge number of people flock to this place especially on weekends.
I love this restaurant for a few factors. The first one is the variety of food they offer. I am a vegetarian and they have a great assortment of vegetable snacks in their menu. They serve around eight snacks along with salads, main course and deserts.
In the main course, there are more than ten items that you can choose. All the snacks and main course items are mouthwatering. Once you are finished with your main course, they offer an abundance of desserts. I am fond of eating sweet items and like their chocolate brownie the most.
Apart from the variety they serve, they also take care of the quality of food that they are serving to their customers. The menu includes different types of cuisines from Chinese, Mughlai and continental. The best part is that you get free drinks with their buffet lunch and dinner. I always order virgin mojito as it is their most refreshing drink.
The ambience of the restaurant is top notch. The seats are very comfortable, and the lighting is a bit dim that compliments the setting very well. Moreover, their staff is very well behaved and always smiling.
This is a newly opened restaurants so the price for the buffet is also not that high. I love going to this restaurant again and again.

A person you know who is beautiful/handsome
How do you think that person is beautiful?
Do you know that person well?
What is the reason behind that person's beauty?
There is a well-known proverb that beauty lies in the eyes of the beholder. The definition of beauty is indeed different for all. God has created all the persons unique in this world.
I have come across many beautiful persons in my life, but the most beautiful person I know in my life is my mom. She is the symbol of beauty and smartness. Her beauty can be seen on her face and her body language too.
She is so fit and active that whatever she wears, she looks so elegant and beautiful in it. Her features are sharp, and I would rather say that she has been made perfectly by God. I have rarely seen her doing any kind of make-up for any party or occasion. Because she looks perfect in natural looks.
Not only she possesses beautiful features, but she is lovely from her heart too. She is very loving and polite. Whenever she comes across a needy person, her heart melts like a candle and she is always ready to help them in any possible way.
From my childhood, I have seen her getting old but there has been no toll on her beauty and skin in any way. Her skin is so smooth and glossy even today. Her color of the skin is very fair, and she looks extremely charming in whatever she wears. But I think that she looks gorgeous in traditional attire.
She is very concerned about her face and body. She takes care of her body and avoids such foods and other things that could spoil her health by any means. She does light workout on a regular basis to maintain this fitness and beauty in her.
I wish for her good health and well-being for her entire life. I hope she remains so beautiful and young like this always.

Describe an important decision you made/ Decision you made with the help of someone

What was the decision

How important was it

Who helped you in your decision making?

There are many decisions that I have taken in my life. A right decision can do wonders, whereas a bad decision in life can cost you a fortune. The one that I will discuss with you today is the decision that I took few days back (or after I cleared my twelfth class/graduation) with the help of my elder sister.

Till now, most of the decision in my life are taken by my parents. They are the well-wishers and they have always taken right decisions for me. Even I always consult my parents and elder sister regarding any decision that I want to take.

After completing my twelfth class, I was in a lot of confusion. I could not make a choice between studying in India and abroad. I thought that it would be good for me if I pursue my higher studies in India but looking at the competition here, I feared of being a failure. On the other hand, studying from a foreign university or college requires a lot of funds. I didn't want to bother my parents about this.

I have never been so jumbled in my whole life. I was not able to make any decision about my future and after some days I started feeling irritated. One day I decided to talk to all my family members regarding my frustration.

My sister understood my situation and calmed me down. She explained me the benefits of studying abroad. She also pointed out that the course I want to pursue will be better suited if I studied from a foreign university. She told me not to worry about the funds as she will talk to the parents regarding this.

My parents agreed instantly and then my sister advised me to go for the IELTS test. This decision cleared the air and confusion in my mind. Now I am really focused, and I have planned to apply in a university in Canada. This decision was very important for me as my whole career was hanging in a balance. I want to thank my sister for helping me to take this decision.

Speak about someone who is a good cook

How do you know him/her?

Why he/she is a good cook

What type of dishes he/she can make?

I have come across many people whom I find to be good cooks. But the one I would like to talk about is my mother. She is a wonderful cook and makes stunning dishes. The reason that she is a good cook is because she likes to cook.

Cooking food is her biggest hobby. In her free time, she likes to watch videos of famous chefs and enjoys copying those recipes. She makes mouthwatering cuisine with minimal efforts. I have no hesitation in saying that she is the best cook I have seen in my entire life.

The reason that makes her a good cook is that she has patience. I think this is one of the qualities that is needed in good cooks. She tries different dishes every day and perfects most of them in a couple of attempts. She is never afraid of failures. Even if the dish is not made according to her wishes, she keeps on trying it again and again till she achieves the perfect texture.

She is expert in making savory dishes. She likes to cook Chinese, continental and north Indian food the most. I like noodles with chilly chicken in Chinese and butter chicken in north Indian category. I get so many different varieties of dishes every day. I never get bored eating food made by my mother.

She has a never-ending desire for making variety of dishes. She does it with great sense of ease and versatility. I like to eat anything that she makes. Apart from making everything delicious, she's expert in plating the cuisines as well.

She has a diary in which she writes all the dishes that she makes. One day I was stunned to see that diary. She told me that she has written around five hundred unique recipes in that. I have suggested my mother to publish a food recipe book soon.

So, in the end I would like to say that my mother is a great cook whom I know.

Speak about something useful you learnt from the member of your family

What did you learn?

Was it helpful to you?

Is there any other thing that you still want to learn?

There are thousands of things that I have learned from my family members since my childhood. I mostly learn from my father as he is a great teacher. He teaches everything with patience and maturity.

I remember when last year I learnt car driving from my father. He taught me this skill in a couple of months. Initially I was very hesitant in learning car driving but my father infused a lot of confidence in me.

It took me a lot of practice to learn this skill as I was very scared of car driving. I can recall that how my father used to wake me up early in the morning so that we could practice in least traffic. On the first day, he gave me some important tips and lessons regarding the functions of different parts of the car.

Then he made me sit with him and he drove the car to show me the things to keep me in mind while driving. I noticed each and everything so that it could help me during my practice. I kept on asking him questions regarding driving a car in different situations. He was patient enough to give me answers for all my questions.

He knew this fact that I am not comfortable in learning this skill, so he took his time in motivating me. He told me about the advantages of learning car driving. He constantly told me not to worry as car driving is a simple skill to learn. His words were really encouraging and helped me to try my hands on driving the car.

Then after a few days, I took the driver's seat and learned the talent of driving under his guidance. After that day, it did not take me more than fifteen days to get accustomed to driving the car in traffic.

I am grateful to my father for teaching me this thing. I still have many things in my mind that I want to learn from my family members but for that I am waiting for the right time.

Describe a stressful day at school/college/university

What made your day stressful?

How did you manage the stress?

How do you deal with stressful situations?

Some days of our lives are so traumatic that they leave an imprint on our brain for the whole life. I was in my school when such an incident happened in front of me. I was roaming around with my friends in the school ground as it was the lunch break time.

Suddenly, we heard a scream from the opposite side of the building and what we saw one boy lying on the floor. He fell from the second floor and was hurt very badly. All the students and other staff members immediately gathered around him. The scene was frightening for everyone as he was screaming in pain and lying in a pool of blood. I was terrified to see him as he was my friend Amit.

The medical staff arrived on the scene and gave him first aid. Then they took him to a nearby hospital. The injuries seemed to be very severe as he fell on the floor from twenty feet. There was pin drop silence in the college after this incident happened. Everyone was praying for his speedy recovery. I was so tensed and did not go to my house. Instead I went to the hospital along with some other students and staff members.

In these kinds of situations, I like to pray. When I do prayers, it gives me peace of mind and strength. I was waiting outside the hospital and kept on roaming here and there. I was in constant anxiety and it was one of the most stressful days for me in the school.

The sigh of relief came to us when we came to know that Amit was fine and out of danger. After some time, we were allowed to meet Amit where he claimed that it was just an accident, and nobody was at fault.

That day was a very stressful one for me as Amit was one of my good friends and I was constantly worried about his life.

A place indoor or outdoor where you can study

Why indoor/outdoor?

Is outdoor a better place to study

Mention the place in detail

Everyone likes to study in a different environment. Personally, I like to study at a place where no one can disturb me. So, the place where I can concentrate more on my studies is my personal room.

I have kept one study table in my room, where I usually study. It is the most comfortable place for me to study as I can focus more on my work rather than things that can distract me. The study table is quite big and can contain a lot of books and stationery in it. The study table is made up of solid wood. It is polished in a tan color. There is a luxurious seat with the table that adds to the comfort of studying on it.

The lighting in my room is also on the brighter side which makes reading books easy. The curtains in my room can be pulled up for more natural light in the room. There is a balcony attached to my room so whenever I need a short break, I can stroll there for a few minutes and recharge myself.

My room is at the backside of our house, so luckily there is negligible outside noise or distraction in my study room. There are all the amenities like air conditioner, mini fridge and computer in my room which makes it easier for me to study for long hours.

If I feel tired studying on the study table, I can sit in a relaxed posture on my bed and continue my study. I am a fan of studying indoor as outdoor noise and activities divert my attention a lot. So, my personal room is the place where I can study better than any other place.

A movie or TV show that made you laugh

Describe the show/movie

Speak about the actors

How this movie or show is funny

I am very fond of watching movies and TV serials as they give us great entertainment. I usually don't get a lot of time to watch TV on the weekdays. So, the only day left for me is Sunday. On Sunday, one of the most famous show is telecasted on TV, The Kapil Sharma show.

I love to watch humorous shows that can make me laugh and give me some stress-free time. Nowadays, I am watching this show regularly. It is a hilarious show that involves various comedians and celebrities that visits the house of Kapil Sharma, the host.

This serial is broadcasted only on weekends for one-hour in the evening and is hosted by a well-known comedian Kapil Sharma. The host of the show is very famous in our country and is well known for his funny satires.

His excellent standup comedy makes him different from all other comedians.

The show is accompanied by various other famous comedians like Ali Asgar, Upasana Singh, Sunil Grover, Kiku Sharda, Chandan Prabhakar, Sumona Chakraborty. All the actors in this show are super funny and makes everyone laugh hard.

This show is witnessed by a huge number of people who are invited to be the audience at the show. Every weekend, some famous personalities visit their show and they do a lot of hilarious stuff with them. This show is a one-hour dose of stress-free time. It is one of the highly viewed shows of all time in our country.

I eagerly wait for this show every weekend. I finish all my work before the show is about to start and I am glued to my TV screen until the show ends. I even love to watch the repeat telecast of this show on weekdays.

So, I feel that this is the show that makes me laugh every week.

Talk about a dish you know how to cook

Can you cook many dishes?

Do you often cook it?

How that dish is made

I am not a cook, but I can make a few dishes. I believe that cooking is an activity that everyone should know irrespective of their genders. Mostly in our country, men are not associated with cooking, but I think that they should also know a bit of cooking so that they can survive in every situation.

I can mostly make Indian dishes. The one that I like to make is rice with kidney beans. This is one of the most popular dishes in the part of the county where I live. This is also known as the royal dish. Most people make this dish to please the guests.

I like to eat it every week especially on weekends. I like to make this dish and serve it to all my family members. My friends are also fond of eating this dish made by me. This is a simple, yet it takes a bit of time to prepare. To make this dish, red kidney beans must be washed and soaked in water overnight. This process helps them to cook faster and brings the best taste.

In a pan, add two tablespoons of oil or ghee. In that, put ground onions and tomatoes. Then add salt and red chilies to taste.

Heat the mixture until it is cooked properly. Then pour the soaked kidney beans and this mixture in a pressure cooker. Add a couple of glasses of water for consistency. Let it cook for thirty minutes. On the other hand, soak some rice for ten minutes and then boil it in a pan and serve hot with kidney beans.

This is a dish that has a lot of spicy curry in it. It is best served hot. I am in love with this dish. I always love to eat it with some salad and curd.

A time when someone didn't tell you the whole truth

When did this happen?

What was the truth that was concealed?

How did you feel when you came to know about the truth?

There are many instances in my life when I was not told the whole truth. Actually, this happened when we went to a private bank to open up a bank account. I had to open a savings bank account, so I went there as it is one of the most renowned banks in our country. I went there along with my father.

I inquired about the opening of the account at the reception. I was escorted by the receptionist to the counter where new customers are directed. I was asked about my age and was given a form to fill. I filled all the details in the form and submitted it to the employee at the counter. The lady behind the tables asked me to tick mark the type of account I would like to open. There were three types of savings account that came with different benefits. The first one was free of charge and had no condition of maintaining a minimum balance in it. Other types of accounts were expensive to maintain but had many benefits.

Since I am a student and there can be times when my account will have not much balance, my father suggested me to open the simple account with zero balance. I told the bank employee to open a normal savings account. They told us to wait for fifteen minutes and asked us to deposit a small amount of money to activate the account. I deposited five thousand rupees that day.

After a few days I received a message about some money that was deducted from my account. I had made no transactions, so I became suspicious about it. I went to the bank immediately and asked them about the deducted money.

They told that the charges were subtracted due to low balance in the account. They deducted one thousand rupees from my account. I argued that this was a zero-balance account and how can they charge me for low balance. I was angry and complained this issue to the manager of the bank. Then the manager told me that it is mandatory to keep at least ten thousand for a month when you open a new account. I told the manager that I wasn't provided with this information when I opened the account and demanded for a refund. But my efforts went into vain as they didn't give me a refund.

I felt betrayed by the bank staff as they did not tell me the whole truth and conditions of opening a bank account. I felt dejected and learned a lesson that day.

Tell about a party you went

What was the occasion

Who arranged the party?

How did you enjoy

I go to a lot of parties that are arranged by my friends and family. The one which I would like to tell you about is the party that I attended last month. It was my friend's birthday party. My friend Amit is of my same age and he celebrated his birthday in grand style.

Three of my other friends were also invited to his party. In total we were five friends and Amit came to my house to pick me up in the evening. Then we picked all the other friends and asked the birthday boy about the party. He smiled and said that it is a surprise, but he disclosed the plan to calm our nerves.

He told us that he has booked a hotel in Kasauli for his special day. We were extremely excited about the party and within a couple of hours of drive we reached our destination. There we were greeted by the hotel staff and were handed over the keys to our room.

It was actually not a room but a villa instead. It was a two-room villa with a private swimming pool in it. I was awestruck by the luxury of that villa. Without wasting any time, we started the party. We ordered some snacks and drinks and enjoyed our dinner. Then we went in the pool and enjoyed a couple of hours there.

My friend had also brought a musical system with him. We played some loud music and danced to its beats. After dancing for some time, we played cards and talked about every useless topic in the world. Then we cut the cake and ordered some more snacks.

We couldn't sleep the whole night as we were so immersed in the party. We were just talking and doing fun the whole night. Suddenly we realized that the sun had risen, and we all started feeling sleepy. We all went to sleep and woke up for the breakfast after four hours.

It was such an enjoyable day that I can never forget my whole life.

Talk about something you taught to a teenager / Talk about something you taught to someone

What did you teach?

How much time it took?

Did the person learn that thing?

There are a few things in my life that I have been able to teach to teenagers. The one thing that I would like to tell you is when I taught something to my cousin. My cousin is only fourteen years old and he wanted to learn to send and receive emails.

He called me one day and asked me if I was available and could teach him this skill. I told him to come over to my place someday. After a couple of days, he came to my house as we had planned previously. I opened my laptop and connected it to the internet. Then I started teaching him the different aspects of email.

First, I told him about the different websites that offer to create free email id. We picked one and made a new account on that. I told him to choose an identity and a unique password for further use. He chose the id and created a new password.

Then we opened the email homepage and I trained him to compose different kinds of emails. I also taught him to send attachments with the email. I could notice that he was very curious when I was telling him all these things. Then he asked me about creating the emails faster. Then I showed him the template section where we can store different templates for different situations.

After that I told him to open the emails received by him and how should he draft the reply. I also taught him the method to save email list and how he can use shortcut buttons to perform different functions to save time. I told him everything about emails that I know. Then I asked him to send me some emails so that he can perfect this art. He spent around three hours with me and learned most of the things that I taught.

At the end, he thanked me a lot and said that it was an urgent need for him to learn how to send and reply to the emails. He was very happy that day as he had learnt a new skill that will help him in future.

When you found something that someone lost
What did you find?
How and where did you find
Did you return that

I have seen a couple of people in my life who find a lot of lost things. I think I am not that lucky but one day I found something that I could never imagine in my life.

Last year I went to a theater to watch a movie. During the movie I opened my shoes and placed it below the seat. After the movie was over, I noticed that my shoes were pushed deep under the seat. So, I had to bent down and look for my shoes.

I got the shoes but to my surprise I also found something lying on the floor. I quickly pulled it and noticed that someone had left his wallet accidently over there. It was a men's leather wallet. It was swollen like a ball and when I opened it, I was shocked to see that it was stuffed with a lot of money.

I inspected further and found some ATM and credit cards as well. I quickly put it in my pocket and brought it home. I had no idea what to do with it. I told my parents about this and showed them the purse. My father told me to check the wallet thoroughly and see if we could find the owner. Otherwise he suggested to return the wallet to the mall authority.

In the side pocket I found some fancy looking visiting cards that suggested a name along with phone number. There was no address on those cards, only name and a mobile number. I called on that number, but no one picked the call. After some time, I received call from the same number, and I asked that person if his wallet was lost.

He acknowledged instantly and told me about the color and belongings of the wallet. I told him my address and asked him to pick up the wallet as soon as he gets time. He came to our house the next day and thanked me a lot. He said that he never expected to find his wallet as there was a huge amount of cash in it.

He was really happy and kept on thanking me for the gesture. He then gave me two thousand rupees note as a token of appreciation, but I refused saying that it is all your money and you deserve all of it. He thanked again and insisted me to keep that. I kept that note but later donated it to a private charity.

So that was the thing that someone lost, and I found it.

A meal you enjoyed at a restaurant

Which restaurant did you go to?
What did you order there?
Did you enjoy your meal?

I love eating out at the restaurants. Whenever I feel bored from the homemade food, I go to restaurants to enjoy my meals I would like to share my experience with you about a meal that I enjoyed at a restaurant. Last week I went to a famous restaurant of my city to dine with my family. It was not a special occasion that day, it was just a family dinner after a long time. The name of the restaurant is China love. This is a Chinese cuisine restaurant and is famous for its authentic taste. We went there at 7 PM and were greeted warmly by the staff.

We took our seats and started skimming the menu. It is very difficult to order food at this restaurant as the menu is so diverse and has a huge number of items in it. In the meantime, we were served with sizzling hot Chinese tea. This is a complimentary drink that they serve to everyone who come to their restaurant. The tea they serve is so soothing and refreshing.

After that we ordered our food and some drinks. The restaurant has a Chinese ambience as the décor of the restaurant is in Chinese theme. Light music plays in the background and the cutlery they serve has Chinese inscriptions on it.

After some time, our dinner was served at the table. We ordered a cheese sizzler, chilly cheese with gravy, noodles and fried rice. Their sizzler is amazing in taste. It contains some rice at the bottom topped with spicy gravy with some boiled vegetables along with fried potato chips. The noodles are not as spicy and has a very authentic taste.

The cheese chilly is made of gravy containing onion and capsicum with chunks of fried cottage cheese. The fried rice was so delicious that we had to order another portion of it. After that we ordered a Chinese sweet dish, custard tart. It is like a cake but tastes like a custard.

We enjoyed our meals to the fullest. That meal at the restaurant was fabulous.

Faraway place you would like to visit
How far is it from your hometown?
Why do you want to visit there?
When are you planning to visit there?

There are many faraway places in my bucket list that I wish to visit. The one that I would like to visit this year is Kerala. It is a state that is in the southernmost part of my country. The flight duration to cochin is about three hours. It is the longest direct flight within our country from the place I live. Kerala is a coastal area and is full of rain all year round.

I have searched about Kerala on the internet and found that it is best to visit from November to March as it is a bit dry, and the temperatures are bearable. There are many tourist attractions to see there. Kerala is also one of the greenest states of our county.

There is a direct flight to Cochin from Delhi. From Cochin, it is easy to travel to all parts of the state. The best place to visit is Alleppey. Alleppey backwaters are a sight to see and there are numerous types of houseboats that one can book for a stay.

Apart from this, Munnar is a must-see place in Kerala. It is a hill station and is one of the most popular destination for honeymoon couples. Munnar is famous for its aromatic vegetation, low-flying clouds, and tea plantation. Munnar has one of the finest tea plantations in India. There are some fine beaches in Kerala. Kovalam is one of them and it is famous for water sports like para sailing. The coastline of this beach is in crescent shape and lined with beautiful palm trees.

Kerala is also famous for its aromatic cuisines. There are many roadside restaurants that provide authentic cuisines. Kerala is home to a huge variety of spices. Most of the spices produced in our country are grown in Kerala.

People from all over the country and world visit Kerala for holidays. It is one of the most prominent tourist destinations in our country. So, this is the faraway place that I would like to visit in my near future.

Describe a beautiful home you have seen

Who owns the house?

Describe the house in detail

Why do you think that house is beautiful?

Recently my friend shifted to a new house. He invited me to visit him on a Sunday. I went there in the morning and what I saw there was nothing short of a great experience.

My friend's new house is like a king's palace. It is built in a total area of four thousand square feet. It is a huge area that has a house in the center and the surrounding area of the premise is converted into a courtyard. There is a huge entry gate at the front that leads to a parking area. The exterior of the house is painted in white colour.

The main door of the house is magnificent. The carvings on the wooden door looks elegant. The main door opens in a common area that has sofas, a table and stairs leading to the upper floor. As soon as one enters in the house, you get a luxury feeling. The lighting on the roof is of warm white colour which perfectly complements the white colour marble on the floor. The floor is of pure white colour but reflects a golden colour with the lights on. There are five bedrooms on the ground floor. I went to my friend's bedroom and asked him to show all the corners of his house. His room was painted white in colour with beautiful design on one wall. The floor was

211

the same as in common room. The room was glittering and was looking fantastic.

I also saw the other rooms in which the colours were a bit different, but the floor was same all over. All the things were chosen according to the taste of the individuals in the family. The roof of the house has a down ceiling. The ceiling has gorgeous led lights that adds to the overall beauty of the house.

Most of the walls of the house on the ground floor are painted in white colour but the walls in the drawing room were colourful and vibrant. The drawing room is big with a seating capacity of twenty. The drawing room is decorated superbly. There is a huge chandelier that hangs in the center of the drawing room.

Then we went on the upper floor where I saw only one room. That room was huge and had all the sports related equipment and a ping pong table. I was so excited to see it and played a couple of games with my friend. The upper floor also had a big terrace garden. I saw such a beautiful terrace garden for the first time in my life.

I felt so good after visiting this house. My friend's house is the most beautiful house that I have seen in my entire life.

A radio program you find interesting
Describe the theme of the program
For how long you have been listening to this show
Do you regularly listen to the radio?
I don't like to listen to radio a lot. But if I get some free time, I like to listen to Radio Mirchi. Mirchi is Hindi for Red Chilli. The tag line of Radio Mirchi is "Mirchi Sunnewaale Always Khush". This radio channel is one of the most famous channels in the country.

I generally listen to the radio when I am in a car, I like to listen to radio program, Mirchi Murga hosted by RJ Naved. RJ Naved is one of the most hilarious hosts on the radio. He has a great fan following across the country. He possesses a great sense of humor and is admired by millions of people in our country.

In this show, he calls random people and plays prank on them. This program is one of the most followed programs in India. They also make video versions of this serial but when you listen it on radio, it is even more hilarious.

There is no aspect of the show that needs to be shown visually. The only thing is conversation between the RJ and the caller. In this show, the RJ picks up a random phone number and calls on it and talks nonsense with the person on the line.

RJ Naved talks in a way that the person gets offended and frustrated. Sometimes, people even start abusing in frustration. Although the abusive language is censored with a beep sound as it is a family show.

Apart from this, RJ also plays latest Bollywood songs on the demand of the callers. He talks directly with general public in this show. People ask him a lot of questions and give answers in hilarious way. I don't spend a lot of time listening to radio, but I love this show very much.

A subject you did not like but now you find interesting
How did you develop interest in that subject?
Why you did not like it earlier
Do you still read that subject?

I did not like most of the subjects in my school time. I thought that mathematics, chemistry, physics and especially history are useless subjects. I was always more inclined towards practical subjects like biology, physical education and computers.

I hated history as a subject when I was in school. I could never remember all the dates and events of the past. I never scored good in this subject and found the history class to be the most boring one. But after all these years I have started to find my interest in history.

I found my interest in history when I read a book written by Mahatma Gandhi. The name of the book is 'My experiments with truth'. When I read the book, I was so impressed to find the history in it. Our history is so rich that we must study it in order to learn from it. This book taught me about the struggles that our past leaders have made so as to achieve freedom for our country.

I have gained a lot of interest in the history subject from the past few years and have read a number of books on it. Apart from reading My experiments with truth, I also read about the autobiography of the former president of the republic of South Africa, Mr. Nelson Mandela. The name of the book is Long walk to freedom. From this book I came to know that Nelson Mandela spent almost thirty years in jail and still came out to become the first black President of South Africa.

History teaches us a lot of things that we can follow to take right decisions in the future. Reading history inspires us to achieve greatness in our lives. I have now made a habit of reading about history every day. I spend around 30 minutes in reading something about the past. I feel that history subject has attracted me a lot in the recent times.

Something you bought but did not use

Do you like shopping

What was the product and why didn't you use it?

Do you regret buying it?

I am a shopaholic person and whenever I get chance I like to shop. Sometimes I also shop unnecessarily and repent afterwards. One thing that I remember that I bought and did not use is a perfume.

I bought this perfume from my trip to Dubai, but I didn't even use it once. I went to Dubai last year with my family and was very excited about the trip. We saw myriad attractions over there and went to a lot of shopping malls. There we came to know that Dubai is famous for its Oudh. Oudh is basically essential oil that has long lasting fragrance. People of Emirate use Oudh in their daily life. This can be called as perfume because Oudh is not known in the outer world by many people. This perfume comes in an endless variety of fragrances and colours.

Someone at our hotel suggested us to visit Meena Bazaar which is a local market in Dubai to buy the perfume. We went there immediately and started looking for shops that were selling perfumes. We got notice of a huge multistoried shop that was designed in a perfume bottle shape. We all were attracted to it and went inside to shop for perfume.

I am not a huge admirer of perfumes, but I use them on certain occasions. So, I thought of buying one perfume as a souvenir from Dubai. The Oudh perfume is packed in a traditional flask made of glass. It is not sprayed but applied gently on to the neck and other body parts directly.

I bought a fancy bottle that contained 50ml of perfume. I tried the fragrance on the neck and like it pretty much. The fragrance was pungent and stayed on the body for most part of the day. After some time, I couldn't bear the smell and had allergic reaction on my body.

It was a non-returnable product so I couldn't return it. The bottle is still kept with me in my dressing almirah, but I haven't used it even once. I have no regret of buying it as I have kept it as a souvenir.

Time when you had to change your plan

What was the original plan?

Why did you change the plan?

Was it easy to change or you faced any difficulty?

I generally don't change my plans. I like to stick to my plans and follow them strictly. But there was one instance when I had to change my plan. This happened last month when we were planning to go to Goa.

We had planned this trip a lot of days in advance. I took the responsibility of booking the flights, hotels and tour. We were planning this trip with my other relatives. In total we were eight persons and I was very excited for that trip.

We booked our flights and hotels from a renowned travel website. I had paid all the amount for the tour in advance. I started preparing for the trip a week in advance. I packed my bag and took all the necessary clothes and items in that.

My other family members also did all the preparations for the trip. We had to leave on Sunday for Delhi as we had to catch the flight from there. Unfortunately, on Saturday my cousin got seriously ill. He was diagnosed with acute fever and viral infection. We were so worried about his health and I thought that trip would be cancelled as we had to depart for the trip on the next day. I was also concerned about the bookings that we had made.

The doctor advised him to take rest for at least five days and suggested not to go on the trip. For this reason, we had to change all our plans. We all decided to postpone the trip. Fortunately, our tickets and hotel bookings were refundable. So, we were able to change the dates of our travel. I contacted the travel website and got the response swiftly. They modified our bookings and gave us new tickets and vouchers.

We postponed the trip ten days ahead so that my cousin could recover properly, and we did not want to go without him. So, this is the time when I had to change my plans.

A person you wanted to be like

Who is that person and what does he do?

Why you want to be like him/her

Have you become like him/her?

I admired a lot of people in my childhood. There were many hero's that I followed, and I always wanted to be like them. There was one person whom I wanted to be like. He is my all-time favourite cricketer Sachin Tendulkar.

I am a great follower of this game. In my childhood I used to watch cricket matches whenever I had free time. I remember that most of my friends were more interested in watching cartoon programs, but I was always indulged in cricket matches.

Most of the youngsters in our country who play cricket were inspired by Sachin Tendulkar. He earns a great respect around the world from cricket lovers. He is considered to be the greatest cricketer to have graced the cricket field till now. He holds great records in the game and some of the records set by him looks so unbelievable. Most of the people reckon that no one will be able to achieve those records.

I was a huge fan of Sachin Tendulkar and always wanted to become like him. I used to imitate his style of batting and, I would do certain gestures that he did while playing. I had a huge poster of Sachin on the wall of my bedroom. I always looked at his poster and imagine becoming like him and play this game for my country.

He has great qualities in him. He is very calm in nature and understands the situations and tackle the difficulties in a mature way. He used his calm nature in his playing days to win crunch matches for our country. This is the quality that I surely wanted to borrow from him.

Not only me, most of the youngsters in that era wanted to become like him. In the playing days he had that charisma which was admired by everyone. I wanted to be similar to Sachin Tendulkar in every aspect of life. Although I couldn't become like him, but he is such person whom I admired the most in the past and I still do.

OR

There are many people in my life whom I want to be like. The person whom I want to be like is Harmanpreet Kaur. She is an Indian cricketer. She plays an allrounder for the Indian women's cricket team.

Recently she was awarded with one of the most prestigious awards, Arjuna Award for cricket by the ministry of youth affairs and sports. She was born in 1989 in Moga, Punjab. Her nick name is Harman. She is a top order bat and bowls right arm slow. She made her debut for the country in the year 2009.

She has set many records in this field. She became first women cricketer to score 100 runs in a twenty over match in the year 2018. She went through a lot of struggles in life before becoming a settled player in the team. She was awarded the captaincy of the team in the year 2018

While she is playing the game, she looks very aggressive. She has an attacking style of play and is famous for hitting the ball long. I like her playing style and most of the young girls follow her and take inspiration from her to become cricketers. Women in our country were not interested in playing cricket previously. Their thinking changed after they realized that cricketers like Harmanpreet Kaur can earn such a great name and fame by playing this game.

I am following her from many years, and I was once a huge fan of her game. Five or six years back, I wanted to become like her and create a niche for myself. She is such an inspiration for all the girls who look to take up this sport.

I was very impressed with her and always wanted to become like her.

Food that people eat on special occasions
What is the food
How it is prepared
Do you like it

India is a land of occasions and festivals. People of our country like to eat special food on special events. India has so many cultures and religions that every other day is a festival.

There is one sweet dish that is consumed by millions of people on special occasions. The name of the dish is KHEER. It is basically made from sugar, milk and rice. These are the main ingredients that form this palatable dish. KHEER is one of my favourite desserts. It is made by boiling milk and condensing it to half. Then rice is added to it and is again boiled for twenty minutes. At the end, sugar is added to taste. This is then cooled and becomes a think liquid. Some people add dry fruits at the top before serving.

There are many versions of KHEER. It varies from region to region. Some people make it thicker and some like it runny or thin. People in some areas like to add saffron to make it more colourful. Some prefer this dish cold and some like to eat steaming hot KHEER. It all depends on personal taste and occasion.

KHEER has a significance in our culture. There are several festivals and occasions that are associated with it. On the eve of EID, people make KHEER to celebrate the festival. Moreover, on the weddings, KHEER is the main sweet dish that is served to the guests. Some people even eat this dish after achieving something.

KHEER is one of the most common and consumed sweet dishes in our country on special occasions. I think the reason behind this is the ease of making this dish. Only few ingredients are required, and it can be made in a short time.

This dish has a rich history. It is believed that this dish has been in existence from thousands of years. People made this dish on the special occasions in the past as well. So, I think that KHEER is the dish that people eat on special occasions.

An occasion when you bought/made a special cake
Why did you buy the cake?
Why is it special
Give details of the cake

I must have bought numerous cakes in my life as there are special occasions every year. Generally, I buy cakes on my friends or family member's birthday. But the time when I bought a special cake was the wedding reception of my brother.

There are many reasons that why this cake was special. The first reason is that it was my brother's wedding and I was really happy on that day. The other reason was that it was going to be the biggest cake that I have seen in my life.

My father put the responsibility of buying the cake on me. So, I went to a bakery where I generally go. It is one of the renowned bakeries in our hometown. I went there a week before the function. I asked the manager of the bakery about the special cakes for wedding functions. He handed me over a cake book in which thousands of designs were printed.

He told me to choose one for the occasion. I was so confused as there were so many cakes in that book. My preferred type of cake is chocolate based. So, I told my requirement to the manager and then he suggested me chocolate mud cake. He explained that the cake is made from hundred percent chocolate topped with more chocolate on the outside of the cake. I finalized that cake, but I didn't tell anyone about the design and type of the cake. I made full payment in advance and they assured that our cake will be delivered on time.

Another reason that it was a special cake is that I had never seen such a huge cake in my entire life. The cake was designed for two hundred people. When they delivered the cake at the wedding venue, everyone was surprised to see the huge size of the cake.

They carefully unwrapped the cake and placed it on the table where the cake was to be cut. The cake was made in several parts and they assembled each part on the table. The height of the cake was around four feet. I had never seen such a wonderful cake in my life.

After the cake was cut, everyone praised it. The taste was fantastic, and the presentation was equally good. Undoubtedly it was the most special cake of my life.

An aspect of modern society that you dislike
Which aspect do you dislike?

Why do you dislike it?

Is modern society better than the older one?

Change is the unchanging law of nature. This line is true in every aspect of the world. I have seen a lot of changes in the perception, customs and culture. But the biggest change has happened in the lifestyle of people and I don't like it at all.

People are now becoming lethargic and dependent on technology for most of their chores. I dislike the intervention of technology in our life. Technology is useful for us but only up to a certain extent. After that it becomes a menace.

These days I see most of the people hooked to their phones. Nowadays people are using internet more than ever and the usage continues to grow in the future as well. This is a dangerous trend as we are disconnected from the real world. People are living in a virtual social world where they interact with people and their friends through social networking sites. But there is no physical contact and emotions.

Apart from this, today's children are staying indoors as compared to the past. They don't like to go out and play. Instead they are stuck in either mobile phones or video games. It is a terrible inclination towards such activities. I don't like when I see kids sitting at home and watching cartoons instead of playing outdoors.

There has been a hazardous invasion of technology in our lives. People in the past used to walk a lot but today people use vehicles to travel short distances. This habit has made people lazy and weak. Due to such lifestyle, immune systems are getting weak.

In my area, I have come across many people who are facing the deficiency of vitamin D. The major reason behind this problem is that people like to stay indoors whereas vitamin D is absorbed from sunlight exposure.

In the end I would like to say that I don't like the overdependence on technology aspect of the modern society.

Describe a famous scientist/inventor you know about
How did you know about him?
What has he achieved?
What made him famous

Scientists have brought the revolution in our world. They are the ones who have given us some of the best things in our life. They have invented so many things on our planet that have made our lives easier. I adore many scientists of our country, but whom I admire the most is Dr. APJ Abdul Kalam. He was born in the small coastal town of Rameswaram.

I came to know about this great man when I was in school. We read many articles describing his achievements and I read his autobiography as well. He has given his expert ideas in the aeronautical field. Not only this, but his contribution to the Defense area of our country is also remarkable. He is widely known as the "Missile Man of India" as he was one of the biggest contributors in the launch vehicle technology in space and missile development program.

He launched India's first missile vehicle in the space in the 1990s, named SLV-III Project after joining the ISRO. He deployed the Rohini satellite in space in the year 1980. His work was so brilliant that he got immediate approval from the Indian government to proceed with his work for the Indian satellite launch vehicles. Being the Director of the satellite program, he hired more engineers for his assistance and launched many satellites successfully over a period of three decades.

Many missile programs were initiated in the year 1980 under his leadership to develop ballistic missiles for the defense of our country. He was also involved in a few manned and unmanned space programs. His contribution to our country not only ends here, but he also served as the President of our country from the year 2002 to 2007. I think he was still unknown to a lot of people until he became the president of our country. He was also known as the People's President for his humble nature and his knack of meeting people casually in public.

I am not only inspired by his excellent work in the technology but from his personal life too. He came from a very humble background. Despite this he was able to study hard and became one of the most eminent scientists that India has produced. Apart from this, he has written myriad books. His autobiography has been read by millions of people across the world. The name of that book is Wings of Fire.

He has received various prestigious awards in his lifetime like Padma Bhushan, Padma Vibhushan, Bharat Ratna and many honorary doctorate awards for his excellence in the aeronautical industry.

I admire him as one of the greatest inventors of our country.

Describe an exciting experience in your life

Why was that experience exciting?

How did you feel

What did you do?

There have been few exciting experiences in my life, but I would like to explain an exciting time of my life when I went to a foreign country for the first time. I asked my parents to take me and my sister to a foreign trip. They were kind enough and told me that after I complete my 12th class, they would surely take us to a foreign trip.

My father decided to take us to Dubai. It is a small country in the United Arab Emirates. It takes only three hours from Delhi to reach Dubai. We were all excited for the trip as it was our first visit to a foreign country. I started preparing for the trip as early as one month in advance. I bought new clothes and shoes for the trip.

I was very enthusiastic when we reached at the Airport. I saw the immigration area for the first time in my life. It took us two hours to get the boarding pass and the visa stamp on our passport. When we reached the Dubai airport, we were received by the tour company and were dropped at our hotel.

The next day we went out for shopping and to explore the city. I had never seen such infrastructure in my life. I saw hundreds of tall buildings and went on to the top of Burj Khalifa which is the tallest building in the World right now. During our stay, we saw desert area, beaches and world's biggest mall.

Every day we would see a new thing. I was stunned by the beauty of the city. The roads were well maintained. There were trees on the edge of the roads. It was surprising to see as Dubai is a desert area and still, they managed to maintain such greenery in the city.

We stayed in Dubai for five days and I could barely sleep at nights. I was always excited about the next day and activities to do. Our hotel was a five-star hotel and was loaded with all the luxury amenities.

I can easily say that this trip was the most exciting experience of my life.

Describe a school you have studied in

Explain the details of the school area

Did you like the school?

I went to one of the most famous schools in my city. I read in Shivalik Public School. The school was situated three kilometers from my house. I used to ride my cycle to the school. Our school was built in a huge area and had all the modern amenities in it.

I will start with entrance. There is a huge gate at the front which is painted in yellow and burgundy colour. These are the theme colours of our school. There is a reception area right at the entrance of the school on the right-hand side. It led to a huge parking area where school buses are parked. There are several buildings in the school premises. The first one is known as A-Block. This block had classes 10th, 11th and 12th. The principal's office is also located in this block. This block was the most disciplined wing of the school at the time I studied there.

Behind the A-Block, there is a smaller building known as B-Block. In that block, classes 5th to 9th were located. In front of the block A and B there is a huge 100 meter by 100-meter square shaped ground. That ground was mainly used for hockey and football practice in our times. Adjacent to the ground is a big canteen area and two basketball courts.

On the other side of the playground, there is the largest building in the school campus. This building is known as block – C. This building houses a boy's hostel and primary classes. The hostel area is not that big, but it is very neat and clean.

Adjacent to the hostel area, there is a big dining hall where hostel students used to have their meals. Opposite to the dining area, there is a huge auditorium where we went regularly to watch educational movies and documentaries.

Right in the center of the school area, there is a huge assembly area where all the students used to gather in the morning and do the prayers. I really enjoyed my time at the school. I was blessed to study in such school where all the amenities were available accompanied with world class infrastructure.

Expensive clothing you have bought lately

Why did you buy that expensive piece of clothing?

Tell about the dress

Do you wear that dress quite often?

I generally don't buy expensive clothing but there are some occasions in life when one needs to buy fashionable clothes. I remember when I had to buy an expensive attire for my brother's marriage.

The marriage party was to be held in the evening, so I decided to buy dark coloured three-piece suit. This was the first time when I had to buy such dress. I went in the market and started looking for a perfect dress for the occasion.

I explored all the branded shops and tried a lot of suits there. But, somewhere down the line I was not satisfied. Some suits were perfect in fit but the colour was not attractive. On the other hand, some had attractive colours but didn't fit well.

So, I decided to get my suit stitched from a tailor. I found a renowned tailor in the town and told him my requirements. He showed me a couple of books containing hundreds of clothing designs. He also recommended me to buy a particular type of cloth for the suit. Hence, I bought a black coloured cloth of five meters in length and took it to the tailor. The cloth costed me around ten thousand rupees.

I wasn't impressed with the design that tailor showed me. So, I browsed the internet and took out a three-piece suit design from there. I showed it to the tailor, and he assured me that he would imitate that design to perfection.

He did a couple of modifications to that design so that it would suit my body type. The stitching cost of the suit was five thousand rupees. Then I had to buy a matching shirt with the suit. That shirt was of white colour and costed me around two thousand rupees.

I don't wear this dress often as it only suits on parties and special occasions. I had never got such an expensive clothing for myself but when I wore that suit, I felt that it was worth every penny.

OR

(For Girls)

I am not very fond of expensive clothing. I always set a budget before purchasing anything new. But there has been a time where I shopped limitlessly which was on my brother's wedding.

In the Indian culture, a lot of importance is given to all the rituals which are performed in a wedding and getting decked up for them is one of the most favourite part of all the girls.

I was extremely excited for the wedding and wanted to look the best, so I bought a Lehenga which is a traditional form of an Indian Gown. It is a Gown designed by one of the renowned designers in our country, Sabyasachi. The dress was great looking but was very expensive. So, I decided to look for more shops.

Then I went to the other shops and saw hundreds of designs, but nothing could match the dress I had seen earlier. So, I went back to the shop I had gone previously and ordered the dress. It was a very expensive dress and I had to pay twenty-five thousand for it.

The dress was royal looking with a combination of vibrant colours. The main colour of the dress was bottle green along with yellow. The detailing and design of the dress was mesmerizing.

The tailor at the shop took my measurements and altered the dress according to my size. I wore that dress on the wedding reception of my brother and everyone at the wedding venue gave me flattering remarks and told me that I was looking like a royal princess.

I had never bought such an expensive dress in the past.

Time when you had to take care of a baby

Who was the baby?

Why you had to take care of him/her

How did you feel about the situation?

I like to play with small kids and babies. But it's not an easy task for an inexperienced person to take care of a baby. It may seem an easy task but from my personal experience I can tell you that it takes a lot of courage to take care of a baby.

There was an instance in my life when I had to take care of a baby for a couple of hours. My sister has a one-year baby whose name is Amit. He is a very adorable and don't cry too much like other kids. He still doesn't walk properly so there must be someone to look after him all the time.

Earlier my sister had applied for a job in a multinational company. She received an interview call and the company was located in the city where we live. She called me and asked if anyone was at home to take care of Amit. I told her that everyone had gone out for one or the other work and I was the only person who was present.

She told me about the situation and rushed to our home. She told me that I had to baby sit Amit for a couple of hours. I was reluctant at first, but I was finally ready to take the responsibility. She bought a bag full of Amit's toys along with spare clothes and baby food.

She quickly explained me how to make baby food and how to feed him when required. I told her not to worry and leave Amit with me. My sister hurried for the interview and I was left alone with Amit.

I stated playing with him as soon as my sister left as I didn't want him to notice that his mother is not there. I made funny faces to make him laugh. After a while he was feeling hungry and started crying for food and made gestures indicating that he was hungry.

I quickly made the baby food by adding boiled water in the oats pack. I fed him all the food and it made him really happy. We continued playing with toys and I spend a wonderful time with my nephew.

After some time, my sister came and thanked me for babysitting Amit. I told my sister that I had a wonderful time with Amit, and she could drop him anytime with me. I bade goodbye to both and loved spending time with him.

Job you think you would be good at OR Describe something you would like to do in the future
Why do you think you will be good at this job?
Would you pursue your career in it?
How will you do your job

I haven't decided much about my future but there are some things that I like to do and one day may pursue career in that. The thing that I love doing is travelling and searching about new places across the world.

I have been to a couple of foreign countries and a lot of cities in India. So, I have a deep knowledge of travel and things to remember before travelling. I like to explore new places and I also like to tell people about those places. I think I would be good at being a travel guide.

Not only I like to travel to new places, but I also want people to see those places and learn about them. I got this habit in my childhood when I was taken to Shimla by my father. He showed me the city and explained each and everything there. I fell in love with travel and discovering new places. I think I would be able to guide people about the places according to their nature and choice. I can make itinerary according to the needs of people. I can be good at guiding them about the important cities and places to learn about our culture and history.

I am very good at planning the holidays. Whenever our family decides to go on a holiday, they always put this responsibility on my shoulders. I always search about the flights and hotels at cheap price

I also seek important information about the places before I visit. I like to make notes of important information such as transport, weather and food of the city I am going to visit. Getting this information really helps at the time of the travel.

Even if I am not travelling anywhere, I still like to collect useful information about the tourist destinations and educate people about them. I think that I can be a good tour guide in future.

Something that you borrowed from your friend or family
Why you had to borrow
Is borrowing a good habit
did you return the thing?

I don't usually borrow things from others as I consider it a bad activity, but I think borrowing from a good friend or family member is not a bad idea. I have borrowed few things from my friends and family in the past. But I remember once I needed a digital DSLR camera for my school trip to a wildlife sanctuary. I didn't buy a DSLR camera as it is very expensive. I am very fond of clicking wildlife photographs and the camera that I own is old and do not click clear pictures.

So instead of buying that thing I called one of my best friends who had this camera. My friend got ready to give me the camera on the first call. He told me to collect the camera from his home and he would also teach me certain functions of the camera that I don't know.

I reached his home and he handed me the camera along with its accessories and safety gear. He explained me how to use the accessories and what are the different modes to get the best picture. Then he packed the camera and equipment in a bag and wished me luck.

I wanted this camera badly as one doesn't get a chance every day to visit wildlife sanctuary and click wildlife photographs. I thanked my friend and promised him to return his camera in the same condition.

I took that camera on my trip and clicked hundreds of pictures. I felt amazing while clicking the pictures. The camera also had an extra lens attached to it which helped in to zoom the far away animals and places. My other colleagues were really impressed with the camera and my photography skills. Some of my mates wanted to borrow the camera from me but I told them it is not mine. As soon as I came back from the trip, I decided to save money and pledged myself to buy a similar kind of camera. After that, I saved all the pictures in a laptop and handed over the camera to my friend with a big thanks.

Describe a shop or store you often go to
Where is the shop/store located?
What do you usually buy from there?
What do you enjoy the most at the store?

There are many shops that I visit regularly. But in this topic, I will describe a store where I go every week and spend a lot of time there. I mostly go there with my mother as we buy fresh vegetables, fruits and daily needs from that store. This store is in the center of my city.

The name of the store is Reliance Mart. It is one of the most trusted brands in our country. They have thousands of stores across India. This is a supermarket that sells most of the things that we require in our day to day life.

I usually go there on Wednesdays in the evening. The reason I go on this day is that there are more discounts and offers on all the products. I also came to know from one of the staff members of the store that they get fresh supply of fruits on Wednesday.

This supermarket is located on the ground floor of a popular mall. If we buy goods worth 250 rupees or more then they refund the amount of the car parking ticket of the mall. At the entrance of the store, trolleys are piled up. I take one trolley and keep my stuff in it.

One must carry a reliance store card in order to buy anything from there. They check the authentication of the card at the time of billing. The store is so big that it contains all kinds of products from clothes, shoes, biscuits, bags, processed food, dairy products and so on.

One can also buy crockery and sports goods. This is the biggest supermarket in my city. There is a canteen area right at the back of the store. One can have food and refreshments over there. Along with the canteen, there is a bakery area that sells cakes, pastries, breads and loafs. I always buy my bread from this store.

I love shopping so I feel rejuvenated after visiting this store. I always find something new there and I can't resist myself from buying those things.

Describe a national day in your country
Why this day is a national day?
Do you celebrate this day?
How do people celebrate this day?
India has three major national days. On 26th January we celebrate Republic day, on 2nd October we celebrate Gandhi Jayanti and my favourite one is the Independence Day that is celebrated on 15th August. Our country got freedom in 1947 from the British Imperial rule. The reason it is our national day is because all the people across India celebrate this day with great joy and enthusiasm.

Thousands of freedom fighters and revolutionaries fought for the independence of our country. On this day we pay tribute to the people who sacrificed their lives to get freedom for our country. There have been many revolutionaries like Mahatma Gandhi, Bhagat Singh and Subhash

Chandra Bose who fought against the British rule and helped India to become a free nation.

On 15th August, massive army parade takes place in the capital of our country. Different regiments and battalions take part in the parade and show their prowess. Navy and Air Force also display their weapons and artillery to the public on this day. The parade is held near the India gate and millions of people come there to see the parade live.

The prime minister of our country inaugurates the celebrations every year at the Red Fort, New Delhi. The prime minister also gives speech to motivate people to fight for the betterment of the country.

I celebrate this day by hoisting our country's flag at the top floor of my house and I also like to call my friends and family members to celebrate this day. We exchange sweets and gifts and fly kites on this day. Kite flying is a popular activity on this day across our country. The reason people fly kites is that flying kite is a symbol of freedom. So, they express this emotion by flying kites.

I wear traditional clothes on this day. White gown with lose pants. I also like to play patriotic songs and watch the parade on TV. All the schools hold singing and dancing competitions to commemorate this extraordinary day.

Describe your favorite flower

What is the importance of flowers in our life?

Why do you like that flower?

Tell something about that flower

I am a nature lover, so I like all the flowers. Flowers are very important in human's life. people exchange flowers on special occasions and flowers also increase the beauty of the surroundings.

The one that I like the most is the rose flower. You will be surprised to know that there are more than three hundred species of rose flowers. The rose plant can grow four to five feet tall and the stem of the plant is often armed with sharp prickles.

Rose flower has large petals with very smooth texture. There are many colours that can be seen like white, pink, black, yellow and maroon. Red is the most common type of rose flower. It smells very good and can be grown in different environments. This plant can be grown in most of the areas with minimum of sunlight and water.

Rose flower has numerous benefits. The petals of the rose flowers are used to extract rose oil. Rose oil is then used to make perfumes and room fresheners. Rose oil is also used in a number of cosmetic items.

Rose water is also one of the most common products. Rose water is used in drinks and to clean the skin. Some people also put rose water in eyes to reduce irritation and redness. There are endless number of uses of rose flower.

Ice creams are manufactured using rose petals. The flavor of rose petal is very palatable. It increases the flavor of any edible item. Some Indian sweets are also made of rose flower. Not only this, rose flower also contains vitamin C. So, it is used by pharmaceutical industries to make medicines.

The petals of rose flower can be directly consumed, and it acts as a natural mouth freshener. Red rose is considered as a symbol of love. Couples give red rose to each other on the valentine's day. Rose has become a universal symbol of love.

I have three or four rose plants in my back yard. One yields red rose and the other produces pink. I love the fragrance, shape and everything about rose flower.

Describe an art and craft activity you did at school

Do you like art and craft

What was the activity about?

Did you enjoy it

I am always at the front of the line when it comes to co-curricular activities. I participated in several activities in my school life. One activity which was related to art and craft was making few posters for a cycle rally. The cycle rally was held to create awareness about the dangerous effects of single use plastic. These days most of the people use such polyethene bags that are non-biodegradable. As a result, these bags cause huge problems in our environment. Since I was participating in the rally, I was instructed by my teacher to make some posters regarding the rally. My teacher emphasized that the posters are very important for the rally and should be made to perfection.

I took the work seriously and started making different patterns on white charts. It took me a lot of time to think the design, colour and slogan for the rally. My brother gave me some ideas and I also searched a bit on internet and started creating the posters. I had to make six posters. So, I decided to make three different designs.

I chose vibrant colours as the background of the poster. I wanted such colour that would attract everyone's eyeballs. Two posters had florescent parrot colour, two had orange colour and the remaining two had bright pink colour.

After painting the background colour, I made a sketch of single use plastic bag in the center. Then I put a bold cross symbol on the bag suggesting to not use these bags. Then I thought a lot about the slogan and finally came up with 'Say no to single use plastic bags.

When my teachers saw those posters, they appreciated me and thanked me for the job. We took those posters and pasted it in front of our cycles. I really enjoyed the rally that day as we gave a wonderful message to the society.

I had done quite a few art and craft projects in my school, but I enjoyed this one the most. Because I had to apply a lot of thinking and it was made for a good social cause.

Describe a noisy place you have been to

Do you live in a noisy environment?

Why was the place noisy?

Did you get uncomfortable

It is not difficult to find noisy places in our country. We have the world's second largest population and there are countless vehicles commuting on the roads. In this topic, I would like to explain my visit to PCA stadium which is situated in Mohali.

I went there to witness a T20 match between India and Australia. This was a world cup match and was held in the year 2016. I had never felt such a huge noise before in my life. The match began at 7 PM and ended at 11 PM. It was one of the noisiest places that I can remember.

As soon as I entered the stadium, I saw the stadium packed with people cheering for their respective teams. The match was held in our country so most of the spectators were supporting India. Even before entering the stadium, the noise of the crowd could be heard outside.

It was a very important match so there were an estimated forty thousand people in the stadium. I had never seen such a huge crowd at one place before. When the match started, people were less noisy. But when the Australia's wickets started to tumble, people began to shout loud in ecstasy. People generally create noise to lift the morale of the team.

India batted in the second innings. The match was a close encounter but a great batting performance from Virat Kohli ensured that India won the match. With every shot Indian player were playing, people were celebrating it like a festival. Some were blowing whistles and others were smashing empty water bottles to create sound.

I was surprised to see that some people had brought blow pipes and other musical instruments to create a noisy environment. I had never heard such noise continuously for four hours. It was such a noisy day.

However, I enjoyed my day as we won the match

Describe a social networking website/platform you use

Do you use social networking sites often?

Which is your favourite one

Why do you like it?

These days, most of the youngsters are engaged in social networking websites. Youngsters use it for the most part of the day to connect to new people and to see what is happening in their friend's life. I use social networking site every day. My favourite one is Facebook.

I have been using this website from a couple of years and I have made many new friends within country and abroad. I have also connected with my old friends with whom I lost touch. I think that I use this website for more than an hour every day.

There are many reasons to like Facebook. The biggest reason is that you stay connected to your friends 24x7. You can post your photographs and you can let people know that what is happening in your life. similarly, you can check what your friends are up to these days.

Apart from this, I have found a lot of my old friends on Facebook. Now, I regularly chat with them and get the updates. Moreover, one can like different pages on this website to get information regarding that page. For an example, if you like cars, you can like pages related to cars. They will show you videos and updates related to latest cars in the market.

One can also watch news and latest trends going in the world. You can also connect with people who are living in foreign countries. Not only this, you can also promote your business on Facebook. You can do advertisements regarding the product you sell. I am very fond of using this website for making friends in foreign countries.

In total I have made around hundred new friends in foreign countries. I chat with them and try to learn about their culture and lifestyle. I also do video calling with my friends and relatives who are living in foreign countries.

All in all, it is a wonderful social networking website.

Describe a personal goal which you have not been able to achieve
What is your goal?
Why have you not able to achieve it in the past
How do you plan to achieve it?

We cannot get everything in our life. There are certain goals in my life that I aspire to attain but I have not been able to achieve them till date. Some are professional while others are personal. One of my most desired goals of all time is to reduce my weight.

I need to reduce some weight and get a healthy and fit body. I have become a bit overweight in the past few years because of my sedentary lifestyle. I sit for several hours to study and I rarely get any time for the physical activity. If I get some time in my daily life, I spent it on various indoor activities like watching TV and using mobile phone, which has made me quite dull and inactive in my daily life.

So, I am planning to start a regime where I can cut on my calories and start some modular workout on a regular basis. I think that I need to spend at least an hour daily on exercise and other workout regimes. I know I can shed my weight easily, but initiation is required. Since I was having exams a few days back, I could not start it, but soon I will stick to this strict routine.

Health is everything for a human being. If we don't maintain our health, it is not worth living. The first thing I need to do is to cut on my sugar intake as I am a sweet lover. Next thing, I will be doing is to join a gym in the evening time and go for some intensive workout.

Sometimes, I feel very ashamed of myself when I look in the mirror as I was never like this. Even my friends and relatives have started taunting me for my overweight. I feel very bad when people centralize me for the discussion of being overweight. But now I have become so determined and I will get back to my toned body very soon with a disciplined lifestyle. I tried to pursue this goal in the past year but haven't been able to make a routine. But this time I am quite sure of achieving it.

Describe the politest person you have come across in your life
How do you know that person?
Why do you think that he/she is polite?
Share your experience with that person

I have come across some polite people in my life, but I would like to speak about a person who is my relative and I think that he is the politest person I know in my entire life.

I am talking about my uncle who lives in Himachal Pardesh. His hometown is Bilaspur and I often visit him in my holidays. I love to go there as it is a neat and clean place with tremendous environment. Himachal Pradesh is one of the greenest places in our country.

I would like to share something about my uncle's personality. His name is Rakesh and he runs a bakery. He is running this business from the past twenty years and he is doing well in it. I have never seen such a polite person in my entire life. He is not only polite to his friends and family, but he speaks in the same way to everyone.

He is never in an angry mood and I have never seen him shouting on anyone. His speech is so polite and direct. He doesn't speak much and gives his opinions in only certain situations. He is always gracious to his customers and I have seen people praising him for his well-mannered speech and behavior.

I remember one instance when me and my uncle were riding through a market and suddenly, we got hit by a speeding car. Luckily, we did not get injured. There were some minor bruises. Suddenly huge number of people gathered there and started criticizing the car driver who hit us.

Immediately my uncle told the crowd to not shout at him and let him go as it was not his fault. The only problem was that his speed was high in the narrow street. My uncle politely solved the situation and we came back home.

That day I learned a great lesson from my uncle that one should remain polite and humble in every situation of life.

Describe a time when you received a good service from a hotel or a restaurant

What type of hotel/restaurant did you go to?

What did you most like about their service?

Would you again go to that restaurant?

I have been to many restaurants which have provided great services. The one I would like to explain is located in a mall nearby my house. The name of the restaurant is Masters of Grill.

This restaurant is located on the top floor of the mall and is opened newly in our area. The reason I visited there was to celebrate the birthday of my cousin. This was my first visit to this restaurant. It is a buffet style restaurant where both vegetarian and non-vegetarian food are served.

We ordered vegetarian buffet and soon the service of the food began. The service was so quick and smooth that we could not believe it. The waiters were well dressed and well mannered. They politely explained the dish before serving it. I had never seen such trained waiters in any other restaurant.

They served us steaming hot snacks along with drinks. The drinks were perfectly made to our requirements. Every now and then the waiters were confirming about the taste and presentation of the snacks. They also offered us to order any other dish apart from the menu. We ordered chilly cheese which was not in the original menu.

During our meals, the manager of the restaurant personally came to our table and asked us about the experience of the restaurant. I was so glad to see that the restaurant staff was so concerned about us. He also asked about the service of the waiters and quality of food.

At the end, they gave us a mobile tablet in which they asked us to fill the feedback form. I ticked all the boxes and gave 10 on 10 as the overall rating. In the form I filled my date of birth and mobile number. After a few days I received a free meal on my birthday.

I have never had such an experience of good service from a restaurant in my life. Now I am a regular customer of that restaurant and I also recommend it to other people.

A polluted city you have visited OR Describe a place you visited that has been affected by pollution

Why did you visit that city?

What sort of problems were there?

Is government doing anything to solve this issue

India is a country that is rapidly developing in a lot of areas. Due to that, there have been many industries opening up that contributes to pollution. I also think that the demand of vehicles has increased drastically which has led to extreme pollution in some of the cities.

The most polluted city that I have visited in my life is Delhi, the capital of India. Although it is one of the most developed cities across our country, but it is also the most polluted one. The main reason of Delhi's pollution is its population. Delhi is one of the densely populated cities in India. People move there from all parts of the country in search of jobs and business opportunities.

I have visited Delhi a lot of times as many of my relatives live there. I face some pollution related problems whenever I visit there. I face difficulty in breathing and stomachache when I visit Delhi. I came to know from an article that 40% of people living in Delhi are suffering from respiratory problems. When you enter Delhi, you can see a huge pile of waste on the left-hand side of the National Highway. That indicates that not many active steps are taken to tackle this issue.

There is also the problem of clean drinking water in Delhi. Many residents don't get access to clean drinking water. Many parts of the city are highly developed, but some are extremely dirty. I have seen many people wearing face masks as a precaution against polluted air.

Last time when I went to Delhi, I had difficulty in breathing. I had to take medicines for five days to get back to normal. I saw millions of vehicles on the roads that continuously create noise and air pollution.

There were some steps taken in the past to curb the pollution in the city. Electric metro and busses were introduced that run on clean fuel. Despite those efforts, the pollution keeps on growing in the city.

Describe a good law in your country

Explain the law

Why do you think that this law is good?

Do you feel that this law is useful?

Indian judicial system is very strong and there are many laws that protect the privacy and rights of the citizens of our country. The laws are written in the constitution of our country and it is the duty of every citizen to abide by the laws.

One law that I think is good for everyone is the RTI Act, 2005. It stands for Right to Information. This act was passed in the parliament of our country in the year 2005. Since then, every day an estimate of 4800 RTI applications are filed by the citizens of our country.

In this act, any citizen of country may request information from a public authority or any government body. The officials need to reply to the RTI within a maximum of 30 days. This Law was an instant hit and 17,500,000 applications have been filed in the last ten years. Now more and more people are getting the information which previously was hidden from them by the government authorities.

RTI is a legal right of any citizen of India. Anyone can file an RTI and ask the government officials about the public related properties and rules. There is a very reasonable fee required to file an RTI. The fee should be sent to the authorities in a shape of a demand draft from a bank. The RTI process can be done online as well as offline. All information regarding the Law is available online. The process is explained in easy steps that can be understood by everyone.

This law has brought a revolution in our country. Previously people were kept away from important information but with this law in place, one can get the details of all the public organizations and establishments.

A talkative person
Tell about that person
Why does he/she talk too much
How do you feel about him/her?
I know a few people who are talkative in nature, but I have never seen anyone more talkative than my sister Pooja.
She simply loves to talk and talk. She is elder to me and works in a multinational company as a website developer. She is tall and has sharp features with fair colour. She looks very beautiful in traditional attire.
No one can get bored when they are in the company of my sister. She can make anyone talk to her. I think that's why she has a lot of friends. She can make friends very easily. Whenever I see my sister, I always see her talking to someone on phone or in person. I have asked her about the reason behind this. She replied that talking is a therapy for her. She feels relaxed while talking.
She always shares her feelings with the family members. She is of a very jolly nature. I think the reason behind her nature is that she shares all her problems and doesn't keep it to her. If she is in a worry, she always tells me. She also encourages other people to speak up.
I remember when she was in the school. Our parents used to receive a lot of complaints from her teachers. All the complaints were regarding the excess talkativeness in the class. Although, she was a brilliant student academically.
I have never seen anybody talk like my sister. Even if she is not well health wise, she can't stop talking. I always advise her to talk less to save energy, but god knows from where she gets all the strength to talk nonstop.

Interesting news you read in a newspaper
What was the news
Where did you read it?
Was the news helpful to you
I have little interest in reading newspapers. I get my news mostly from the internet. But sometimes I pick up a newspaper on weekends and read the main headlines.

I borrowed a newspaper on a weekend from my sister as she reads it regularly. I generally read the main headlines and skip some of the pages. However, on that day I decided to read the newspaper thoroughly. I took Hindustan Times newspaper from my sister.

I came across one column of a page that I found interesting and I would like to share that news article with you. That news article was given by the government of our country and it was an announcement of a scheme that was initiated by the prime minister of our country.

The name of the scheme is 'Pradhan Mantri Awaas Yojna'. In this scheme the government announced that people of our country will now get quality housing at very low cost. In that article, the government announced that the scheme will be available to every Indian who qualifies for it.

In that news, the prices of two-bedroom apartment was also given. The prices were unbelievable as it was a government backed scheme. The price was around twenty lacs for a two-bedroom apartment whereas a normal apartment in a private colony would cost double.

In the news, the site of the project was also mentioned. They also provided the details of the banks that would be approved for the finance of the apartments. The government opened the applications for the apartments and mentioned the last date of application for the scheme.

I was so impressed with the news article that I showed it to my whole family. So that was the interesting news article that I read recently.

Talk about an instance when you invited a friend for a meal in a restaurant or at home.
Why did you invite him/her?
Where did you invite him/her?
What sort of meal you had?
I have invited many friends to my home and restaurant for meals. One instance I would like to share with you is when I invited an old friend of mine to a restaurant.

Few days back I met one of my childhood and school friend on a social networking website. I got his number from there and called him immediately. I came to know that he has now shifted to a different city. I had discussion with him after a long time. I invited him to visit the city someday.

After a few days I received a call from him, and he told me that he is coming to the city the next day. My parents had gone out for a couple of day for some work and there won't be anyone to prepare meals at home. So, I decided to call my friend to a famous restaurant of our city.

Next day I reached at the restaurant and reserved a table. He came there after ten minutes. We shook hands and gave each other a tight hug. I was a bit emotional that time as he used to be one of my best friends. Soon we ordered some snacks to eat. We talked all the time about the things we did at school and discussed about our old friends.

After the snacks we ordered the main course. I ordered Chinese as I remembered that my friend likes it. We ordered noodles along with vegetable Manchurian. The meal was served hot and fresh. This restaurant is famous for authentic Chinese food.

We had fantastic time talking and the meal was also wonderful. After that I insisted him to stay at our home for a night, but he had to go back.

Describe a meeting or discussion about fake news

What was the news about?

What did you discuss about it?

Was the news fake or real?

Due to globalization, it has become very easy to access information. Most of the times the news that we receive is correct but there can be times when we receive fake news and we believe in it blindly.

Three years back, a fake news circulated on the TV and the internet. The news was that the new currency notes in our country contains nano GPS chips. Even the big media houses and all the news channels in our country circulated this news.

I was at a party with my friends and suddenly this news popped out on the TV. Soon it was all over the internet. Everyone started believing in that news without realizing this kind of a thing is not possible. The news channels were showing that the Nano chip has been embedded inside the 2000 rupee note to detect the location of it.

The news anchors stated the reason that government has done so in order to track black money and raid people who store huge amounts of notes illegally. This news was shown in all the channels and people were posting about it on the social media.

There was an intense discussion between me and my friends about the news. Some of my friends were backing me and supported the idea that it was a fake news. Some of my friends believed what they saw on TV. They argued that there must be some truth about the news that's why all the news channels are showing it.

One of my friends also explained that a nano chip is not so small and thin that it can fit a currency note. He told that it is impossible to inject such chips in millions of notes as it would drastically increase the production cost of the currency notes.

At the end, we all decided to wait and see if the news was true. After some days some news channels claimed it to be a fake news and apologized to people for that.

Talk about a job one of your grandparents did
What type of job it was?
Did he/she enjoy it?
Would you do the same job

I was very close to my grandfather and I have taken a lot of inspiration from him in all aspects of life. He has always guided me to the right path. Right now, my grandfather enjoys a retired life but still does voluntary odd jobs to pass his leisure time.

My grandfather is a well-qualified man and has a master's degree in literature. He worked as a head Librarian in a public library for more than thirty years. He did his job with utmost sincerity and never complained about it.

He retired eight years ago but he still misses his job. He still goes to the same library to read books and relive his working days. He spends around two to three hours in the library whenever he goes there. He told me that he used to work from 8AM to 4PM.

He was the head librarian, so his responsibilities were to take care of the condition of the library and to maintain records of the book in the library.

He was also responsible for the preservation of the old books that were not in good condition.

My grandfather tells me that he had to work really hard to get this job. He told me that he cleared an entrance exam and there were only seven posts, but the number of candidates was in thousands. He got the job and immediately liked it.

My grandfather reads a lot of books and he tells me that he developed that habit while working there as librarian. He started as a librarian but after some time he was promoted to the post of head librarian. His life has been like this. He was and still very sincere towards his work. He is very punctual and hardworking as well.

He told me that he enjoyed every bit of his work as a librarian. But if I am given a job like this then I don't think so that I would be able to do justice with it.

Describe a family business you know

Why do you think that it is a family business?

What sort of business do they do?

Are you inspired by them?

One of the biggest business family in India is the Ambani family. Their family business is named reliance industries. The reason that it is a family business is that all their family members are involved in some sort of business responsibilities.

They are multi-millionaires and they run hundreds of industries across India. The Reliance Industries was founded by Shri Dhiru Bhai Ambani. Then he handed over the business to his two sons Shri Mukesh Ambani and Shri Anil Ambani. Both the brothers parted their ways a few years back and now run their independent industries.

Mukesh Ambani is married to Mrs. Nita Ambani and they both have two sons and a daughter. All the five members are in business and they manage it superbly. Reliance industries is dealing in hundreds of products across the world. Their main business boomed due to the success of their Petro chemical industry.

All the family members are involved in some or the other kinds of business. Mrs. Nita Ambani owns a cricket team franchise named Mumbai Indians.

She manages everything related to that team and is also seen motivating players throughout the matches.

Recently the reliance industries launched a telecom company by the name of JIO. This company has taken over millions of people. Most of the people are now using this company's mobile connection rather than other brands. This company is managed by Mr. Mukesh Ambani's sons. This family works together very well, and I hope that they keep growing like this in the future as well.

I am so inspired by all of them and I aspire to follow the footsteps of Mr. Mukesh Ambani and would like to become a successful businessman in the future.

Talk about your favorite movie star

What type of personality is he/her?

Has he/she influenced you in your life?

Do you feel that actors can make good role models?

Indian film industry has produced many film stars who have earned name and fame throughout the world. But for me one name stands out. He is Akshay Kumar or some of his near and dear ones call him Akki.

His real name is Rajiv Hari Om Bhatia, but he changed his name when he came into film industry 30 years ago. He belongs to India, but he is now a permanent resident of Canada. He has appeared in more than 100 movies and has won myriad awards, including the National Film Award for the best actor and a couple of Filmfare awards. He is married to another famous actress Twinkle Khanna.

He is one of the most successful actors in the Bollywood film industry. Most of his films are on the top of the charts and inevitably does great business. I like him personally because the kind of films he has done over the past few years. He has portrayed incredible history and sacrifice made by our Army men in the films like Kesari, Holiday and Baby.

He also makes films on social problems so that he can inspire people to change for better. His recent movies like Toilet and Padman earned him a great respect from every corner of the world for raising social issues that are still prevalent in our country. Not only this, he is a super fit actor and does most of his action stunts himself.

He always inspires people to remain physically fit. He makes videos and post them regularly on the social media sites regarding the importance of being healthy and fit. He knows martial arts and practices yoga in the morning. I have taken a lot of inspiration from him regarding the importance of health and fitness in our lives.

I think that actors can be great role models. The reason is that people watch them in movies, and they follow them from heart. So, actors can easily inspire people to do well in life and they can be great role models as well.

Describe a period in your history that you would like to learn about

Why you would like to learn about that period

Have you read something about that period?

Do you feel that history is an important subject?

I am fond of reading history and events that happened in the past. A few days back I got a chance to know about Stone Age period of the history. I saw a video regarding this on the internet.

I was so impressed with the video that I curiously wanted to learn about the Stone Age. So, I ordered a book on the internet but due to its unavailability I could not get it. After that I didn't get a chance to read more about the Stone Age.

From the video I got the certain aspect of that era. Stone Age was a prehistoric period during which mainly stone was used to make tools with an edge. This period lasted for more than three million years. The Stone Age period ended with the discovery of the metalworking between 8700 BCE and 2000 BCE.

I also read in the school time about this period. We were taught that the main artifacts like tools used by humans were made of stones. Some historians also say that in this period, tools were also made from bones of the animals.

Stone Age is the first of three-age system of archaeology, which divides human technological prehistory into three periods. The first one is Stone Age, the second is The Bronze Age and the third one is The Iron Age. After knowing these few points about the Stone Age from that video. I became very curious and decided to learn about this period more in the upcoming time. I imagined that how the humans would have survived by depending on the stone alone. History is a very important subject for everyone. I think that without the knowledge of history, one can't move forward. There is so much to learn from our wonderful history.

So, this is the time period in history that I would like to learn about in detail.

A person who has encouraged you recently

Who is that person?

How has he/she encouraged you

Do you feel that we should have role models in life?

There have been many people in my life from whom I have taken inspiration to do well. Recently I was encouraged by a person named Amit. He is my neighbor and a good friend of mine.

He is six years older than me, but he is one of my well-wishers. He lives down the lane and we often hang out together. He is working in a Bank as a manager. I learn a lot of things in his company.

We often go for evening walks in the local area. Recently I discussed something with him about my career. I told him that I was looking to study in one of the renowned institutes in Delhi. To which he politely disagreed and suggested me to get my degree from a foreign university instead of studying in India.

I asked him about the reason behind it. He explained that universities and colleges in India these days are charging almost same fee as the universities and colleges in Canada and Australia. So, it is better if you study abroad as you will get more exposure to different environment and culture. Further, he suggested that the study pattern in Canada or Australia is more practical that the study pattern in India.

He also told me that those countries are also offering students to work part-time along with studies. He said that working along with studies will make me more industrious and intelligent. He explained me at length about the other benefits of studying abroad. That day I felt really encouraged and took the matter of pursuing my further studies in Canada. That's why I am taking the IELTS exam.

I think that it is important to have role models in our lives. Instead of looking for inspiration from celebrities one should find role models in people nearby. Like I found mine in my friend. So, Amit is the person who has encouraged me in a great way in recent times.

Describe a time when you were outside, and rain started
Why had you gone outside?
What did you do when the rain started?
Do you like rain
I remember a situation in my life when I was roaming around the city and suddenly it started raining. That was a tricky situation as I had no umbrella with me that day.
I had gone out to buy a couple of novels. I went to sector 17 market. It is one of the renowned markets in our city. There is a huge open area in the center of the sector and rest of the surrounding area is filled with branded shops, local shops, restaurants and cafes.
This incident happened in the month of December. Generally, there is no rain in this month and December is considered as the driest month of the year. Most of the rain falls in the month of July and August. I went there on a bike and went to a shop to buy the books.
As I was looking for books, I heard a loud thunderclap. I thought that it must be something else but when I came out of the shop, I observed that a huge dark grey cloud cover was coming from the western side.
I decided to rush from there and reach home as soon as possible. My home was about a fifteen minutes ride from there. So, I hurried and started my journey towards home. Shortly after that, light raindrops started to pour down. I didn't stop as it was not much of a threat. I continued my journey, but it was short lived.
A heavy gust of wind hit me, and it started pouring heavily. I had to stop on the side of the road and parked my bike on the pavement. Then I quickly looked for a shelter and found myself under a bus stop roof. You won't believe that I had to wait there for two hours as the rain wouldn't stop. After two hours I came back home but thankfully I didn't get wet. Getting wet in a month like December would have been dangerous as the temperatures in the day are well below ten degrees.

Talk about a practical skill you have
Which skills do you have?
Explain one practical skill you have
Is it important to be skillful?
I have a few practical skills that I have learned over the past few years. I can swim and I can drive a car. I think that practical skills are very important to learn as these skills are important to grow in life.
One skill that I think everyone should know is the computer skills and how to operate all the functions of a computer. I learned this skill when I was in my school. I learned most of the practical skills of computers from my teachers at school, but I also took computer classes in my summer breaks for two consecutive years.
I think that this skill is one of the most crucial skills to learn in life in this era. Most of the work is done using computers these days. It can be seen in every field that the integration of computers is inevitable. We can't imagine an office work that is done without computers.
From mailing important data to the companies from receiving and downloading important files, computers have come a long way. We can maintain records of millions of people in a small computer. We can even control machinery through computers. Most of the industries these days are dependent on computers and robots to perform mechanical tasks.
I know a lot of things about computer. I can send and receive emails on computer. I can also maintain data using Microsoft excel software. I know how to use power point software and create slides and business presentations. I can also use editing software for altering pictures and videos. It is not that difficult to learn all this. I learned all of this in a period of only four months.
I think that it is very important to be skillful as it separates you from others. Even in the job interviews these days mark sheets doesn't matter. They look for people with more practical skills and prefer offering jobs to them.

Describe an unusual vacation you had
Do you like vacations?
Why was the vacation unusual?

Did you enjoy it?

I am the kind of a person who loves to go on vacations from time to time. I plan vacations after every three months. One day, I was surprised by my father when he announced to all the family members that he is taking us to a vacation this summer holidays.

That holiday was unusual in many ways. The first reason that why this holiday was unusual is that I had never been to a beach area. I had never seen a seashore in my life before. Due to that reason, I was very excited for the trip.

There were many types of landscapes and things that I found very unusual. I am talking about the time when I went to Phuket. I found that place extremely beautiful but very unusual as well. Phuket is an island that is a part of the republic of Thailand. It is situated in the southern part of the country. Phuket is surrounded by sea and I was very surprised to know that weather remains constant all year round. I live at a place that has ever changing weather and variating temperatures.

I live in a plain area where sea is far away. I saw ocean and mountains everywhere in Phuket. The landscape and trees there were very different from the place where I live. The other unusual part of the holiday was food. We couldn't find Indian food easily. The food there was dissimilar from what we eat back home. There was more sea food and other items that were unfamiliar to us.

People there were different looking, and their body language was quite unusual as well. But they were very friendly and amicable in nature. There were many other noticeable things that differed from the things from my hometown and country. We did a lot of activities there that are not easy to find in our country. I think the reason I found that holiday unusual was that I visited a foreign country for the first time. I saw things that I had never seen before.

I absolutely loved that vacation and would like to go there again if I get a chance.

Describe an irritating person in your neighborhood

Who is that person?

why does he/she irritate you?

Do you like his/her company?

Most of my neighbours are very good in nature. I love to spend time with them occasionally. They are very welcoming and generous. But there is one guy whom I don't like as he is very irritating and cunning in nature.

He works in a gym as a fitness trainer and I had my first interaction with him last year. In the first meeting I thought him to be a decent guy but after a few meetings I found him to be mysterious, cunning and over smart. He is always praising himself for what he has achieved. He always says that he is the best and he doesn't like people in the neighbourhood.

I don't usually meet him these days and other people in the neighbourhood don't like him either. He does some irritating things that annoy me and other people living nearby. He goes to gym early in the morning and comes back in the afternoon. After he comes back, he plays extremely loud music on the speakers.

This irritates everyone in the locality and many of the neighbours have tried to explain him about that situation. But he has showed no courtesy towards people. Nowadays he plays it intentionally at night and early in the morning. Many elderly people and kids get disturbed by it.

He also calls his friends late at night and parties by playing loud music. This habit of his irritates everyone and nobody likes him in the area. Last month all people in the neighbourhood gathered and asked his landlord to tell him to vacate the house so that everyone can live in peace.

I think he always did that deliberately to irritate people. I have never seen such an irritating person in my life. No, I don't like his company at all.

Describe a surprise party you organized for your friend

Why did you arrange the party?

How did you plan the party?

What was your friend's reaction?

I have been a part of many parties and I love to surprise people by throwing parties. I have a very special friend in my life and I always celebrate mine and his birthday together. The name of my friend is Amit and he lives near my house.

Last year I told Amit that I will not be able to party with him this year. He was upset and asked the reason. I told him that I had to go to one of my relative's marriage party out of the town, so I won't be able to celebrate his birthday with him.

That was my plan to surprise him with a birthday bash. I deceived him by making an excuse as I wanted to surprise him this year with a grand birthday party. The reason I planned the surprise was that one of our common friends Anuj was also coming from America to visit the country. So, I planned the surprise party along with Anuj.

First, I had to make sure that Amit was present in the town and would not go anywhere else otherwise the surprise would have been of no use. I booked a party hall in a restaurant for twenty people and made all the selections of food and drinks. I also selected a special cake for him.

On the day of the birthday, we all gathered in the hall and one of my friends went to Amit's house to take him to the restaurant. As soon as Amit reached the hall, we all surprised him with a loud greeting and hugs. He was shocked and expressed his happiness by thanking us all for making his day wonderful.

He was also surprised to see Anuj who had come from America. We all enjoyed the party and the memories of that day are still fresh in my mind.

Describe people who raise awareness about the environment
Who are they?
How do they create awareness?
Do you feel that they are effective?

I came to know about this group of people who raise awareness about the environment a couple of years ago. But now I follow them actively on social media and I know a couple of members personally. The group is working in our city from the past four years.

The name of the group is Go Green. People in that group are mostly environmentalist and they care about the environment seriously. They arrange a few awareness programs and events to make people aware about the environment.

They make sure that people living in our city take care of the environment. They arrange cycle rallies on Sundays and raise slogans against the use of single use plastic bags. Recently, they gathered hundreds of people from all walks of life and swept the roads and other dirty parts of the town.

They also publish a newsletter and leaflets to aware people about the necessity to maintain environment. They also focus on saving drinking water. Last year they had organized a big event that focused on saving precious drinking water. In the event they told that how people can save water by using sustainable methods.

Not only this, this organization has also raised slogans against the excessive use of vehicles in the city. More vehicles contribute to pollution so they suggested that people should focus more on carpooling methods. They emphasized that this will not only save the environment but will also save your hard-earned money.

Yes, they are extremely effective as they get so many comments from people on their social media posts. A lot of people come there and express their appreciation and offer help to the organization.

They do a lot of work locally and has gained a lot of popularity over time. Many people especially youngsters have joined them in this campaign, and I am also thinking of joining them soon.

Describe an experience when children made you laugh
What was the situation
How the children made you laugh
Is laughing a good activity

I can recall one instance from my memory when some children made me laugh out so loud that I was not in my control. This happened when I was strolling in a park and saw some kids making a lot of noise.

There were around twenty kids who were approximately aged between six and ten. When I went near, I noticed that someone was guiding them to act. When I spend some time there, I came to know that they were rehearsing a comic skit for their school's annual function.

I sat on a nearby bench and started observing their performance. Slowly other people gathered and soon there were around twenty people who were watching the practice. The kids were looking well trained and followed every instruction of their coach.

They were speaking dialogues that were very funny and complex. They were divided in two groups and one by one each member of the group would taunt each other by using a funny line or conversation. It was an extremely hilarious act that made everyone laugh.

They spoke their discourses in such a way that they were sounding really humorous. They were addressing each other in a very funny way. They practiced that skit for about ten minutes, and I found it hysterical. Those children made me laugh out so loud with their every act and dialogues. I couldn't believe that how they managed to speak in such a way despite their young age.

I feel that laughing is a great activity. Some doctors also suggest that laughing loud can cure cardiac issues and it also contributes in increasing the blood flow of the body. I have seen that people don't laugh whole heartedly. They should do this activity more often to maintain happiness in life.

Describe the greatest success of your friend that made you feel proud

Speak about your friend

Tell about his/her achievement

How does the success of your friend make you proud?

I am going to speak about one of my best friend Amit. He lives near my house and I share a tremendous relationship with him. He recently completed his 12th class and decided to join the Indian Army. Nature wise, he's a disciplined person and speaks less. He is slim and handsome looking. He is tall and has fair colour.

I know Amit from my childhood and I also know that he always dreamt of joining the Indian Army. From childhood, he was very passionate about serving the country through Army. He always told me that he wants to wear that Army uniform and use those guns to destroy the enemy.

After completing his 12th class, he joined the best coaching classes to clear the NDA (National Defense Academy) entrance exam. This exam is one of the most difficult exams to clear and millions of youngsters appear for this exam every year but very few of them crack it.

Every year there are a lot of vacancies in the Army, but they never chose quantity over quality. They only select the deserving candidates. I remember he used to study day and night to crack the NDA exam. He studied for more than ten hours a day apart from the tuitions.

He was so indulged into studies that he never played with other kids and he never showed up at any party from friends. He was always into his studies and never bothered about anything happening outside of it.

I feel very proud of his success as he is serving our country and placing his life in danger for the citizens of our country. I have utmost respect for the Army men, and I feel proud that my friend is doing the duty that many people only dream of doing.

Talk about a situation when you complained about something and got good results

Why did you complain

How much time was taken to get the thing resolved?

Do you often complain about things?

I have complained to a few departments over the past years. This time it was a very serious issue that needed to be addressed to the local authorities for prompt action.

Generally, governments in our country don't act quickly over complaints so at first, I was reluctant to speak about the problem but when it got over the head, I wrote several letters to the local authority about the situation.

I live in a colony and it is well maintained in most of the aspects. But the condition of roads and footpaths is terrible. There are large potholes in the roads everywhere. Recently the holes have become worse and have become quite big. A couple of accidents happened due to these potholes. Few days ago, a biker slipped due to the potholes and sustained serious injuries.

Many people in the past have complained about this situation but no one has looked upon it yet. Then I realized that I must do something about it. So, I wrote several letters to the municipal council and District Commissioner office about the issue. I sent an email containing the photographs of the condition of the roads. I was hopeful that my complaints would bring some results after some time.

To my surprise, they took the action in a week and the government team arrived in our colony to analyze the issue. The team met the people of our colony and promised to take the action soon. After a week all the roads were laid, and footpaths were maintained. I was so happy to see that government took the action in such a short time and resolved the problem. No, I do not complain about things too much but whenever I see something wrong happening, I always complain about it. I think that if your complaint can solve problems then complaining is a good thing.

Describe an outdoor activity you did for the first time
Which outdoor activity did you do for the first time?
Why did you do that activity
How did you feel about it?
Recently I went to a lake that is situated in my city. It is one of the biggest man-made lakes in our country. I generally go there to walk in the evening. Most of the people come there to rejuvenate themselves. One can see Shivalik hills in the backdrop of the lake. It is a beautiful site in the north part of the city.
I went there with my friend one day to take a stroll. We were walking on the track and admiring the beauty of the lake. My friend was visiting the lake for the first time as he came to meet me from Delhi. He saw boats sailing in the lake so he suggested to do boating.
I was hesitant initially but thought of giving it a try. We bought the tickets for a two-seater boat and waited for our turn. We stood on the platform made in the lake and the instructor gave us information on how to paddle the boat. He also tied safety jackets on our waist.
We started with the boating and saw each part of the lake. I was doing this activity for the first time, but I felt good. While boating I realized that it takes a lot of efforts to peddle the boat. There was a steering in that middle that took control of the direction of the boat.
I had seen many people boating before, but I never thought of doing it. That day I thanked my friend for insisting me to do this activity. I felt rejuvenated and inspired after doing this activity. I think it is a fantastic activity that involves a lot of strength in legs. It is a good way of doing exercise as well. That day I really enjoyed the boating time.
So, this is an outdoor activity that I did for the first time.

Talk about a part of city that is changing
Why has that change happened
What is changing and which part is involved
Was the change necessary

Recently our city was declared in the list of the smart cities by the central government of our country. Under this scheme the cities will be enhanced with the facilities that are commonly prevalent in a developed city. There are certain parts of our city that required considerable development.
The government opened the tenders and the work began in full swing. There were many areas of the city that developed in this time period. The commercial area was face lifted and the residential areas got more parks and green areas. Many government clinics and institutes were constructed within the city and on the outskirts as well.
But one change that was required the most was the development of the international airport. There was already an airport in the city, but only domestic flights were operated from there. Now, government has upgraded that airport to cater the needs of the international passengers. The airport was made to work 24 hours as opposed to 12 hours previously for the passenger flights. A new terminal has also been added at the airport for the comfort of the passengers. Now the airport has also advanced equipment and runway that can support the landing and take-off of any type of aircrafts.
The government provided a separate route for the airport and named that road as airport road. Several other projects have developed along the airport road. The airport was also renamed as the Mohali International Airport. Many people of our state live in foreign countries. The nearest international airport was situated 250 kms away.
So, the change was required badly in this part of the city. I want to thank the government and local authorities for bringing this wonderful change in the airport area. I think that our city has changed a lot and has far better facilities than the past.

Talk about a job that helps make the world a better place
Explain that job
Why do you think so?

How has that job changed the world?

There are many jobs that make people's life better. Those jobs make the world a better place to live. I think that doctors and teachers are the professions that are very important in developing the world. But I reckon that people working as scientists are the ones who are making the world a better place.

In my perception, scientists work constantly in improving our lives. There have been millions of inventions in the recent past that have led to improvements in the life of people. Scientists have contributed immensely in making our lives better.

Right from the invention of the light bulb to the discovery of an LED light. We have seen so many new things coming in the market every other week as a result of hard-working scientists. They are constantly occupied in improving the existing technology and developing the new one.

Scientists have been instrumental in developing new drugs that cure diseases that were incurable in the past. As a result of developments in the field of medicines, the life span of humans has also increased.

There have been several scientists who made a mark on the society. Scientists such as Nikola Tesla, Thomas Alva Edison, Einstein and APJ Abdul Kalam have made this globe a better place to live. I have a great respect for the scientists living around the world. They sacrifice their personal lives for improving people's lives.

I think that this job has made the world a better place to live. The inventions made by the scientists have made people's work easier. Scientists don't often get the credit for putting their efforts in the field of science. This job is one of the thankless jobs in the world.

A famous person you would like to meet

What makes a person famous?

Why do you like to meet him/her?

What will you do after meeting him/her?

There are many people in this world who are famous, and I want to meet them desperately. But if I need to pick one person then it would be Narendra Modi. He is the prime minister of our country and it is not easy for everyone to meet him. He is the most important person in our country.

He became the prime minster of India in 2014. Before that he served as the chief minister of Gujrat for 13 consecutive years. He is the member of parliament from Varanasi. In his childhood he left his home after completing high school. He spent most of his later stages of life as a worker of RSS and gradually rose in the ranks.

He has numerous qualities as a politician and as a person. He is a wonderful speaker and speaks in a unique way that is liked by the people of our country. He is very hard working and dynamic. I think that he is the most hard-working politician of our times.

He was awarded as one of the most powerful persons in the world by the Forbes Magazine. He has achieved several awards in India and abroad. Many people regard him as the best prime minister that India has ever produced in terms of decision making. Recently as the prime minister of our country, he took several decisions that previous governments were unable to take. These decisions have proved to be good.

He recently posted a video on the internet. In that video he was doing Yoga and he inspired others to follow it in order to remain fit and healthy in life. I would like to meet him because I want to learn that how we can develop such qualities in life. When I will meet him, I will ask him about the things that we can do in life to become successful like him.

If I get a chance to meet this brilliant personality, then I will not miss it.

Describe a person you know who likes to help people in free time
Who is the person?
How does he/she help people
Why does he/she help people
I know one person who lives in my neighborhood. His name is Mr. Vishal. He is around 60 years old. He recently retired from a government post. He is the one who helps people living in our colony in every possible way.

He is very active despite his age. He is always seen doing something in our area. If anyone needs any kind of help in the colony, they go to him. The reason he helps people is that he likes it. He once told me that he has earned a lot in life and now wants to give something back to the society. He lives in a big house and has also made an office on the ground floor.

There he meets people and listen to their problems. Then he explains them about how they can get their work done. If they are unable to do that, then Mr. Vishal provides them assistance and he doesn't even charge the fee for it.

Recently Mr. Vishal made a committee that would look after the cleanliness and maintenance of the colony. Now the committee takes one thousand rupees each month from all the households to save the funds for the maintenance.

He is always available whenever someone needs him. He keeps an eye on things that needs improvement. He never cares if it is day or night, he looks after the work tirelessly. He always asks people to keep the surroundings neat and clean. He is an environmentalist and is seen growing plants and trees every weekend.

Recently there was a problem regarding the roads in our colony, but the local authorities were not looking to solve the issue soon. Mr. Vishal took the job in his hand and visited the government offices regularly to convince the authorities and got the work done.

He is so inspiring and amicable that one can learn many things by spending time with him.

Describe a person who speaks foreign language very well
How do you know that person?
How can that person speak that foreign language well
From where he/she learned it

I know a lot of people on Facebook who are from another country and speak different languages. But I would like to speak about my uncle who is living in Spain from the last ten years. He is working as an electrical engineer there.

His family is also living with him and he visits India every year and lives with us for 15-20 days. He is a very intelligent person and talks very sensibly. His both sons were born in Spain hence they don't speak a work of Hindi. They either speak Spanish or a bit of English.

He couldn't speak Spanish fluently earlier as he was still learning the language. But from the past three or four years he speaks that language like natives. When he comes to India, he talks with my cousins in Spanish. I don't understand a word of it, but I like to listen to their talk. I try to understand their conversation, but I can recognize only a few things that too from their gestures.

When he came recently, I asked him to speak the language and teach me some words and phrases. He taught me some common phrases and some greeting words in Spanish. For example, Hola is hello and adios is bye. I also learnt that gracias is thank you.

My uncle told me that he took the basics of Spanish classes in Spain and gradually learned the language. He said that it is important to live in a foreign country to learn their native language. He took five years to learn the language properly.

I found this language very interesting and I have planned to learn this language in future. Spanish is also one of the most popular languages all over the world.

Tell about your recent free time you had and how you spent it
Do you often have free time?
How did you spend that time?
Did you utilize that time in a constructive way?
I usually don't get a lot of free time as I am working hard from my future. Even on weekends I am always busy in studying something and improving my life. I don't like to sit idle, but I do like to spend my free time in learning something new.

Recently I was free for a week as my tuitions were off due to the festive season. So, I decided to learn some cooking skills. I think that irrespective of your gender one should know cooking. I know a couple of simple dishes, but I wanted to learn about some more.

I joined cooking classes near my house and from the first day found it very interesting. Our teacher Mrs. Neha is a great cook. She is a homemaker and teaches cooking in her free time. I used to go there from 9 to 11 in the morning. She taught us a lot of cooking skills and numerous cuisines in a matter of a week.

She is very knowledgeable and a great teacher. I learned Italian and Chinese cuisine. I was taught how to make pizza and pasta in the Italian class. In the Chinese class, I had learnt to make Manchurian and soup. The class was amazing as there were six other students. We all were given prior instructions in the class and then we did the practical. Our meals were inspected daily, and feedback was also given.

Mrs. Neha gave us a homework in which we had to make a dish from home. I always made those dishes from home and would take them to the class for everyone to taste. I would say that I didn't become perfect in making these cuisines, but I surely improved my cooking skills there.

I always utilize my time in learning a skill. I never waste my precious time in watching movies and T.V. I think that utilizing time in a constructive way contributes to the holistic development of a person.

When was the last time you enjoyed with your friends?

Speak about the time

How did you enjoy it?

Do you often go out with your friends?

Recently I was feeling boredom from my fixed routine. So, I decided to go on a road trip with my friends on a Sunday. I called a couple of my friends for the trip. We all planned to visit Shimla and come back the day after. All of us gathered at one of our friend's house and started the journey early in the morning.

We started our excursion at 5 AM in the morning. On our way we saw incredible sights. Shimla is situated at the top of the hill at a height of about 7000 feet. It is very green area with cold temperatures all year round. Shimla used to be the summer capital of India in the past when British ruled our country. They liked the weather and serene nature there. In the middle of our journey we stopped at a roadside restaurant to do breakfast. We ordered traditional potato stuffed bread with curd and butter. After that we continued with our journey in the car and reached Shimla. It took us five hours to reach there. We checked in to the hotel and got fresh. After that we strolled the streets of Shimla in the evening. The weather was really cold as compared to our city.

We took our dinner in one of the famous restaurants in Shimla and got back to our rooms. There we had conversations that lasted for more than three hours. That night we got very late and slept at 4 in the morning.

Next day, we got up late and did our breakfast at the hotel. At 1 PM we checked out of the hotel and started our journey back home. On our way back we clicked a lot of pictures of the surroundings and made funny videos.

I usually go out with my friends at least once in a month. I enjoyed a lot on this trip. This excursion acted as a much-needed break for me. It rejuvenated my mind for a long time.

Talk about a time when you had to wake up extremely early
At what time you had to wake up
What was the case
Were you able to wake up and complete the task?

There have been many instances in my life when I had to wake up early in the morning. But once I had to wake up extremely early because I had to catch a flight to Dubai with my family. Our flight was scheduled to fly at 7 AM in the morning from the Indira Gandhi International Airport, New Delhi.

I live in Chandigarh which is a five-hour journey from Delhi. Our flight's departure date was 24th December at 7 AM and we reached Delhi on the 23rd. We stayed at a hotel and slept early to make sure that we wake up on time in the morning. We had to reach the airport by 4 AM. So that meant that we must wake up at 3 and leave the hotel at 3:30 AM.

We were very nervous as getting late would prove to be detrimental for us. We all made sure that everyone set the alarm on their phones and we also informed the hotel staff to give us a wakeup call between 2:30 and 3:30 AM.

I was so excited for the trip that I could hardly sleep. But somehow, I managed to sleep at 1 AM. That meant that I had only about 2 hours of sleep. When my alarm sounded, I got up with swollen eyes and severe headache. The reason of my condition was the lack of sleep. I quickly got up and took bath and got fresh. After some time, I took a cup of coffee and I felt better.

We were able to wake up on time and reached the airport early. We boarded our flights and enjoyed the trip.

Describe an app you use on your mobile phone
How did you come to know about the app?
How often do you use it?
Has it helped you in your daily routine?

I use many mobiles apps in my free time. Some apps are gaming based and others are helpful in making payments and booking taxis. The app that I use the most is YouTube. I came to know about this app five years ago from one of my friends.

My friend told me that there's an app from where you can view videos of any kind. I downloaded the app in my phone and started using it. The app requires you to fill some personal details so that you can make an account in it. They ask for your email id and phone number. You can also upload your profile picture in the app.

Making an account allows you to watch all the videos available on YouTube. With this you can also create your own channel on the app and can upload videos of any kind. The video should however meet the guidelines of the app creators. I have also made a channel by my name, but I haven't uploaded any video yet.

I use this application for two to three hours a day. Whenever I am feeling anxious, I play motivational videos. If I am in a sad mood, then I see comedy videos. It is not like a TV in which you can only watch fixed programs telecasted on it. You can choose whatever you want to view. You can pause the video anytime and you can download some of the videos as well for later use. Some people are even earning millions of dollars by posting videos on YouTube. They earn according to the number of views on the videos and by supporting advertisements of big brands on their YouTube channels.

It has helped me immensely in my daily life as I can learn an unlimited number of things from It. It Is a source of information and news. One can view unlimited videos on different topics of their own wish and choice.

Describe a night when you could not sleep
What was the reason behind sleeplessness?
How did you spend that night?
Did you feel tired the next day?

There have not been many nights in my life when I couldn't sleep. I generally sleep easily but there was an instance in my life when I couldn't sleep at all. This happened last year when my sister met with an accident. Actually, I had planned a trip with my sister and two other cousins. We planned to visit Goa for a leisure trip. The trip would last three days, and we were scheduled to do a lot of activities near sea. On the second day of the trip we went to the Baga beach and did a lot of water sports.

Something unfortunate was about to happen that day. My sister was doing para sailing and I was making a video of her. At the time of landing she couldn't manage to keep her feet properly on the platform and slipped to the side.

Her helmet fell off and her head hit the platform hard. She felt unconscious and sustained injuries to the head. I was shocked and worried. People gathered in a blink of an eye and we called a taxi to take her to a nearby hospital.

The doctor suggested for a minor operation to treat the head injuries. I didn't called home as it would make everyone worried there. The doctors performed the surgery and told me that the injuries were serious but now we have treated her well. She was still unconscious, and I was still worried about her health. I couldn't meet her as she was kept in the intensive care unit.

I was wandering in the hospital lobby and couldn't sleep all night. I was concerned about my sister's health and prayed to God for the whole night. I was so anxious that many negative thoughts were crossing my mind.

Early in the morning I received good news from the warden that my sister is conscious, and I can meet her. I rushed to the room and hugged my sister in happiness. I told her about what happened the previous day. She was discharged in a couple of days and we safely returned back home. That night was very difficult for me and I couldn't sleep at all.

Describe someone who is your online friend
How did you become friends?
Tell about your friend
Are you in touch with him/her?

I am a very active person on the social networking websites. I use Facebook, Instagram and Tiktok. I mostly use Facebook as I like the ease of using this website. I can upload photos easily and I can chat with my friends.

The best aspect of Facebook is that you relate to the whole world. You can make friends from any part of the world. I have more than twenty friends who are from other countries. I would like to describe one of my online friends who live in Russia. She became my friend last year.

I generally find people on Facebook with similar interests as mine. Then I send them a friend request. After they accept my request, we try to share our culture and knowledge. We became friends last year through this website and share a very good relation. Her name is Guzel. She is of Catholic religion, but she doesn't believe in God.

She is a student of History and lives in Saint Petersburg, Russia. Currently she is studying in Moscow state university in Moscow. She told me about her college and friends. We both shared pictures of our family members and friends. I told her about my country and religion. She was very impressed to know about the diversity of our country.

I invited her to come to India and stay with us. She has accepted the invitation and is planning to visit India this year. Now she has become a very good friend of mine. She is tall with blonde hair and her eyes are of blue color.

I am regularly in touch with her from the past one year. We chat almost every day for ten minutes or sometimes I speak to her on video call. She speaks English very well. She told me that most of the Russians don't speak English at all.

She has become a very good friend of mine. I am planning to meet her next year when she comes to India.

A time when you had to wait in a traffic jam

When did it happened and how did you manage it?
What was the reason behind the jam?
Are traffic jams common in your country/city

Last month I got stuck in a traffic jam when I was going to my home. I was driving a car and suddenly I saw a lot of cars jammed on the road. I thought it to be a regular jam, but I was about to witness something that I have never seen before.

I stopped the car and noticed that the vehicles were not even moving an inch. Even after thirty minutes there was no movement. So, I decided to play songs to get rid of my boredom. I was surprised to see that the jam was growing with every passing minute and there was no way out. Everyone came out of their vehicles and were looking at each other in frustration. I was trying to find out the cause of the jam. One person coming from the other side of the road told us that an accident that happened half an hour ago was the main cause of the jam. After waiting for another one hour, the traffic started moving slowly and soon the jam was cleared.

After moving ahead, I noticed two big busses lying sideways. This was the reason for the jam. It was horrifying to see the accident site. There was some blood spilt on the road. A lot of glass was scattered as well. I was praying for the victims of the accident.

Next day I read in the newspaper that three people were killed in the accident and rest of them sustained minor injuries. I was relieved to read that only three people died because one would assume from the magnitude of the accident that many people would have deceased.

Traffic jams are quite prevalent in our county. Most of the traffic is found in the cities of our country than towns and villages. Most of the cities are overcrowded that leads to a lot of traffic on roads. Other reason of traffic on road is poor driving habits. Government is making efforts to reduce the traffic, but no results are seen.

Describe an important year in your life
Why that year was important
Did you achieve anything that year?
What did you do well in that year?
I always consider every year important in my life. I feel that the year I completed my 12th class was the most important year from a lot of perspectives. Many events happened in that years and as a result of that I consider that year to be the most important year of my life.

In that year I completed my most anticipated milestone of life. I got good results in my 12th class examinations. The year was also crucial because I had to decide about my future. I was confused between studying in India or to go to a foreign university for my further studies. My father helped me in making right decision at that moment.

An important event happened in the same year that changed my life. My elder sister got married that year. I share a great relation with her. Although I miss her very much, but we remain in regular contact with each other. She is a great friend of mine and I share everything with her. She lives happily with her husband, so I feel that made my year great.

After receiving the 12th result I was looking for career counselling. One of my uncles suggested me to appear for the IELTS exam and apply a study visa to a foreign university. He told me about the benefits of studying abroad. He emphasized that one gets great exposure while studying in a foreign country.

At that moment I was inspired from my uncle and started research about the foreign studies. I found that it would be better for me if I study in Canada. From that day I decided to pass my graduation from a foreign university. That moment made that year great for me as I had the aim for my future now.

I achieved many things that year but what makes that year important for me Is the marrlage of my sister and the decision of my career.

Describe a happy family event from your childhood

Do you remember events that happened in your childhood?

What was the event about?

Is it important to celebrate events in life?

I remember most of the events that happened in my childhood. I guess my memory is strong. There were many events that happened when I was a child, but I would like to tell you about an event that I remember well.

I am talking about my aunt's wedding. My mother's sister got married when I was six years old. I had a fantastic relation with my aunt. Her name is Nisha. She is a great person who always smiles in every situation. She is the youngest of the siblings, so her wedding was celebrated in a grand fashion.

I remember that many arrangements were made for the wedding. There were three functions in total. The first one was held at the residence of the bride. The name of the function was Sangeet. In that function all the friends and family members gather to sing traditional songs and to perform old style dance as a ritual.

The second function was held at a hotel. All the relatives and friends from both bride and groom's side gathered there for the Ring ceremony. The couple exchanged the rings, and everyone clapped with joy. That was a great memory as we danced all night and had great food there.

In the last function all the religious rituals and ceremonies were held. We all gathered at a temple where the proceedings took place. After the ceremony got over, all were served with traditional meals in the temple. After that it was time to bid goodbye to the bride. I recall that I was very emotional at that moment.

It is very important to celebrate events in our life. It creates a chance to meet relatives and friends. Also, it provides a break from the monotony. People can relax and enjoy the moment.

Describe your favorite way to relax

Why are people under stress these days?

Describe your favourite way to relax

Do you get stressed

Recent results have shown that more than 40 % of people working in private sector are suffering from stress related problems. There are numerous factors that cause stress. The main reason I think is the high expectation that people carry and if they are not able to make it, they get stressed.

Sometimes I get stressed, but I get out of it quickly. There are many ways through which I keep myself relaxed. The first one is listening to songs. I also like to play some outdoor games to get out of anxiety. I also like to go out and do shopping in this kind of a situation.

But my favourite way to relax is to go out with my friends and spend time with them. When I meet my friends, I forget all my worries and tensions. Whenever I am with my near and dear ones, I feel great. I have many friends who are always available when I need them.

I generally go out with my friends in the evenings. I also like to spend night at my best friends' house. I have been very fortunate to have such friends in my life. One of my friend lives near to my house who is always present with me when I am in trouble.

I remember that once I was going through a rough time. I was feeling very low and couldn't share anything with anyone. But my friends came to know about it and came to my house. They helped me to get out of that situation by supporting me. I am very lucky to have such friends in my life. Yes, I get stressed when I am not able to complete anything on time. I get anxious sometimes when I am confronted by a problem in my life. But every time I can manage stress in some way or the other.

Your favorite means of transport
Do you use public or private transport?
Speak about your favourite means of transport
Why do you like it?
I use both kinds of transport in my day to day life. I use public transport like bus and train when I need to go for a long journey. On the other hand, I use my private car/bike in my daily routine. Both have their own advantages and disadvantages.

I also like to board planes as they is fast and convenient. But in regular routine I think that car is my favourite means of transport. Whether I use my own car, or I hire a taxi, car is undoubtedly my preferred mode of transport.

Car has several advantages over other means of transport. It is one of the most luxurious ways to travel short and long distances. One can easily travel for long periods of time by taking regular stops. Cars are generally quite efficient. It is a weatherproof vehicle. You can travel nonstop in any kind of weather.

Hot weather can be tackled by the air conditioner and cold weather can be suppressed by the heater in the car. In a single car four to five people can travel together. There is also boot space to keep your luggage. Moreover, cars can travel on most of the terrains.

I have a car which I use in my daily life. It's my dad's car but I can use it whenever I want. I go out with my friends in my car. I enjoy long drives in the car with them on weekends. Cars don't require much maintenance. One can get it serviced after every six months. It is the most reliable vehicle of our times.

I have been to many trips on a car. The best part is that we can stop anywhere and get the feel of the surroundings. I would like to conclude the topic by saying that out of the other modes of transport, car is my favourite one.

Something you have learned recently from the internet
Do you use internet every day?
What have you learnt and is it useful to you?
Can we learn skills from the internet efficiently?
We can learn myriad skills from the internet efficiently. Most of the people these days find internet the best place to learn anything. People are more dependent on internet to learn anything more than ever before.

I have learnt many things from the internet but one thing that I would like to share with you is the art of playing guitar. From my childhood I was very keen on learning guitar. I tried many times but couldn't get enough time to learn this musical instrument. I love to listen to the sound of a guitar.

I made up my mind to learn guitar one day. But the main issue was that I didn't had much time back then. I was busy in my studies and only got free at night I bought a guitar and downloaded a few lessons for practice. I used to see the downloaded videos everyday but couldn't grasp much of it.

One day I came to know about a YouTube channel in which a person named Jack teaches people how to play guitar free of cost. He has uploaded hundreds of videos related to playing guitar. There are numerous videos that are tailor made for the beginners. I used to open the videos and would hold guitar in my hands.

He thoroughly explained in the videos about holding the guitar and which string should be pressed to play a certain note. I followed all his lessons carefully and learned the techniques of playing guitar. I made notes of the things he told in the videos. He taught everything patiently and creatively.

I am not an expert in playing guitar, but I can play a few basic notes that I learned from the internet. I am very thankful to the internet for teaching me so many things.

270

PART THREE

Follow up Questions with Solutions

Sports

Do you like to play sports?

Yes, I like to play a lot of different sports. I used to play cricket in my school time. Nowadays I like to watch cricket matches and play it whenever I get time.

Which sports is most famous in your country?

Our country invented hockey but the most followed spots is cricket. People follow cricket as a religion in our country. They get very emotional during the matches. Most of the kids also like to play cricket in their free time.

What are the advantages of playing sports?

Playing sports is a great activity as it involves us physically as well as mentally. There are many advantages of playing sports. It teaches us teamwork and it also keeps us fit. One can also opt sports as his/her career.

Is there any disadvantage of playing sports?

I don't think that there is any disadvantage of playing any sports. However, if one doesn't play it with proper safety equipment then it can be harmful. Also, there can be serious injury or fatal accidents while playing sports. This is the only disadvantage I can think of.

Which sports are generally preferred by women?

I think these days women are playing all the sports. There is no sport that women are not playing. Even recently, women were seen playing cricket matches at international level which is a great sign of equality.

Do you think that sports bring people together?

Yes definitely, in a country there can be a lot of different opinions among people when it comes to politics and other things. But when it comes to sports, everyone supports one team and I think that sports do bring people together.

Plant

Which plant do you like the most?

I like basil. It's a wonderful plant and has numerous qualities. A lot of people believe that the leaves of basil can relieve fever if consumed directly or in tea. Some people in our country consider the basil plant as sacred and often worship it.

Which is the most common plant found in your country?

272

I guess rose plant. I can see it everywhere. I think it is because that this plant doesn't require a lot of watering and sunlight. And it also gives beautiful flowers. That's why people like to grow this plant.

What are the benefits of growing plants at home?

I think the first advantage is that it purifies air. Some plants have natural scent which suppresses foul smell nearby. I think that plants look beautiful regardless of their variety. These are the major benefits of growing plants at home.

Do you like gardening?

To be honest, I am not very fond of gardening as it requires certain skills that I don't have. You need to have a lot of patience and will to do gardening. My father is very fond of this activity, but I never developed any interest in it.

Do you think everyone should grow plants?

I think at least once in a lifetime; everyone should grow a plant. It's a noble cause, moreover growing plants have a lot of advantages so I think that everyone should grow plants.

Food

Speak about your favorite cuisine.

I love Chinese cuisine. It's delicious as well as healthy. Most of the Chinese dishes are either stir fried or steamed. I like steamed food as it has less calories. Whenever I get a chance to eat outside, I prefer Chinese.

Which is your favourite dish?

Vegetarian haka noodles are my all-time favourite. I can eat this dish 10 times a week. I can't resist myself wherever I see Chinese food. I like to have my noodles mild spicy with some extra mushrooms and soya sauce.

Which is the traditional food of your country?

I live in the northern part of the country so the staple food here is wheat. So, anything made of wheat is the traditional food on the north side. If we move towards the east and south side of our country, then rice is the traditional and most common food.

Any dish that you like to cook?

I like to cook vegetable fried rice. It is an easy dish to cook. We need to take some vegetables and mix them with boiled rice and add some spices

273

and sauces to make it palatable. It hardly takes 30 minutes to prepare this dish.

Do you like to eat fast food?

As the name suggests this food is cooked fast. I like to eat it occasionally as it is delicious and cheap. But mostly I prefer homemade and traditional food as it has all the nutrients and essential minerals needed. Fast food may look attractive but is not very good for the health.

Education

Do you like the education system of your country?

Yes, I feel that education system of my country covers almost all the basis but there is one area where we can improve a lot and that is curriculum. The syllabus is very old and needs an immediate restructuring. Most of the students are learning certain things that are out of date and things that are not at all practical.

What changes do you want to make in the education system of your country?

I would like to make a couple of changes to the system. The first one is to make the education more practical rather than cramming hundreds of theory books. The second change will be in the curriculum. It needs to be more diverse and should develop a student holistically.

How many hours a student should read books apart from his studies?

I think it is unfair to them. They are under a burden of so many books already. But reading is a great habit. If students can take out some time to read about great leaders or personalities, then I think it is a good idea. In my opinion, students should spend around 3 hours a week on reading material apart from the curriculum.

Which was your favourite subject in school time?

My favourite subject was science. I liked the diversity in subjects and how the subjects such as physics, chemistry and biology were so different from one another yet so same. I used to be so active during my science class as we would learn new things every day.

Any subject that you didn't like?

I never liked mathematics. I used to get confused when I saw all the questions and calculations. That was the subject that I never understood completely and not once scored well. I got a lot of headaches while solving the problems in math's.

Which type of education is better, distance learning or regular schooling?
In my opinion, both types of education have their advantages. If a person is in a job or a business, then distance education is the best solution for them. But if the student has ample time to study then he or she should go for the regular education.

Leisure activities

What do you like to do in leisure time?
I generally like to listen to music and surf the internet. I like to browse about new places around the world and new songs that release every week. I also like to watch cricket matches whenever I get time.

What kind of leisure activities do the women do in your country?
Women generally prefer to watch sitcoms and movies. These days a lot of females are involved in watching fashion related shows and documentaries. They have feminine choice when it comes to the free time activities.

What kind of leisure activities do the children have in your country?
Children in our country like to play games and sports. Cricket is the most popular sport, so children watch it and play it with their friends. Video games are also popular among the kids.

Do you feel that one should read books in leisure time?
Why not? I think it's a great habit to have. I like to read books and I think that people should read books too. It gives us a lot of knowledge as well as understanding of life.

Who has more leisure time in your country, men or women? Why?
I think if the women are home maker then women have more leisure time than men. On the other hand, if a woman is working then it's the other way around. In that case, men have more leisure time as women will be busy in household chores as well as work.

Wealth

What is more important, health or wealth?
I think both are integral in life. Health comes first because a healthy person can enjoy all the stages of life. Wealth is also one of the most important

aspects in human's life. So, I feel that health and wealth are not equally important, health comes first and then wealth.

How will you spend 1 crore rupees?

If I am given this much money, I will like to make my dreams true. First, I will donate ten percent of money to a charity. Then I will buy a small house for myself. With the remaining money, I will tour the whole world.

Why do you think wealth is important?

I think that wealth is the only thing that can make our dreams true. If we want good education, great medical care or want to travel the world, wealth is required. Wealth fulfills most things in life.

What are the advantages and disadvantages of being wealthy?

There are many advantages such as one can travel the world, one can buy whatever he or she wants. Wealth can let you buy big houses and cars. But I don't think that there is any disadvantage of being wealthy.

Weather

How is the weather like in your country?

Weather is quite diverse in my country. India is a big land and all parts have different weathers. In north, you will find summers and winters. In eastern side, you will find more rains than any other part of the country. In the south, weather is almost same throughout the year as its mostly the coastal area with tropical climate.

Which is your favourite weather?

I like summers because you can wear light clothes. Moreover, you can have loads of ice creams and cold drinks. The best thing about summers is that one can enjoy long days. Summers gives us an opportunity to visit swimming pools and amusement parks. This fun can only be enjoyed in summers.

Do you dislike any weather?

I don't like rainy season. There are two major reasons for that. One, it gets wet everywhere and people without cars and private transport struggle a lot in our country. Secondly, it gets very humid after the rain stops. I don't like to sweat a lot.

Do you feel that weather affects the mood of a person?

Yes definitely, if the weather is nice and dry, I like it very much and if it is rainy then I feel depressed. Similarly, if a person doesn't like summers or hot weather, he or she might not feel great in that kind of weather.

What kind of weather is good for the crops in your country?

I think it depends on the kind of crops one grows. Mostly dry weather is good for staple crops like wheat. On the other hand, rice requires a considerable amount of water. It depends on crop to crop.

Celebrations

speak about a recent celebration you attended?

Recently I went to my cousin's house to celebrate his 18th birthday. He was very excited on that day and we enjoyed a lot in the party. I met all my relatives after a long time. I enjoyed the food as well as did a lot of dance that day.

Is it important to celebrate important days?

Yes, its integral to celebrate important dates as it reminds us of our past and achievements. Celebrations bring confidence and it motivates us to achieve more and more in our life.

Is it a good idea to invite neighbours to our family functions?

Yes, why not? If we have good relations with our relatives, then we should surely invite them to our family functions as it will further enhance our bonds. It also shows the trust you have in each other.

Do you celebrate your birthdays?

Yes, I celebrate my birthday every year. I go out with my friends to a restaurant and we order food and drinks. I also like to do some charity on this day. I usually donate some amount of money to the needy.

Do you think that some people waste a lot of money in celebrating weddings?

It is true in our country and especially in the part of our country where I live. People spend huge sums of money on wedding ceremonies and celebrations. I think it is a complete waste of money and resources. Instead they should save it for the future of the couple.

Travelling

Do you like travelling?

I absolutely love travelling as it breaks the monotony. I like to go out whenever I get time. It relaxes me and recharge me for the days to come. I go out with my friends on weekends and especially in the month of December.

How does travelling makes you feel?

It makes me feel wonderful. When I travel, I feel tranquility which no other activity gives me. I feel complete on terms of wisdom and satisfaction when I travel.

What are the benefits of travelling?

There are many benefits of travelling to the traveler. The first one is that a traveler learns behavior pattern of people from different societies. Moreover, it gives a chance to visit new places and eat different types of cuisines.

Is travelling costly in your country?

No, I think travelling in my country is not that expensive. If you travel by air, then it can be a bit costly but if you chose to travel by bus or train then I think that you can travel at a low cost. Our country is well connected by rail so I believe that it will be the best and cheapest option.

What are the things that a solo traveler should keep in mind before travelling?

Before travelling solo, I think there are couple of things that the traveler should keep in mind. Firstly, he or she should carry all the first aid medicines and should have enough funds in case of an emergency.

Animals

Which animal you like the most?

I like cow the most. It is one of the sacred animals in our country and is worshiped by a lot of people in our culture. Cow gives us milk and its dung can also be used as a fuel in traditional homes.

Should animals be kept as pets?

Animals should be kept as pets as they are our true friends. Animals such as dogs are widely regarded as the best pets across the world. Millions of people keep dog as a pet due to its loyalty and vigilance qualities.

Should we eat animals?

I think this is a debatable topic. In my personal view I reckon that it is up to an individual whether to eat animals or not. Across the world, billions of people eat animals and there are many who don't. it's on the personal choice of the humans.

Do you feel that animal products such as leather shoes and bags should be banned?

Yes, I think there should be a complete ban on the killing of animals for making leather products. Our science is so advanced that we have already invented alternatives. So, I don't think that there is a need to kill animals to produce such products.

Which is the most common animal that can be found in your country?

India is such a big country and we can see all types of animals here. The most common ones I would say is the cows and dogs. A lot of people in rural area keeps a lot of cows as pets. Moreover, dogs are also kept as pets by many people in my country.

Birds

Which bird do you like the most?

I like peacock the most as it is also our national bird. It is a big bird that can fly for a limited period and to a limited altitude. Its color is mesmerizing. It has a long neck which is purple in color and it dances in joy during the rainy season.

Do the birds have any importance?

Yes, birds are important for the smooth operation of the eco system. They are responsible for the controlling of insects and other bugs that would otherwise increase if there were no birds.

Do you feed birds?

I have never fed birds to be honest. I have seen it in movies and in the zoos as well. If I would ever get a chance, I would love to feed birds.

What can we learn from birds?

I think one thing that we should learn from the birds is their patience. Birds are so patient while they make nests. I have seen the process and it can take a lot of days or even weeks to make a nest. Birds never get frustrated instead they keep on piling whatever they get to build the nest.

Happiness

Is it important to remain happy?

Yes, it is very important to be happy as it can treat several problems as well as it can elevate your mood. Being happy is one of the biggest challenges these days. I think a person who's happy is always healthy.

What are the factors that influence happiness?

There can be a few factors that can influence happiness. It depends upon an individual as to what makes him or her happy. Some people are elated by earning more money and some simply feel happiness while travelling.

How can a person remain happy?

A person should never try to control the things that are beyond control. Also, one should try to wake up early in the morning and practice a bit of meditation. You should also try to watch comedy movies or accomplish small tasks on time to remain happy.

Do you think that happiness is linked to good health?

I totally believe that our health is linked to our happiness. I have seen a lot of people who are not happy, and they tend to be mentally more disturbed than people who are always in a joyous mood. Happiness has a direct impact on our health physically as well as mentally.

Law

Describe a law in your country.

I would like to speak about the child labor law. No child under the age of fourteen years can do paid work anywhere in our country. If someone is found engaging a kid who is under fourteen, then he or she might be put behind bars or imposed with a heavy fine.

Do you feel that laws are strong enough in your country?

I think the laws are very strict and strong in my country. If anyone breaks the law, then he stands for a strict punishment by the penal system. The laws can be improved in certain areas but most of them are fine.

Is it important to follow all the laws?

Yes, the laws are made for the betterment of all the citizens of a country. It's essential to follow the laws as it keeps the running of the social machinery smooth.

Is there any law that you want to introduce in your country?

Yes, I want to make a law under which it would be compulsory for every citizen of the country to get education up to senior secondary. Under this law the government will provide the funds required for the education of people.

School

What type of school did you go to as a child?

I went to an English medium school which was located near my house. The school had all the facilities that are needed for the overall development of the students.

Which type of schools are better, government or private? Why?

I think in my country most people prefer to enroll their kids in the private schools because they are more concerned about student's progress. They also focus on the co-curricular activities. Moreover, private schools have the right sort of infrastructure and environment of study.

Do you feel that schools should be allowed to charge the tuition fee according to their standards?

No, I think that government should make a law as these days private schools are charging huge amounts of fee to enroll the kids. Under this law the schools should not be allowed to charge more fee than a maximum limit set by the government.

How do you think that government schools can be improved?

According to my notion, government should take the initiative and responsibility to take care of the quality of the government schools. The government should hire professionals that can revive the condition of the government schools in our country. They can add more facilities and infrastructure with low fees to attract more people.

Do you feel that school plays a major role in the development of a person's life?

Unquestionably, schools are like temples and students worship the books and their teachers. Schools teach us a lot of things in life. We make our first friends at the school. We come to know about the etiquettes we need to have in different situations. It plays the biggest role in the development of a child.

Teachers

What is the role of teaches in our life?

Teachers play a great role in our life. They guide us in every possible way. I have had so many great teachers in my life over the years. Teachers are the best role models to have.

Has any teacher influenced you in your life?

Yes, one of my teachers in 10th class had a big influence in my life. His name is Mohinder Sir. I can recall that I was very weak in mathematics and I needed a lot of help in that. I asked him for the extra classes, and he was kind enough to help me.

Would you like to become a teacher in your life?

If given a chance I would certainly like to become a teacher. I would like to enjoy the responsibility of being a teacher in my life. It is a very tough job though as the teachers handle many students at one time.

Do you feel that a teacher needs to be highly qualified?

In my perception teacher must be very much qualified. He or she needs to be updated with the latest knowledge as to keep their student's knowledge up to the mark. A teacher should have an ocean of knowledge so that the students can be benefitted from that as much as possible.

What should be the qualities of a good teacher?

A good teacher is always there for the students. A good teacher should have patience and good listening capacity. A teacher should always be punctual and hardworking.

Dance

Do you like to dance?

Yes, I like to dance. I like to do bhangra and I also dance on the Bollywood songs. I like to do free style dance as I am not a professional dancer. I generally dance in the weddings and celebrations with my friends and family.

What type of dance is popular in your country?

We have so many types of dances in our country. Kuchi pudi, Bharat Natyam, Bhangra are one of the most popular dances across our country. Different regions have different styles of dancing.

Why do people dance?

I think dance is a way of expressing one's feelings. Just like music and writing, people like to dance to express themselves. I mostly dance when I am happy. In our tradition, people dance on weddings and other celebrations.

Is the dance different for men and women?

I believe that up to a certain extent the dance is different. Although the dance type will be the same, but the steps and hand moments will be different for men and women. There is a subtle difference in the expressions of the dance for both the genders.

Wedding

What is the wedding like in your country?

As India is a big nation, we have several styles of weddings in our country. Most of the people in our country like to celebrate weddings with a great enthusiasm and excitement. They like to buy expensive jewelry and like to buy a lot of dresses.

Have you ever been to a large-scale wedding?

Recently I went to the wedding of my friend's brother. It was the best wedding celebrations that I have seen in my entire life. There were unlimited cuisines and the wedding venue was decorated like heaven. The bride and groom were wearing expensive dresses and there were all the things that you can expect from a big fat wedding.

What is the importance of marriage in our life?

I think that marriage is an association between the couple and their families. Marriage enlarges the family and you know that you have more people in your life who will be there in your thick and thin.

Do you feel that marriages in the past were better organized than today's marriages?

I learnt from my elders that the marriages in the past were long and simple. There used to be a couple of dishes to eat and relatives would gather at the home of the groom and bride and be there for more than a month. So, I think that marriages in the present are better as no one has enough time and the events are also managed in a better way.

What changes will you see in the marriage celebration after 20 years?

I reckon that there will be a lot of changes in the celebrations in the coming 20 years. People have now become more conscious of the spending they do on organizing the functions. There will be less show-off in the marriages and people would rather spend more money on buying the assets than organizing big functions.

Sleep

How many hours do you sleep every day?

I sleep for 7 – 8 hours every day. I get to bed by 11 and wake up at 6 AM. I feel that I need at least 7 hours of sleep to get my body back to full potential. On weekends, I take a nap in the afternoon sometimes.

Do you like to sleep?

Everyone likes to sleep, so do I. I like my sleep very much. Whenever I am feeling tired or frustrated, I go to sleep. If I am not feeling well, I prefer to sleep more. In a way, sleep is like a medicine if used in a proper manner.

Do you dream?

I usually don't have dream while I sleep but I dream occasionally. I have very unusual dreams at night. I get dreams of meeting my idols, achieving my goals and some wired ones as well. Once I had a dream in which I was falling from a building.

Do the people in your country discuss their dreams?

I have never shared any of my dreams with anyone. Neither any person has shared his or her dream with me. I think this is a personal thing, so people feel hesitant to share their dreams with others.

What are the disadvantages of sleeping long hours?

In my opinion, it's very dangerous to sleep for more hours than usual. First, it destroys your productive time and it is not good for the health of a person. More sleep leads to obesity and obesity leads to several diseases.

Family

What type of family do you live in?

I live in a joint family. I think I enjoy living in a joint family as we have more members who can be there for us when we need them. There is more harmony when you live in a big family. I have 9 members in my family. I like every one of them.

What are the advantages of living in a nuclear family?

I think the only advantage that you have while living in a nuclear family is that you don't have a lot of interference. There are a smaller number of members, so it gives you freedom to do whatever you want.

What are the disadvantages of living in a nuclear family?

I think the only disadvantage of living in a nuclear family is that a person has very few people to go to when he/she feels troubled or depressed. A person can sometimes feel lonely in nuclear family.

Do you feel that families are disintegrating day by day?

Yes, the families in my country are disintegrating as a result of some factors. These days people don't like interference from others, and they like to live in their own way. That's why this situation has occurred.

If given a chance, would you like to live in a nuclear family?

I don't think that I can live in a small family. I like to have people around me as I am a talkative person. I think we learn a lot of things from people around us. Moreover, I am the kind of a person who likes to live in a joint family.

Friends

Do you have one or two or many best friends?

I have only two friends who can be called as best friends. I can share every part of my life with them. I think it's never good to have too many friends. One or two good friends are enough.

Do you feel that there are advantages of having a lot of friends?

I think that few friends are enough. You don't need to have a lot of friends in order to fulfil your social needs. Having a lot of friends can lead to trouble sometimes. If you have a greater number of friends, then you must give them time. That means you have very less time for yourself which is not a good sign.

What do you do in case you have a misunderstanding with a friend?

I always call my friend up and try to talk to him or her. That's the best way to approach if you have any misunderstanding between friends. I will share my point and will listen to his or her point as well and try to find a way out.

What can be risky among friends?

I think there can be one thing that can be very risky. We share a lot of things between friends and sometimes we trust a person who's not worth trusting. The information can get leaked which can lead to a lot of problems.

Do you feel that we should invite our friends to family functions?

I think it's important to invite our friends to the family functions as friends are also like family. Friends know everything and they are the part of our lives. So, it becomes important to call good friends to our family functions.

Hometown

Tell something about the place where you live.

I live in Mohali. It is a neat and clean city. There is no scarcity of greenery in my hometown. There are numerous gardens and parks which are made for the public. Infrastructure is great and all the facilities like education, shopping complex and hospitals are in abundance.

Is there anything you would like to change about your hometown?

I will like to change a couple of things about my hometown. The first thing that I would love to have is increased frequency of public transport. Ours is a developed city but lacks public transportation. Secondly, I would like to see more cycling tracks around the city.

Is there anything that makes your hometown special?

Yes, greenery makes my hometown special. It is one of the greenest and cleanest cities in my country. This is also a planned city, so everything is well lined up and easily accessible.

Which place in your hometown is special to you?

I like going to the PCA cricket stadium. It is an international stadium situated in the heart of the city. It has a club and I am a member of it. I like to go there for swimming and doing exercise in the club gym.

Is there any famous personality that lives in your hometown?

There are many famous personalities that live in Mohali. Many Punjabi singers live in my hometown and I have come across many of them while roaming around the city. Some famous sports personalities are also dwelling to my hometown.

Neighbours

Do you have interesting neighbors?

Yes, I have very interesting neighbors. They have a joint family and in total they are 9 members. We always celebrate the festivals together. We also go on picnics once or twice a year.

How are neighbours important?

They are very important as they are the first ones to respond to any situation. If we have an emergency, then neighbours will respond first. If we require any help in that situation, we will not call a distant relative but the neighbours.

Have you ever helped your neighbours?

Once one of my neighbours went to the market where he slipped and hurt his ankle. There was no one at his house that day as everyone had gone to work. So, I picked him up and took him to the doctor for treatment and escorted him back to his home.

Do you also call neighbours to your personal celebrations?

Yes, we always call our close neighbours to our family functions or personal celebrations. They are very close to us all the time, so it won't be a good idea to not call them. Neighbours are often very generous and help us in arranging things for the celebrations.

Who's an ideal neighbour?

An ideal neighbour would be like a friend who will always be there when needed. He or she should not hesitate to come to your house, and you should also be not be shy of going to your neighbor's house without invitation.

Colors

Which is your favorite color?

I like blue the most. It is a symbol of calmness and keeping cool. I like this color as its sooths my eyes whenever I look at it. I also look good in blue colored clothes. I like this color so much that I got the walls of my room painted in blue color

Do you feel that a color can change a person's mood?

Yes, colors can change a person's mood. If someone is feeling down and out, then I think they should wear bright or vibrant color as it will elevate the mood. On the other hand, looking at dull colors can depress the mood.

Do the colors have religious importance?

In our culture and country, color has a lot of significance in religion. For example, at the time of worship, red color is sacred. While in some communities, white color is a sign of purity.

Is there any color that you don't like?

There is no color that I don't like but I can say that I don't like light or dull shades. I am an optimistic person; hence I like vibrant colors. Dull colors make me feel annoyed.

Which color is mostly preferred by women in your country?

From my few interactions with women, I conclude that most of them like pink or red color. I think it's because of the reason that pink color gives a feminine look, that's why women like it.

T.V

Do you watch TV?

Yes, I watch TV in my leisure time. I like to watch discovery channel and music channels. I like to listen to the latest songs, so I always tune into such TV shows and channels. Watching discovery is like studying in a university as it gives an abundance of knowledge.

For how many hours do you watch TV?

I watch TV for around one and a half to two hours. I love to watch TV as it gives us a lot of knowledge and we can literally watch anything on it. It is also like a stress buster for a lot of people.

What are the bad effects of watching TV?

There are several bad effects of watching TV. I think a person can get addicted to it and may watch it for long hours. This can affect eyes as well as the overall health of a person.

How many hours should the children watch TV?

I feel that children under the age of two should not watch TV at all. And children above the age of two should be allowed to watch TV for not more than two hours per day.

Do you watch News on TV?

I only watch news when there is something interesting or there's an incident that has happened. Otherwise I generally don't watch news channels.

Culture

Is it important to preserve our culture?

Its indispensable to preserve our culture as it reflects our past and history. If we are unable to preserve our culture, then the upcoming generations will not be able to learn the traditions and values from the past. Preserving culture should be the main priority of people these days.

Is the culture in your country different from other cultures?

Our culture is very different from the rest of the world especially the western countries. I reckon that the culture in my country is like some neighboring countries, but I still feel that every country has its own culture. Is there any culture that you like the most?

In our country, the culture of celebrating festivals is the best culture and I like it the most. The reason is that when we celebrate the festivals together, it increases harmony and respect between people of different cultures and religions. Diwali is such festival which is celebrated across all religions and regions.

Do you feel that people should change their culture when they move to a foreign country?

I don't think that it is a good idea to change the culture after moving to a new country. One should never forget his or her own ethics, practices and customs. I think they should try to adopt the new culture without forgetting their own.

Do you feel that there has been a cultural mix in some countries?

Yes, there has been a lot of cultural mix in some countries across the world due to globalization. This is not a bad thing at all. I believe that it brings people from different castes, races and regions together.

Business and jobs

Would you prefer to do job or a business?

If given a chance, I would like to get a job first. After taking experience of four to five years, I will plan to start a business of my own. I feel that before starting a business one should do job.

Which one is better, job or business?

According to me, both have their own advantages. Where jobs have secured income, business can offer you unlimited earnings from it as it has no limit. Jobs have fixed working time, but most businessmen work for long hours.

If given a chance, what kind of business you would like to start?

If I am given a chance, I would like to start a business related to import and export of certain products. I like travelling so that's the best possible business which can offer me more travelling.

Is there any job that you dream of doing?

I dream of working in the parliament of India or in a big politician's office. I am very curious to know how the life of big politicians is and how they work for the country. I would also like to contribute to the country's development through this kind of a job.

What kinds of jobs do women prefer in your country?

Women generally prefer to do white collar jobs in my country. Most women are highly educated, so they prefer to do managerial jobs. They also like teaching jobs so that they can spare out time for the families.

Globalization

What are the positive effects of globalization?

Due to globalization, more and more people are connecting with each other. There have been great improvements in terms of transportation and communication. It has brought a lot of positive changes in the world.

What are the negative effects of globalization?

Globalization has proved to be beneficial for humans, but it has also created some chaos. Due to globalization, many people have lost their jobs to technology and internet as most of the work is now done by robots and computers.

How has globalization changed your life?

It has impacted my life in a positive manner. I have now access to my friends who are living in abroad. I can make a video call to them in a blink of an eye. This has been possible only through globalization.

Speak about the biggest advantage of globalization?

I think improvements in the transportation has been the biggest advantage of globalization. Nowadays we can travel in fast trains and aero planes and we can reach our destination in a relatively short time and more comfortably.

How can globalization change the future?

I think globalization will change the future quickly. We can already see a lot of developments in the field of transport, medicine and technology. In future, the focus is on the communication and to take it to the remotest of the areas due to which more people will connect with each other in a better way.

Magazines

Do you read magazines?

I don't read magazines regularly, but I have read a magazine recently. The name of the magazine is Autocar. This magazine has an abundance of knowledge regarding the recently launched cars and about the best cars in market. It also has customer's reviews for selected cars. I liked this magazine very much.

What type of magazines are popular among women in your country?

In my perception, women like to read fashion related magazines. These kinds of magazines are helpful to them to get updates regarding the latest fashion in clothes and accessories. I often see my sister reading this type of magazine.

Do you feel that men read more magazines than women?

I think that women tend to read more magazines than men as there is more variety of magazines for women rather than men. Moreover, I have read a survey in a newspaper and it suggested that in our country more women prefer to do reading than men.

Do you feel that magazines can teach us something?

Yes, magazines teach us a lot of things. We can learn from magazines if we absorb the knowledge given in it. There are some magazines such as Competition Success Review which is read by thousands of students across India. They learn the latest trends in competitive examinations and education.

Are the magazines better than newspapers?

I think magazines and newspapers are very different from each other hence should not be compared. Magazines are better in terms of visuality and printing quality. On the other hand, newspapers are best for getting current news.

Newspapers

Which is your favourite newspaper?

I love reading Hindustan Times newspaper. It is one of the oldest newspaper's in our country. Its pages are well laid out and different type of news is divided into different sections. There are a couple of supplement newspapers in it as well.

Do you read newspaper every day?

No, I don't get this much time, but I feel that one should have a habit of reading newspaper every day. This is an excellent habit as it keeps you updated about the happenings. I read it weekly especially on the weekends.

Do we learn anything from the newspaper?

Yes, we learn a lot of things from it. People mostly learn a lot of new words and latest news. We also learn how to arrange such huge amount of information in such a compact way.

Is there any page of newspaper that you like the most?

I like reading the sports section of any newspaper. In my favourite newspaper, the sports page is always the second last page. I get a lot of knowledge about different sports events and about sportspersons.

Do you feel that newspapers print fake news?

I don't think that newspapers print fake news as they have a huge responsibility on their shoulders. Although some news editors try to print exaggerated or spicy news to attract more readership. But most newspapers have genuine news.

Buildings

Speak about an interesting building.

I have seen numerous buildings in my life, but I find the Elante Mall's building very interesting. It is very huge, and the architecture is also marvelous. The building is one of the most famous buildings in my city.

What type of buildings are found in your city?

Our city has an army-based airport so constructing tall buildings are not allowed in most parts of the city. Weather you see residential apartments or the commercial settings, most of the buildings are not tall. Generally, 2 to 4 floors are constructed, and this is what I feel is the beauty of my city.

What type of buildings do you like?

I love tall buildings. I always dream of living in a city with many tall buildings and get very excited when I see skyscrapers. Once I visited Dubai and went to Burj Khalifa which is the tallest building in the world. It felt amazing while on the top of it.

Have you ever visited a strange building?

I have been to a few strange buildings. Burj Khalifa can be termed as strange for its size and design. But I would like to speak about Amer Fort

which is in Rajasthan. It is strange because it's so big that anyone can get lost in that easily. That fort is centuries old but us still intact and beautiful.
Speak about a public building in your locality.
There are several public buildings in my area. They are either banks or public service departments. I would like to speak about the post office building. It is situated in the center of the city and has a huge parking area in front of the building. The building is modern and well planned. It has a lot of place for public to get their work done comfortably.

Library
Have you ever been to a library?
Yes, I have been to many libraries. The one which I liked the most is the British library, which is situated in Industrial area, Chandigarh. It is one of the most modern libraries in the city. It holds a large variety and collection of books for its members.
Should there be an entry fee to the library?
No, I think that entry to the library should be free for the public. This encourages more and more people to come and get themselves educated. This will also inspire the habit of reading which is diminishing day by day.
Do you feel that books should be given on loan for free?
No that's not a good idea. I think that there should always be a minimal fee for the book lending. If the library lends books for free, then there can be a loss to the finances. In order to maintain the running costs and books, reasonable fee should be charged.
Do you feel that introduction of computers in the libraries is a good idea?
I feel that computers have changed the way people live. They are also very helpful in libraries as computers can store huge number of electronic books and volumes which are rare, or which are in bad physical condition. People can simply open the readable file in the computer rather than reading from a physical copy.
Do you feel that number of libraries should be escalated across the country?
The count of libraries should be increased everywhere in the world. In my perception book reading is the best way to pass the leisure time and to get knowledge. If the number of libraries is risen, then more people will begin to show interest in reading books which will be great for the mankind.

Zoos

Have you ever been to a zoo?

Yes, I have gone to Chat Bir Zoo which is located near to my hometown. It takes around 30 minutes to reach there from my home. I have visited this zoo more than ten times. It's a big zoo and has a variety of animals. The entry ticket to the zoo is very reasonable and is worth visiting.

Which is the best time to visit zoos?

One of the care takers at the zoo told me that the best time to visit zoo is March and April in summers and November and December in winters. At this given time of the year, most of the animals are active and playful. One can see all the animals in great mood.

Have you seen any strange animal in the zoo?

I have seen a lot of animals in the zoo over the years but the strangest of the animals that I have seen are the Alligators. They are very lazy in nature. I have seen them from close quarters, they remain in the same position for hours and don't even move an inch. But when they are hungry and they are ready to be fed, they are very active.

Should there be an entry fee to the zoo?

I think there should be a decent entry fee to the zoo. There are several expenses that the zoos bear in order to take care of the animals. They feed the animals, pay the salary of the staff and other miscellaneous charges. So, I think that the zoo can utilize their earnings in this way.

Do you feel that zoos are the best place for animals?

I think that zoos take care of the animals in every possible way, but it is not the best place for them. I feel that forest is the best habitat for animals. Forest is the natural and more interesting habitat for them. They can roam freely, and they can hunt and eat on their own. Forests provide more resources to animals than zoos.

Museums

What is the importance of museums in life?

Museums are an integral part of life. From museums we can gain so much of knowledge about the past events and society. It's always good to visit a museum as it reflects the past of ours and inspires us to take the legacy forward.

Have you ever been to a museum?

Yes, I have seen two museums in my life. The first one I saw was the Chandigarh museum which has primarily textiles and tools from the past, the second one is the Ripley's museum in which I saw strange collections from all over the world.

Have you seen anything interesting in the museum?

Indeed, once I saw the skeleton of a whale fish. I never thought that I would be able to see such thing in my life. The structure was massive, and each part of the skeleton was explained nicely. I think that it was really an interesting thing to see.

Do you feel that museums are boring?

Not at all, I think museums are one of the interesting places to visit. One can learn so many things from museums. These kinds of places have abundance of knowledge and I feel that information is never boring.

Do you feel that children should also visit museums?

Absolutely, I feel that it is a great place for children to visit. There are many museums which are solely dedicated to kids and the learning there has been made simple especially for kids. I think it's a great idea to take children to museums.

Vegetarianism

Do you eat non-veg?

No, I am a vegetarian. I used to eat non-veg but from the past 6 years I have given it up. I think that eating non-veg food can be unhealthy sometimes. That's why I left eating it

What are the benefits of being vegetarian?

There are a few benefits of being vegetarian. The first one is that your digestive system remains neat and clean. Vegetables improves the metabolism of the body. It also fulfills the nutrition and essential vitamins required in the body.

Do you feel that meat consumption should be banned?

No, I don't think that meat consumption should be banned. I strictly think that it is up to an individual's choice whether to eat meat or not. There are numerous people who depend upon the meat industry. So, I think that it's not a good idea to ban the consumption of meat.

Do you feel that meat eating is not good?

I left eating meat a few years back as I thought that it is not a good habit. Moreover, I believe that killing animals for consumption is cruel. So, I think that meat eating is not good.

What are the drawbacks of being vegetarian?

There are no such drawbacks of being a vegetarian. Nevertheless, vegetarians can find it very difficult to survive in some western countries where vegetarian dishes are hard to find. Other than that, I don't think that there is any disadvantage of being a vegetarian.

Computers

How have computers helped us?

Computers have helped us in every possible way. Nowadays, computers are used in every field whether it is medical or engineering. Computers have overtaken numerous operations in big industries. They have also helped us in our daily chores and needs.

Is there any negative side of computers?

Indeed, computers have taken over manual labor in most of the fields, but it comes with some disadvantages. Computers have killed a lot of jobs in certain fields. It has made us lethargic and too dependent on them for every small task.

Do you use computer in your daily routine?

Yes, I use computer every day. From searching latest news or anything on the internet, I use computers. I also use computers to play video games and watch movies. It's a helpful device in daily routine.

Have we become slaves of computers?

Certainly, we have become slaves of computers and it has become our master. We look forward to computer for most of our needs. We are fully dependent in most of the tasks whether it is related to work or leisure.

Do you know someone who does not use computer at all?

Yes, my grandfather does not use computer at all. Although he uses mobile phones, but he never uses computer. He is very smart and knows everything about latest gadgets, but I have never seen him using computer once.

Internet

What are the advantages of internet?

Internet holds abundance of knowledge and we can access it anywhere but for that you need a data pack or an internet connection. The biggest advantage of internet is that we can talk to our near and dear ones who live thousands of kilometers far away from us.

Do you often use internet?

Yes, I use internet every day for two to three hours. I use it for getting updates on latest news and to talk to my friends and relatives living in foreign countries. Sometimes I use internet to operate my e-mails.

Do you feel that kids should also be allowed to use internet?

I think that kids should be allowed to use internet for their schoolwork and leisure time. One thing important is that parents should set a time limit for the use and they should also install a browser that is compatible for kids which does not show adult content.

What are the changes that have been instrumental due to the invention of internet?

The biggest change due to internet is the way we can connect with people from all over the world and the other one is the internet browsers from where we can get knowledge of anything within a blink of an eye.

Do you feel that government should provide the internet for free?

I think more than a luxury; internet has become a need in today's world. If it can be under the budget of the government comfortably then why not? In some countries, the governments are already providing internet facilities for free.

Sky

Do you see sky?

Yes, I see sky. I generally see the sky briefly when I go out of my home for the first time in the morning. The first thing I do is to see the sky.

At what time of the day do you see sky?

I generally see the sky in the morning as well as at night when the stars are shining. In the daytime, it's too bright to look at the sky. So, I feel that early morning and evening is the best time to observe sky.

Have you learned anything after seeing the sky?

I have learned that we are so small, and nature is so big. When I see the sky, it looks unlimited. It looks never ending just like God. I think seeing the sky makes us humble and thankful.

How do you feel when you see sky?

It feels extraordinary. I just admire the beauty of sky and I also praise the lord for wonderful things that he has given us. I feel energetic and ready to rock when I see sky.

Do you also see stars?

Yes, quite often I see stars. Whenever I stroll in the evening or at night, I see the stars. I try to find the constellations of stars that we studied in the primary classes. I see that all the stars have different level of brightness and they look pretty among the Moon at night.

Cars

Which is your favourite car?

My favourite car is Toyota Fortuner. It is an SUV car. SUV stands for sports utility vehicle. This means that this kind of car can be run on any terrain without breaking a sweat. I love this car as it is powerful and big as well as it looks amazing.

What is the importance of having a car in life?

It is indispensable to own a car these days. A car can accommodate four or five members of the family and it doesn't matter whether it is raining, or the sun is burning hot, you can travel in the car comfortably and safely.

Do you feel that number of cars is increasing on the roads rapidly?

Absolutely, the number of the cars are escalating day by day. I think easy payment options have made people buy more and more cars. Now almost everyone can afford a car, that's the main reason behind the growth in the traffic.

What should be the mandatory features in the car?

There should be a couple of compulsory features in the car. The first one is that, the installation of airbags should be a standard inclusion in the car. The second one is the advanced braking system which is very helpful in emergency breaking. I think these two features should be mandatory for every car manufacturer to provide in every car variant for safety purposes.

Have you ever seen a strange car?

Recently I saw Mahindra Eco for the first time. It was a beautiful looking car but the strange thing about that car was that it was very small in size. On searching about that car further I found that it's an electric car and the size was kept small intentionally for smooth driving in the city.

Tourism

How has tourism evolved society?

Tourism has bridged the gap between cultures and languages. More people nowadays are learning new languages and eating new cuisines. The society has formed a mixed culture due to tourism and it has also increased the understanding among people.

Do you feel that tourism generates income?

Tourism generates a lot of income for the people involved in it. when tourists go to a certain place, they rent a car, hotel, guide and they also buy souvenirs and try local food. This is great financially for the people of that place.

Have you ever met a tourist?

Yes, I met one tourist last year when I went to Rajasthan. I saw a lot of tourists there especially from the foreign countries. I got a chance to talk with him. I shared a lot of information about my country and he told me many things about his own country and background. I felt amazing after conversing with him.

Have you been to a tourist place?

Yes, I have gone to a few tourist places. I would like to tell you about Goa. It is a fabulous place for everyone. Goa's coastline is lined with wonderful beaches and restaurants. The food over there is delicious and people are super friendly.

Do you feel that tourism has increased from the past time?

There has been a great increase in the number of tourists these days. This is primarily due to the ease in transportation these days. Many flights have been introduced due to which the price has reduced. Therefore, more people are encouraged to travel.

Crime

Why do you think that crime is increasing day by day?

There are a few reasons behind the increase in the crime rates. The biggest reason I feel is the unemployment in our country. Due to unemployment, many youngsters are forced to sit idle, hence they commit crime.

Do you feel that there should be strict punishment for every crime?

No, I think that punishment should be given according to the severity of crime. Some crimes are hardcore, and some are forgivable. Hardcore criminals should be treated with strictness whereas in case of a small crime, the criminal should be given counselling to change their behavior.

What are the most common crimes in your area?

There are very few crimes that are reported in my local area as there is a lot of strictness. But most of the crimes that are happening are snatching and robbery.

How can the government control crime?

Government can do anything; I think that they can also eradicate crime from the society. Government should have harsh punishment and zero tolerant policy for dealing with crime. The criminal should think twice before committing a crime.

Have you ever been affected by a crime?

Yes, unfortunately I was affected by crime last year when my phone was snatched from the roadside. I was walking on the pedestrian and suddenly a motorcycle came from behind at full speed and the person sitting on the back snatched it from me while I was talking on the phone.

Health

How do you keep yourself fit?

I do light exercise in the morning. I like to do jogging and running. I think it is the best way to keep yourself fit. I also follow a lenient diet plan in which I have reduced my sugar intake to keep myself fit.

What is the importance of good health in our life?

I think there is a huge importance of good health in our life. A healthy person can enjoy all the facets of life. Good health enables a person to work and earn more. A healthy person is also mentally strong.

Do you feel that good diet leads to good health?

Without a doubt. I think when it comes to maintaining health, most experts say that its seventy percent diet and thirty percent exercise. Therefore, diet plays a bigger role in maintaining good health.

What is healthy food according to you?

Any food that covers up all the essential nutrients, vitamins and minerals is a healthy food and food which does not have a lot of fat content but full of proteins. Lentils, eggs and green vegetables are the perfect example of healthy food.

Do you like to eat healthy food?

Yes, mostly I prefer to eat healthy food. Occasionally I also eat fast food and junk food but most of the times I eat cereals in breakfast and lentils in the dinner. I think these two food items are healthy to eat.

Exercise

What kind of exercise do you do every day?

I like to do yoga and breathing exercises in the morning. If I do some rigorous exercise, then I choose to do it in the evening. I think that morning is the best time and I mostly do exercise at that time.

What type of exercise do the people do in your locality?

In my locality, I see people doing every kind of exercises. Youngsters like to do cycling and running, whereas most of the old people prefer yoga and light exercises.

Is there any exercise that we can do without any equipment?

Indeed, there are a few exercises that we can do without using any sort of equipment. Yoga is one and the second is running or jogging. People can also do breathing exercise without using any type of equipment.

Do you feel that exercise can be harmful?

I don't think that exercise can be harmful because it is a great activity which keeps our body fit and fine. The only drawback that I can think that exercise can have is that it can be harmful and dangerous if you are doing any exercise without prior information and guidance.

How much exercise should everyone do in their daily routine?

According to me, everyone should spend at least thirty to forty-five minutes in doing exercise. WHO suggests that every person must take a minimum of eight thousand steps in order to maintain good health. Forty minutes of exercise is equivalent to walking 8000 steps.

Foreign language

Do you speak any foreign language apart from English?

No, I don't speak any foreign language apart from English. However, I am keen to learn Spanish language as it is widely used throughout the world.

Why is it important to learn English?

It is essential to learn English language as it bridges the gap between most of the people. English is the world's most widely spoken language. English opens a lot of opportunities as it enables a person to take his/her thoughts to millions of people.

Is it good to learn a language of the country where you are travelling?

It's not mandatory that you need to learn the language of the country where you are visiting but you should try to learn some important phrases as it can help you in desperate times. Some people learn the basics and main phrases because they like to indulge foreigners in conversation.

Do you feel that regional languages are important?

We can never preserve our history if we don't have regional languages. It's essential to protect such languages and make our next generation learn it. it's good to learn foreign languages but regional languages are of huge importance.

Do you feel that there should be only one language in the whole world?

I think it is not possible. There are numerous countries that don't speak the same language. There are remote places on Earth that don't have access to internet and outer world. So, it will not be easy to teach them a universal language. Although I feel that if there is only one language in the whole world then the world will be a much better place and people will understand each other in a better way.

Space exploration

Do you feel that governments around the world are spending unnecessary money on space exploration?

I feel sad when I see huge sums of money being wasted on space exploration. It's a real waste of precious money. I think instead of investing money on space exploration, governments should spend money to develop the undeveloped parts of our planet and make it a better place for people on Earth rather than finding other planets and aliens.

What are the benefits of space exploration programs?

I am strictly against these kinds of programs as I don't think that it brings any kind of advantage. Its only wasting money on certain observations that may or may not exist.

If given a chance, would you like to travel to space?

If given a chance, then I would love to go to space as it is a rare experience. I think very few people on Earth have been able to spend time in space, so I would not deny this opportunity.

What will you do when you will reach space?

The first thing that I would like to do when I reach space is to find my country on Earth. It would be great to see my home country from space. I will also try to locate other countries on Earth and try to test my geographical knowledge.

Is space tourism a good idea?

I feel that space tourism will be a reality soon. I also perceive that it is definitely a good idea as it would be possible for masses to be in space. This type of tourism will still be rare as it will be very costly and not everyone could afford it.

Future

Do you plan your future?

I try to plan it but sometimes it doesn't happen the way I think. I think it's better to leave the burden of future on God and one should concentrate on present. If present is executed well then, the future is taken care of.

Do you feel that future can be seen?

I never believe in such things and I feel that it's foolish to think that one can see future. It's all myth and should not be believed.

What things are you planning to buy in future?

I am planning to buy a house before I get married. I will also buy a big car and some property.

Where do you see yourself in the next ten years?

I want to see myself well settled in Canada / Australia .... in the next ten years. I want to have a happy life for me and my family.

Are you too worried about your future?

No, I am never worried about my future. I always keep myself in present and leave the rest in hands of the almighty. So, this way I am never anxious about my future.

Hotel

Have you ever stayed at a big hotel?

Yes, I have stayed at a five-star hotel once when I went to Dubai. The name of the hotel is Taj Palace which is in Deira city center. It was a massive hotel with luxury rooms and extra ordinary interiors.

Which is your favourite hotel?

My favourite hotel is Taj Palace as it is nothing short of a wonder. There is a jacuzzi tub and a big swimming pool at the roof of the hotel. The rooms are spacious and luxurious with all the facilities that one can dream of having in a five-star hotel.

What type of hotels are there in your city?

In my city, there are all types of hotels. From one-star to five-star hotels. The most prominent one's are JW Marriot, The Lalit, Hayat Regency and Mount View Hotel. These hotels raise the standard of the city.

Why do people stay at hotels?

There can be a few reasons behind this. The main reason is that if people go to another country or any city where they don't have a friend or a relative where they can stay, in that case people book hotels. Apart from this people stay at the hotels when they go out for holidays.

Is staying in hotel costly in your country?

It completely depends upon where people want to stay. If you stay at a decent three-star hotel then I think that India is a country where you will find cheap hotels. When it comes to five-star or luxury hotels then the prices are beyond most people's budget.

City and village

Which place is better to live, city or villages?

I think better place to live is city as it offers more things than living in a village. Most of the rural population is moving towards city these days as they vouch for more opportunities in education and employment.

What things you can improve in the city you live?

I think that there can be improvements in the transportation system of our city. There is hardly any public transport that one can find. People use their own vehicles which is a huge burden on their pocket.

Have you ever visited an important city/village?

Yes, I have visited many important places in my life. A city that is very important in our country is Jaipur which is in Rajasthan state. It is important as it has preserved a lot of history and it is also a tourism hub of our country. It generates a lot of tourism and employment for the locals.

Do you feel that village is a better place to live?

I feel that cities are always better than villages due to number of reasons but there are a couple of advantages of living in a village as well. People are more friendly in villages. Also, the environment is free from pollution and contamination.

Speak about a city that is very well developed.

In my viewpoint, Chandigarh is very well-developed city in our country. It was the first planned city of our country. It is designed in a way that every part of the city is easily accessible from anywhere and the amenities such as education and medical facilities are located nearby the residential area of every sector of the city.

Childhood

Share any fond memory from your childhood.

I certainly have a lot of childhood memories in my life. The one which I remember is when I was selected as the most intelligent kid in a competition. I remember the event as I was five years old at that time and I still have the pictures of that event with me.

Is childhood the best stage of life?

Indeed, childhood is undoubtedly the best stage of life due to number of reasons. A kid is free from any burden whether it is of education or it is of getting job and earnings for the family. All the kids are stress free and euphoric in nature.

Do you feel that children have less burden than adults?

Children have less burden than adults. Older people are under immense pressure these days. Whereas, children have no responsibilities on their shoulders.

Do you feel that childhood is the best stage to learn things?

I fully agree with you as children have more ability to learn than adults. Their mind is fresh, and they have more time to practice things. Research shows that children catch things easily than adults and they take less time to adapt to anything.

305

How was your childhood?

My childhood was probably like most people's childhood, stress free, burden less and full of enjoyment. I feel that I am lucky to have parents who never stopped me from learning anything.

Jewelry

Do people like to wear jewelry in your country?

Yes, there is a custom and tradition in my country to wear jewelry. Mostly women adore the ornaments and jewelry in neck, ears and wrists. Some men are also fond of wearing jewelry items.

What type of jewelry is popular among women?

I think every type of jewelry is liked by women. They mostly appreciate earrings and neck pieces. I have seen a lot of women wear anklets in my country. Basically, they relish every kind of jewelry.

Do you feel that spending money on expensive jewelry is good?

In my perception, spending on expensive jewelry is not a bad idea. Most people in my country like to buy jewelry made of gold and diamonds. These materials have a great exchange value. Hence, jewelry can be exchanged for cash in crunch times.

Does jewelry have any religious importance in your country?

Yes, in my country there is a religious importance of wearing jewelry. Women in India wear Mangal Sutra, which is a necklace made of gold and other materials. It represents that women wearing it is a married woman.

Do you wear jewelry?

No, I don't like to wear any jewelry item. I tried it once, but I don't like the feel as it interferes a lot in some body postures. So, I never thought of wearing any jewelry again.

Songs/music

Do you listen to songs?

I am very fond of listening to songs. My favourite singer is Sonu Nigam and I hear all his songs in my leisure time. I generally listen to Hindi Bollywood songs and English songs.

Which is your favourite song?

My favourite song is Heal the World song by Michael Jackson. This song became the best song soon after the release. The meaning and lyrics of the song are beautiful. The video is also great to watch.

Which type of music do you like?

I like Pop music the most. I also like to listen to Trance, Rock, Jazz and Classical. Every type of music is unique, but I feel that Pop songs are the best.

Who's your favourite musician?

My favorite musician is Shankar Mahadevan and he's a singer as well. His music is so unique and fresh. He's one of the most respected musicians in our country. He also judges the popular show, Rising Star.

How do you feel when you listen to songs?

I feel tranquil and calm. Songs relaxes my mind and gives me energy to do more things. In a way, music inspires me to do well in life.

Art and craft

What is the importance of art and craft in our life?

Art and craft release the emotions in a beautiful way. It triggers our creative side and encourages us to do better. I think that without art and craft, our life will be very much dull.

Have you ever participated in an art and craft competition?

I have participated in a lot of art and craft competitions in my school time. I remember how the staff of the school used to take us to the open parks where the competition would take place. Hundreds of students competed together for three spots.

Do you feel that art and craft is dying out due to the developments in technology?

I don't deny the fact that art and craft is losing its importance with the advent of technology. These days art and crafts are also designed by computers. Human interference in this field is minimal. Today's youngsters are not patient enough to be interested in art and craft.

Do you think that art and craft should be a compulsory subject in schools?

I am completely in favour of having art and craft as a compulsory subject in the school. This will enhance the creative side of the students and will widen their horizon.

Do you feel that art and craft is a waste of time?

Not at all, art and craft are the way to go. Most people these days don't give importance to it, but the fact is that without art and craft, our traditions will die out.

Parks

Do you like visiting parks?

I love visiting the parks very much. I feel close to the nature when I visit the parks. I have a lot of parks near my home. I generally go in the early morning or late evening to enjoy the fresh environment.

Which is your favourite park?

My favourite park is the garden of silence which is in sector 1 of Chandigarh. It is a big park with lots of green areas. In the center of the park, there is a huge idol of Lord Buddha. I often go there to relax myself.

What kind of people go to parks?

I have seen every kind of people in the parks. I see kids playing with their friends. I see youngsters doing exercise and running. I also see old people there roaming from one end to the other.

What are the activities that people do in the parks?

People generally go to parks for walk and exercise. Some youngsters go to play different games and some sports, but most people visit parks for leisure walks. I have also seen few people going there for reading books while sitting on the benches.

Should there be an entry fee to the parks?

No, there should never be an entry fee to the parks. This way less people would be encouraged to go there. I think it is the basic duty of the government to provide parks in every locality for free of cost.

Book

Do you read books?

Yes, I read books in my free time. I read at least three to four books every year. I feel that we get a lot of knowledge regarding certain things from books that we don't get at school or college.

Which is your favourite book?

My all-time favourite book is Long walk to freedom by Mr. Nelson Mandela. This book is his autobiography and was written by him after he came out of the prison.

Which genre of books do you like the most?

Mostly I like to read autobiographies and biographies of prominent leaders and celebrities. In this way I get to learn about their secrets to success.

What are the advantages of reading books?

There are many advantages of reading books. The first one is that it enables you to learn a lot of vocabulary. Secondly, it increases your knowledge and reading speed. Moreover, reading books is a great free time activity.

Is there any disadvantage of reading books?

I can't see any disadvantage of reading books. The only drawback that I can think is that it takes a lot of time to read books. For example, if you read a book of five hundred pages then it would take around a couple of months. Whereas a movie made on that book or an audio version of that book would be absorbed in three to four hours.

Festivals

Do you celebrate festivals?

I love celebrating all the festivals. India is a land of festivals as we have so many different religions in our country. I like to celebrate Diwali, Holi, Christmas and all other prominent festivals. I believe that celebrating festivals together with your friends and neighbours, increases the harmony in society.

Which festival do you celebrate every year?

I always wait for the Diwali festival. This day holds a great importance in the history of our country. On this day, Lord Rama returned to Ayodhya after fourteen years of exile. So, people on this day celebrate to commemorate the return of lord Rama.

What is the importance of celebrating festivals?

The biggest importance of celebrating festivals is that it promotes love, peace and harmony among everyone in society. Celebrating festivals also keep us attached to our customs and traditions.

Is it important to spend huge amounts of money to celebrate festivals?

No, I think there is no need to spend huge sums of money in celebrating festivals. Celebrations can be simple yet enjoyable. Friends and family members can gather, and they can have a meal together. That will be a good enough celebration.

Do you also celebrate the festivals with your friends and neighbours?

I always celebrate all the festivals with my friends and neighbours. I remember, last year on Diwali our neighbours had arranged a function in which all the people of locality and their relatives came to celebrate. I can never forget that celebration.

Accident

Have you ever seen an accident in your life?

I have seen one accident when I was going to my friend's house. I was on a bi-cycle and suddenly a speeding truck rushed from my right-hand side. It hit a bus on the side while it was crossing the intersection. The bus and truck collided causing a lot of injuries to the people in the bus.

Why do you think that accidents happen?

I think that rash driving is the main cause behind the occurrence of accidents. There is another reason that cause many accidents in my country and that is drink and drive.

Do you think ease in issuance of driving license cause accidents?

I think that in my country it is not easy nowadays to get a driving lesson. One goes through a rigorous process, theory and practical tests in order to get a driving license in India. So, I don't think that it is the reason behind accidents.

How can we prevent accidents?

First, government needs to make very strong laws against the people who drink and drive as it is the most prevalent reason behind accidents. Secondly, people should aware their offspring about the consequences of the accidents.

Do accidents happen too often in your city?

I read a lot of reports of accidents these days due to negligent driving and cases of hit and run. There used to be less accidents in the yester years but have increased considerably now.

Politics

Who's your favourite politician?

I like the prime minister of our country, Mr. Narendra Modi. He was the BJP party's candidate in the 2014 elections and became the prime minister of our country. He has taken up a lot of issues in his own hands and ensured that our country moves in the right way.

Do you follow politics?

Yes, I follow politics but not every time. I like to listen to the debates of some of the prominent leaders of our country and I try to absorb as much information as I can.

Do you feel that being apolitical is good?

Being apolitical is not good for anyone. Humans are naturally political as it is our right to be political. For the betterment of any country, everyone needs to be political.

Do you think that politics have changed over time?

Politics and politicians have changed a lot over the past few years. Previously, politics was not so commercialized but these days, politics is advertised, and politicians are much more dynamic and vocal in their opinions as compared to the past.

Have you ever met any politician?

No, I have never got a chance to meet any political leader in my life. If given a chance, I would love to meet the Prime minister of my country.

Children

Do you know any child?

I know a lot of children and all of them are unique in their own way. I would like to tell you about my niece, she is only three years old. She's very adorable and cute. I was surprised to see that she can operate a mobile phone on her own. She likes to dance on the beats of songs.

Do you feel that we can learn something from children?

We can learn a lot of things from kids. I think kids don't take much stress and they forget their past instantly. I think these are the two traits that everyone can learn from the kids.

Do you feel that all children are naughty?

No, it's not the case. I know a lot of kids and I feel that most of them are naughty in one way or the other but some of them are not. I know one of my neighbour's kid, he's not at all naughty and does everything that his parents tell him to do.

Should children under the age of 16 be allowed to use mobile phones?

I feel that using mobile phones have become a need more than a luxury these days. I think that parents should allow their kids to use mobile phones but only for urgent purposes and not for leisure.

Are there any children at your home?

311

Yes, I have a niece at my home. She is so charming and attractive. She's always running here and there in the house. I like to play with her in my free time.

Superstitions

Do you follow superstitions?

No, I don't follow any kind of superstition. I feel it's not necessary in life as we are in the modern era and believe in science. I think there is no place for superstition in this world.

Speak about a superstitious person?

In my neighbourhood, there is one middle aged woman. I find her very superstitious as she performs a lot of rituals. I always see her feeding the stray dogs and cows. She told me once that she doesn't wash her hair on Tuesdays and Thursdays as she considers it sinful. I find it very strange.

Do you feel that superstitions are a waste of time?

Absolutely, there's no doubt that superstitions are a complete waste of time and efforts. It keeps us confused and distracted throughout the day. I feel that one should stay away from superstitions.

Why do people follow superstitions?

There are a couple of reasons that why people follow superstitions. The first one is that they don't have confidence in their abilities and hence they rely on superstitions. Another one is that they are stressed and are not able to find solutions to the problems, in that case they are inclined towards such activities.

What are the common superstitions in your country?

I have seen some people not washing their hair on certain days and some like to eat curd before leaving their home. Some people like to recite some religious hymns, and some like to offer certain food items to animals and birds. People also like to wear certain colors depending on occasions. There are endless superstitions that people do in our country.

Fashion

Do you follow fashion?

Yes, I follow fashion sometimes and like to be updated in terms of my clothing. I like to look for latest apparels and designs in the market. In a way you can say that yes, I follow fashion.

Do you like to be aware of the latest trends?

As I told you that I keep myself aware of the latest trends in clothing, accessories, shoes and other stuff. It gives me pleasure and joy in looking for new items.

Who is more inclined towards fashion, men or women?

I think if you would have asked me this question ten years back then my simple answer would have been women. However, these days men are not far behind as they indulge themselves into latest fashion more than women.

What type of fashion do people do?

People like to wear fancy dresses and shoes. Women are fond of different accessories whereas men mostly like to state fashion through shoes, belts and watches.

Why people do fashion?

People follow fashion to make their presence felt in the crowd. Some people do fashion to conceal their insecurities. Also, some people look up to the celebrities and try to mimic their style.

Gifts

Have you received any gifts in life?

Yes, I have received a lot of gifts in my life. I generally get gifts on my birthday and special occasions. I love receiving gifts as it gives me a lot of happiness while opening it.

Speak about a special gift you received?

I have received myriad gifts but the most special was the Samsung galaxy watch that I received from my sister. It's a smart watch which tells about the number of calories I have burnt in the whole day. It also gives me a lot of details about my current health and what needs to be done to get myself fit.

How do you feel when you receive gifts?

I feel on the top of the world when I receive gifts. I feel enthusiastic when I receive gifts from my near and dear ones. I never have the patience and I open the gifts as soon as they are given to me.

What kind of gifts you give to other people?

I usually like to give the gifts which can be kept by them for a long time. I give wall clocks, photo frames, expensive pens and note diaries. It also

313

depends on whom I am giving the gift. If it is a kid, then I like to give an educational toy.

Do you feel that it is important to give gifts on weddings?

It's a great idea to give gifts to the wedding couple. They are about to begin a new life and I think that it is essential to give them gifts. We must gift them home appliances or stuff related to furniture so that it helps them to set their new life.

Name

What is the difference between name and surname?

Name is an individual's identity of a person whereas surname represents the family background. Surname in our country depicts the family from where a person belongs.

What is the meaning of your name?

Meaning of my name is _____

Who gave you this name?

This name was given by my grandfather. I like my name very much and I think that it is a blessing from him.

Would you like to change your name in future?

Not at all, I won't change my name in future. It is the name by which I am identified over the past so many years. It is a huge part of my life.

Why do people change their names?

There can be a few reasons behind that. Some people have long names, so they cut short it to form a new name. Some people change their names when they move to a foreign country as their name is sometimes difficult to pronounce.

Nature

Do you love nature?

I think that nature is only meant to be loved. I love every aspect of nature when it comes to the different landscapes. My favourite one is white sand beaches and warm ocean water.

Is there any threat to the nature these days?

There is a huge threat to nature in a lot of ways. The coral reefs of certain parts of the world are diminishing at an alarming rate due to water pollution and human activities. Also, there has been a huge threat to the eco system of some delicate parts of the world.

How can we solve the environmental problems?

I think we need to come together to solve the growing issue of the environment. We should make people aware of the consequences and we should encourage them to spread this message and contribute towards the maintenance of the environment. We should set an example for others by doing something in this regard.

Is nature kind or harsh?

Nature has both the dynamics. Nature can be really kind sometimes whereas it can be life threatening as well. A good weather is a kind gesture of nature. On the other hand, earthquakes, typhoons and other natural disasters are harsh. Nature is very unpredictable.

Do people often enjoy nature?

Yes, some people enjoy nature more than others. Some people do gardening, go for walking in the woods or admire the beauty of a garden. However, some people these days are more inclined towards materialistic things. They don't like to spend time with nature.

Shopping

Do you like to go out for shopping?

I love to do shopping whenever I get a chance. I buy clothes and shoes for myself. I also like to shop the accessories and other electronic items. I think that shopping acts as a stress buster for me.

Who tends to shop more, men or women?

It's difficult to answer, I think that both genders shop equally. The interests can be a bit different. Men like to shop electronic gadgets and shoes whereas women generally prefer to shop clothes and make up kits.

What kind of shopping is popular in India?

People do all sorts of shopping. From buying vegetables and fruits for consumption to buying luxury cars and expensive jewelry. People buy according to their pockets. I have seen that most of the people in my country like to do shopping.

What's the future of shopping?

I think that people will continue to buy things in the future as well. One thing will surely change, and that is the way of shopping. People will prefer to shop online rather than going to the shops physically.

Technology

Do you feel that technology has evolved humans?

Indeed, technology has evolved the beliefs and lifestyle of human beings. They have now become more prone to technology rather than practicing traditional beliefs. I feel that it has brought both good as well as bad changes.

Is technology boon or bane?

It works both ways. Technology has advanced a lot in the recent times and it has been a great boon for the mankind. On the contrary, it has brought a lot of disadvantages as well. It has made people lazy and dependent.

Speak about a recently invented technology?

I love smart watches. It is recently invented in the past five years. It's the best gadget to have. You just need to tie it to your wrist as you would tie a traditional watch. But the difference is that it will not only show you the time but will also tell you about your health and other notifications.

Is technology dangerous?

In some cases, technology can be dangerous. If we use it in excess, then it can have myriad negative effects on us. Technology like x-rays can be harmful if a person is exposed to the rays.

Do you feel that we should limit the use of technology in our daily life?

I think there is a huge need to curb the amount of technology that we use every day. We should only use it when it is required. Needless use of technology is injurious for us.

Bicycle

Do you own a bicycle?

No, I don't own a bicycle, but I am planning to buy one. I feel that it has numerous benefits. We can use it to commute from one place to the other without burning fuel. It also keeps us fit.

Is cycling good for health?

It is great for our health. When we cycle, we are not only going from one place to the other, but we are also using our body to pedal it. it's a great form of exercise.

Do you feel that we should observe a bicycle day every year?

I my perception, we should surly observe a bicycle day every year. I would rather say that it should be celebrated every month across the globe so

316

that people can be aware about the rising pollution and can get inspiration to use cycles more often.

Can bicycles solve the traffic and pollution problems?

I am a firm believer that the use of bicycles can solve the traffic and pollution problems to a great extent. If more and more people start using bicycles, then others will also follow the precedent. This way there can be a lot more improvements in certain issues.

Are there any bicycle tracks in your hometown?

Yes, in my hometown most of the main roads and the leading roads have the facility of a separate bike lane. This encourages more people to ride bicycle. This also ensures safety for the riders.

Work

Do you feel that work is worship?

I am a believer of smart work more than hard work. I think that work should be considered as work and should not be mixed with worship. We do work to earn bread and butter, but worship is done for the peace of mind.

What kind of work you do every day?

I do a lot of different works every day. I mainly study my textbooks and read other than my syllabus as well. I also like to help my mother and father in the daily chores such as dish washing and cooking.

Do you feel that working for more than eight hours is a bad idea?

As I told you earlier that I believe in smart work and I usually don't prefer to work for long hours. I think that an individual has a lot of other things to do as well except work. One should focus on work but for a limited period and then devote rest of his time to family, friends and leisure activities.

How many hours do the people work in your country?

Most of the people work eight to ten hours in a day. I have seen some people working more than that. According to me, working for 7 to 8 hours is an ideal scenario.

How many working days are there in your country?

Most of the people work from Monday to Friday. There are some private organizations that work on Saturdays as well. Some businesses are run seven days a week. There's no fixation to working hours.

Studies

Do you like studies?

I like studies very much. I study for around three hours a day in which I also study apart from my curriculum. I like to read material related to technology and science.

How should we plan our study?

We should plan our study according to the time we want to devote on studies, and we ought to plan in a way that we don't get tired of studying. I think the best way to plan the studies is to study for an hour early in the morning, one hour in the day and one hour at night. This way we will not feel bored by the studies.

Do you feel that students often study trivial subjects at school?

Yes, we have a lot of subjects in school time which are of little use in our real life. We should not be taught the difficult historical dates for the previous event; we have the computers for storing our data. More practical subjects should be taught in the schools.

Is it important to study hard?

Yes, it is necessary to study hard. Whatever time you can give to your studies, you should study with full concentration and efforts. You are only going to get good grades if you study hard. There are no shortcuts to it.

What is smart study?

Smart study means studying in a way that you learn everything in less time. There are an array of mobile applications and software that teach you in a very practical way. This type of learning is much better and effective than theory learning.

Email

Do you write e-mails?

I write emails occasionally or when I need them to write. Till now I think that I have not sent any personal email to anyone. All the mails have been professional, and work related. Exchanging study material with friends or some important documents with someone.

Do you receive e-mails?

I receive a lot of emails in my daily routine. These days, if you visit someone and you drop your email over there, then get ready to receive promotional emails every day. All the mails that I receive are mostly promotional and of very little use to me.

Have you ever received an important e-mail?

Yes, once I received an important email from a friend. He sent me the list of important questions for the final exams of my 10th class. I was very excited to receive that email, but the material was of little use in the examination.

Are e-mails helpful?

Emails are very helpful for everyone. We can send and receive important information and data. Email helps us to store our work and attachments electronically. We can open old mails and information anytime without breaking a sweat. We don't need to store the files anywhere as it is already on the mail.

Speak about a recent e-mail you sent.

I sent an email to my friend. In this email, I send him a lot of photographs that I clicked on our trip to Jaipur. I attached more than 50 pictures that I clicked and send him through email.

Daily routine

What is your daily routine?

I wake up early in the morning then I get ready for my classes. After the classes I like to have lunch and a short nap for 15 minutes. Then I go out in the evening to play with my friends and after taking the dinner I hit the sack at 10 PM

Is there anything in your daily routine that you would like to change?

I would like to have some more time for book reading. I love reading books and I think that with my busy schedule, I don't get enough time to read books.

Are you satisfied with your daily routine?

I am pretty much satisfied with my daily routine. I can perform all my duties and I also take out enough time for rest of the things. I also get time to spend with my family.

Do you get enough leisure time in your daily routine?

I get some leisure time in my routine which I cannot complain of, but I would like to have some more time. I will utilize that time in reading books and play some video games to relax my mind.

Which is the best time in your daily routine?

The best time of my daily routine is the early morning. I feel that this time is pure, and the mind is fresh and away from any negative thoughts. This time is the best time to reflect upon yourself and to plan the whole day.

Films

Do you watch movies?

Yes, I like to watch movies in my leisure time. I like to watch action movies the most. I am also a fan of comedy movies. I prefer watching movies in theater as it has much better sound effects and the movie goes on uninterrupted.

Who's your favourite actor?

I like watching movies of Amir Khan. He's one of the highest paid actors in India. He always strives for quality in his movies. He does a single movie in a couple of years which is invariably a superhit.

What type of films do you like?

I like to watch all kinds of films like action, romance, comedy and drama. Recently my liking towards movies on real events has increased significantly.

Tell about a recent film you have seen?

Recently I saw the battle of Saragarhi. This movie is based on true events which dates to the nineteenth century. The movie is made with wonderful effects and graphics. Lead role was performed by Akshay Kumar. He's one of the best actors in India.

Has the technology improved the quality of movies?

If we compare it to the past then yes, technology has improved a lot of things in the movies. Now, the audio and visual part are much clearer. Technology has also introduced the three-dimensional effect movies with tremendous animations and graphics.

Hobbies

What are your hobbies?

I like to play and watch cricket. I also like to read books in my leisure time.

From where did you learn your hobby?

I learned my hobby from my elder brother. He is also very fond of reading different kinds of books. I used to watch him read books of different genres in the evening. Slowly and steadily I also got into the knack of reading books.

Do you feel it is essential to have hobbies?

A person ought to have hobbies in life. No one can survive without hobbies; life will be so dull. I think one should have at least two or three different hobbies so that their leisure time can be utilized in a better way.

Do the hobbies of a person change with growing age?

Yes, hobbies of a person change at every stage of life but there are some hobbies that don't change. For example, if someone plays a sport then he or she will not be able to continue that hobby for long as sports requires fitness and one cannot remain fit after a certain age. So, people give up some hobbies and take up the new ones.

Do you have the same hobbies that you had ten years back?

A decade before I used to have different hobbies. I remember I had a habit of cycling for a couple of hours. Now I don't even have a cycle. I used to play a lot of video games in my childhood, but I don't do it anymore. These days I am more interested in reading books and travelling.

Smoking

Do you agree with the statement that smoking should be banned?

I agree that smoking should be banned completely at the public places as it harms general public. Otherwise the sale of cigarettes should not be barred as it is a right of a person whether to smoke or not.

What are the ill effects of smoking?

Smoking is very harmful for the lungs. There is a caution sign on the pack of cigarettes that suggests that smoking is injurious to health. It also causes different types of mouth cancers. All in all, smoking is a deadly habit.

Should there be dedicated places for smoking?

Yes, government should try to make dedicated spaces for smokers so that the smoke does not affect the normal public. This way, smokers can enjoy smoking without disturbing anyone.

Are there any smoking chambers in your city?

Yes, there is one smoking chamber that I have seen in a mall. I went there recently and saw a small chamber where a couple of men were smoking.

Do you feel that government should advertise heavily against smoking?

I think that government is already advertising against smoking at a lot of platforms in our country. Whenever we go to watch a movie, there is always an advertisement regarding the negative effects of smoking. That advertisement reaches millions of people every day.

Your country

Speak about a specialty of your country?

The biggest specialty of my country is its diversity. In India, you can see all the religions and culture existing happily together. We have all the different types of landscapes that are found all around the world. We have all the seasons that can possibly occur.

Do you like your country?

I love my country very much. We have done impossible things as a country over the past few years. Our country is developing at a rapid speed. We are one of the most popular nations in the whole world due to our achievements.

Do you feel that India is developing faster than ever?

I have no doubts in this statement. I think that we are in the race to become a developed nation. Our country is witnessing the most rapid developments since previous years. I hope that we get the results soon.

Speak about a place where every foreigner should visit in your country.

There are numerous places where foreign tourists can visit in India. In the northern part of our country we have the tallest mountain range, the Himalayas. It is untouched and serene. A lot of people from our country and foreign as well visit these mountains for relaxation and to observe the beauty of nature.

Are the ties of your country strong with your neighbouring countries?

Yes, my country is surrounded with a lot of neighboring countries like Pakistan, Myanmar, Sri Lanka China, Bhutan, Nepal and Bangladesh. We can even enter Bhutan and Nepal without obtaining a visa. This shows that how good the ties between India and these nations are.

Going out

Do you like to go out in the evening?

I love to go out in the evenings. I feel rejuvenated and relaxed at this time of the day. I like to go for a walk on my own or play cricket or football with my friends

Which is your favourite place to hang out in your city?

I like to go to the Sukhna Lake most of the times. It's a beautiful lake lined up with numerous varieties of plants and trees on one side. There is a track for walking as well as for jogging. One can view the Shivalik hills at the backdrop of the lake.

Do you like to go out with your friends or family members?

I like to go out with both, it depends upon the situation. If I am going out for a party, then I like the company of my friends. If I am going for a picnic or holiday, then I like to go with my family.

Which places do you visit on weekends?

I mostly visit hill stations and lakes. I live in Chandigarh and Shivalik hills are only an hour drive from there. Whenever I feel jaded, I like to visit Kasauli hills.

At what time of the day do you like to go out for fun?

I like to go out for fun at any time of the day. Mostly I go out in the evening and sometimes early in the morning as well. If I plan to enjoy the nature, then I go in the early morning. If I want to enjoy the parties, then I prefer evenings.

Clothes

What type of clothes do you wear in daily routine?

I generally wear casual clothes in my daily routine. If the situation demands, then I change to the formals. If I am at home, then I like to wear comfortable clothes

Do you like fashionable or comfortable clothes?

I prefer both depending upon the occasion. If I need to look good, then I wear fashionable clothes whether they are comfortable or not. But generally, I am the kind of a person who prefers comfort over fashion.

What type of clothes do the people wear on weddings?

People in my country wear heavy clothes on wedding functions. They like to spend huge money on buying clothes for the wedding ceremonies. The colors they wear are vibrant and bright.

Do you prefer branded clothes?

I prefer branded over local clothes. There are two reasons behind that, first one is that the branded clothes last long and the second one is that the designing of brands is unique.

323

From where do you buy your clothes?

I usually buy my clothes from the brand outlet or in the shopping malls. I also order some of my clothes online from the trusted e-commerce websites.

Trains

Are trains the mode of transport in your country?

Yes, trains are widely used by almost all the people in my country. We have all the kinds of trains ranging from cheapest to the most luxurious in the world. India is a big country; hence train travel is the most preferred one.

Have you ever travelled in a train?

I have travelled uncountable times on the train. I generally travel by Shatabadi Express and Rajdhani Express. These two are the fastest and most convenient trains in our country.

Is travelling in trains safe in your country?

Travelling in train is very safe in my country. There are many security personnel that are deployed to ensure the safety of the passengers. Also, there are advanced CCTV cameras these days which also contributes to the security factor of the trains.

What are the advantages of travelling in a train?

There is a bundle of advantages of travelling in a train. The first one is that you can move freely as the trains are more spacious than a bus or a plane. Another one is that we have the option of sleeper class at very cheap rates in which customers can travel first class without burning a hole in their pocket.

Do the trains get late in India?

It happens a lot in our country and it can get frustrating sometimes. This aspect of the railway system is not yet improved. Once I got stuck at the station for about seven hours waiting for the train. Sometimes it can get even worse.

Time

What is the importance of punctuality in our life?

I think that being punctual is one of the most important attributes to have in life. Being on time shows that how dedicated you are towards something. Punctuality is a trait that all successful people have.

Do people value time?

No, I don't want to say this, but it is truth that in our society people usually don't value time. Most people are not true to their commitments and appointments. This shows that they don't value punctuality.

Do you make timetable for your future?

Yes, I tend to make a timetable for my future. It allows me to plan my work accordingly and I mostly finish my tasks on the planned time schedule. It is very helpful for people who are not able to manage their time in a proper way.

Do you feel that we should value time?

It's crucial to value time in our lives otherwise the time will not value us. Once the time has passed, it never come back. So, it's necessary to respect time.

Were people more punctual in past time?

I think yes, people were more loyal towards time in the past as compared to the present. People nowadays are lazier due to the advent of technology.

Transportation

Is public transportation in your city good?

No, there is very limited public transport in my hometown. People either take out their own vehicles or they depend upon the auto rickshaws that are privately run and are a poor mode of transport.

How do you travel every day?

I travel by my personal bike/car or you can say that I travel by bus.

Which type of transport is most popular in India?

Trains and buses are the most commonly used transport in my country. Bus and train are both comfortable and have reasonable prices. The connectivity of trains in India is amazing.

Is the transportation cost high in your country?

No, I think that transportation cost is not that high in my country when it comes to the private vehicles, buses and trains. However, the prices of domestic flights are skyrocketed.

Is it easy to transport goods in your country?

Yes, its easily available. People can transport their goods across the country using the services of movers and packers and the transport companies. India is well connected with roads and rail network, so it is not a difficult job to transport goods in any part of the country.

Reading

Do you like reading?

I love reading very much. Most of the times I read self-help books and auto biographies of famous politicians and sportsperson. I read at least for one hour every day.

What kind of material do you like reading?

I prefer reading all sorts of material. I chose a book by its cover and title. The one that attracts me, I pick that book. I don't care what sort of book it is. I feel that every book teaches you something.

Do you feel that reading can be addictive?

Yes, it can be very addictive. I have seen people reading novels and books for hours and hours continuously. Reading books for too long can have negative effects. The most common is insomnia.

What are the benefits of reading?

There are numerous of benefits of reading books. We learn a lot of vocabulary and phrases. It gives us huge amount of knowledge. Reading increases our memory and ability to debate on certain topics.

Have you seen anyone who's a good reader?

Yes, my elder brother is a wonderful reader. His reading speed is incredible, and he also remembers everything that he reads. He can complete a two-hundred-page book in four or five hours.

Restaurant

Describe your favourite restaurant.

My favourite restaurant is Bar-b-cue World. Its located at multiple locations in my city. It is a restaurant chain and only serves buffet lunch and dinner. I like going there as they have tremendous variety of food items to choose.

Do you often go there?

I go there once a month or if there is a special occasion. I like to celebrate my birthday with my friends and family at this place.

Which dish do you generally order there?

I don't order anything as it is a buffet restaurant. It's up to us to choose the dish we want to eat. I like honey chili cauliflower and grilled mushrooms.

Is restaurant food good for health?

No, restaurant food is not good for health. We should avoid it as much as we can. On the other hand, it does not harm too much if we consume it occasionally.

Why do people visit restaurants in your area?

People visit restaurants when they celebrate an occasion with their family and friends. They also visit there sometimes when they are tired of eating homemade food and don't want to cook themselves.

Pollution

What are the causes of pollution?

There are several causes of pollution like garbage waste, industrial waste, generation of electricity through coal and vehicles. These are the main sources that creates pollution in the environment.

How can we overcome this issue?

We can overcome this issue by creating awareness among people about the ill-effects of pollution. Government can take several steps to create a neat and clean environment.

What can government do to control the pollution?

Government can make strict rules against the people who create unnecessary pollution. Heavy fines should be imposed and in severe cases, imprisonment should be given. In some countries, there is a heavy fine for littering.

What are the major problems caused by pollution?

There can be serious issues that can be caused by pollution. Thousands of marine species are dying due to dumping of plastic into the ocean. More people than before are suffering with respiratory problems.

Which type of pollution is most common in your country or city?

In my city, the most common pollution is the air and noise pollution. These days, there are a huge number of vehicles running on the roads. The exhaust emissions have led to air pollution.

Population

Is population a problem in your country?

It's a big problem of my country. A lot of people in my county are unemployed because of the population explosion. Job creation and demand is not there but the population is increasing by leaps and bounds.

What are the causes behind the increase in population?
People are not educated enough and don't know the consequences of huge population. Illiteracy also plays a part in the reason behind growing number of people.
Is one child policy the solution?
No, I think that it is not the right solution. China did it few years back, but it didn't work well. Initially they were able to control it but after some years, the old age population increased, and young people's population declined. This became a major problem in their society after some years.
How can we curb the population?
The best way to control the population is to create awareness among people on public platforms. Government should encourage people to give birth to not more than two kids and give incentives to those who follow the instruction.
What are the disadvantages of an overpopulated country?
The biggest drawback of huge population in a country is that the unemployment rates shoot up. More people will struggle for one position of a job. Another problem is that the demands are more than the production, this results in inflation.

Home

In what kind of a home do you live?
I live in a big house as I put up with all my cousins. I live in a joint family. Our house consists of eight rooms, four at the ground floor and rest on the second floor.
What type of homes are there in your locality?
We have generally similar kind of homes in our locality. It differs from size to size. The width and length can be different, but the height and number of stories allowed are the same for everyone. People are not allowed to build more than a three-story house in my locality and whole city.
Is it important to have a parking space in the home?
Yes, I think it has now become a basic requirement of everyone. To have personal parking space at the house is a blessing. I think that every house should have a parking space.
What is the difference between living in a house and an apartment?

A house comes with a lot of advantages. In house we can modify anything, we have more space and we can add multiple floors to it. In apartment, more security is there, and the cost is less. Both have their own merits.

What type of home do you prefer to live in?

I prefer to live in a big home that is an independent house. I like to have more space hence I don't like to live in apartments. I love to live in a house that is also big from inside and should have multiple floors.

Mobile phones

Do you use mobile phone?

Yes, I use mobile phones. I use a Samsung smart phone. I use it for a variety of purposes. I like to play games sometimes and I also watch movies on it. I also like to read e-books in my free time. The main function that I use in mobile phone is calling and messaging.

Should school children be allowed to use mobile phones in schools?

School children should never be allowed to use mobiles phones in schools. That is their time to study and being thoughtful in the classroom. Mobiles are a great distraction for kids or for anyone.

How has mobiles changed our lives?

Mobiles have changed our lives in a lot of ways. Previously we used to have a separate alarm clock to wake up, a camera, radio and TV. But, with the advancements in the technology of mobile phones, we don't need any of those devices. Everything can be done by using mobile phones.

What are the negative effects of mobile phones?

The biggest effect of mobile is on the health. People use mobiles for a longer period. We are always hooked up to mobiles for any task. It would not be wrong to say that we have become slaves of mobile phones.

Are mobile phones expensive in your country?

There are certain brands that are expensive in India but most of the mobiles are not expensive. One can get quality and feature loaded mobile smartphone at a low cost.

Drink

Which is your favourite drink?

I love to drink mango shake. Although I wait for summers before the mangoes can become available in the market. I drink it almost every day in the summer season. I like it chilled and sweet.

Can you make a drink?

Yes, I can make a couple of drinks. I can make mango shake and cold coffee. You just need to mix one teaspoon coffee powder and some sugar in chilled milk to make cold coffee. Just shake it to get a wonderful cold coffee. You can also add vanilla ice cream to enhance the experience.

What benefits do the cold drinks have?

There are not many benefits of cold drinks as they can cause cough and are very sweet. But, at the time of extreme summers, one should drink soda or cold beverages in order to avoid heat stroke.

Do you also drink fruit juices?

Yes, I like drinking all sorts of fruit juices. My favourite ones are the pomegranate juice and black current juice. I think that fresh juice is great for the digestive system and our skin.

Do you take hard drinks?

No, I don't take hard drinks.

Malls

How are malls better than shops?

I feel that malls are more spacious and have more variety under one roof. In summers, it's good to go to mall as the entire shopping complex is air conditioned. Malls have other activities to do as well.

Are there any malls in your hometown?

There are more than 7 or 8 malls in my hometown. I live in a modern city so there is no scarcity of malls. Some are of small and medium size but Elante mall and VR mall are massive.

For what purpose do you visit mall?

I visit malls to shop for my clothes and I also go there to watch movies. I also go to malls to dine as there are numerous top restaurants.

What is the future of malls?

The future of malls is very bright. Nowadays, more and more people are shopping from malls and shopping complexes. People get more variety and convenience while they are in mall.

Do you feel that shops in malls generate more income than shops in the markets?

Indeed, shops in the mall generate more income than shops in the market. It is due to additional foot fall in the malls and other benefits that malls bring. Malls are fully air conditioned and there are many other amenities in the same building.

Swimming pool

Have you ever visited a swimming pool?

Yes, I have been to a lot of swimming pools. The swimming pool I like the most is the one which is made in the sports complex of my city. The pool is indoors and is built according to the Olympics standards. A lot of people of all age groups come there to learn swimming.

Do you know swimming?

I am still learning the art of swimming. I took lessons last year but was not able to learn proper swimming in deep water. I can dive and float for a couple of seconds and that's it.

Do you feel that swimming should be taught in schools?

I think that swimming should be taught in schools because it is such an activity that everyone should know. I don't think that all the schools will be able to provide this facility, but they can aware kids about the benefits of swimming.

Is it a good idea to learn swimming at an early stage of life?

Anything that is learnt at an early stage of life is well learnt. Swimming is such an activity that can be learnt properly at young age. At this age, the child can learn and adopt anything easily.

What are the advantages of swimming?

There are numerous advantages of swimming. The first one is that it is a complete exercise as all the body parts are involved while swimming. Secondly, it can be a life saver in emergency.

Fruits

Which is your favourite fruit?

I like to eat all the fruits except papaya. My favourite one is mango and banana. I also like watermelon in the summer season. Mango is very sweet and delicious and is also known as the king of fruits. Banana gives more minerals and nutrients than any other fruit. It is also very filling.

What are the health benefits of eating fruits?

There are many health benefits of eating fruits. It clears up the digestive system thoroughly. Eating fruits also helps in preserving our skin. Fruits contains a lot of antioxidants that ensure good health for all our organs.

331

What type of fruits are there in your country?

There are all types of seasons in my country, hence we get all sorts of fruits. We have bananas, mango, apple, orange, watermelon, sun melon, musk melon, guava, kiwi, strawberry and so on.

At what time of the day do you eat fruits?

I mostly eat fruits in the evening after the dinner. This is the best time to eat fruits as it helps to digest the dinner and I generally take light dinner, so the fruits compliment it well.

From where do you buy fruits?

I accompany my mother when she buys fruit. We buy fruits from Reliance mart. It is one of the biggest supermarkets in our area. Fruits available there are fresh and cheap.

Photography

Do you like taking pictures?

Yes, I like it very much. I have a decent camera in my smart phone so whenever there's an occasion or something special, I take out my phone and click photos and make videos.

Which camera do you use to take pictures?

Mostly, I take pictures from my mobile phone as it is quite handy and its always in my pocket. I also have a Sony digital camera in which I take pictures when I go for an excursion.

Do you feel that we should click photos more often?

I think when we click pictures more often then we miss the real moments. We should click the picture once or twice in the event and rest of the times, we should enjoy the moment.

Speak about a special photo.

I have a special photo that hangs in the drawing room of our house in a grand frame. The photo was taken on my cousin's wedding and is of a big size. In that photograph there are all the maternal family members of mine. All my cousins, my uncles and aunts. I really love that photo.

Does photography require special skills?

No, I don't think that there's any rocket science in clicking pictures. You just need to fit everything in the frame and just click the button. Although one should be trained enough for professional photography.

Role model

332

Do you have a role model in life?

Yes, I have a role model and he's my grandfather. He has achieved a lot of things in life. I have learnt a great deal of things from him. During his young days, he struggled a lot and eventually reached heights of success.

Do you feel that we should have role models for inspiration?

Yes, we should have role models in life. We can look up to them for inspiration. We should have role models in life who are our near and dear ones so that it gives us a chance to learn things from them.

What kind of role models do the people choose?

People mostly prefer famous personalities and celebrities. Some people like to choose sportspersons as their role models. I think people generally look for successful people as their role models.

Do you feel that actors can make good role models?

I don't think that actors can be great role models as what they are on screen doesn't mean that they are the same off screen. We can't judge their real personalities so I think that one should not make actors as their role models.

What type of people can be good role models?

Scientists, politicians, great teachers, spiritual leaders and writers can be good role models. These people are the ones who reform societies and influence the thinking of people. They will make wonderful role models.

Women

What is the position of women today?

I think that position of women today is very strong. Women of today is independent and takes decisions at her own will. In some societies the plight of women has not improved but at most places the change is occurring.

Do you feel that women are empowered enough in your society?

I feel that in most of the developed countries and in countries where literacy rate is high, there has been a huge improvement in the position of women, and they are empowered enough to make their own place in society. In my country this is happening gradually.

Should women serve in police and army?

They should serve in police and the army as they are not inferior to men. In my country, women are already serving as women cops and commandos. They are as good as anyone.

What should we do to empower women?

We should encourage girls from a young age about having their own choices so that they can take decisions on their own. The feeling of inferiority is induced in women from childhood. If we can stop it then we can empower women.

What do you think about women?

I think that they are smarter than men. If you see the current trend in matriculation and 12th results, you will see that there are more girls who top the rankings than boys. That's a clear sign that they are intelligent enough and we don't need to take decisions on their behalf.

History

Is it important to preserve history?

It's essential to preserve history as it reflects on our past and inception. If we preserve history, then only we will be able to make our children learn about the sacrifices and struggles that our ancestors made to bring us to a position where we are now.

Why do schools have history subject?

Schools have history subjects because children need to learn about the important events and dates of the past. History has great value and they can form interest in reading it if they learn from childhood.

Do you like reading history?

I love reading history and historical events. I prefer reading about past scientists and about the events such as Mahabharata. This enhances our knowledge about past, and we can also share our knowledge with others.

Should history be made compulsory throughout the education?

Today's generation hardly know any facts about history. It's an old saying that we can't win present without knowing history. I think yes history should be taught throughout the educational years and it should be the compulsory subject.

Do you feel that we should teach current history rather than the old one?

Yes, we should teach current history more than the older history. Both have equal importance, but I feel that kids will take more interest in learning the 21st century history than the older history.

Media

What is the role of media in shaping our society?

Media plays a big role in shaping our history. It has a huge impact on the lives of people from all walks of life. Everyone is hooked up to media every time for latest updates.

Do you feel that media has become a part of our life?

It's a crucial part of our life these days. We are attached to media for the most part of our day. We rely on it for valuable information and entertainment every day.

Do you feel that media is powerful?

Media is a powerful medium which can either bring all people on the same page or it can start wars on the difference of opinions. Media is the most powerful weapon in this era.

Should media interfere the personal lives of celebrities?

I think it is a bad idea. Famous celebrities have their personal lives and they have the right to enjoy it without anybody's interference. Sometimes, media takes it too far in the coverage of a story. That can be really irritating for celebrities.

Should there be a check on media?

No, I think that media should be an independent body and there should not be any check on it. India is a democratic country and media in our country is independent and I think that it should be like this everywhere.

Boats/ships

What is the purpose of boats and ships in your country?

Boats and ships are used to commute from one place to the other. It is also used to ship the cargo and goods. India is a country where extensive use of boats and ships is there.

Have you ever travelled on a boat or ship?

I have travelled once on a ship in Goa. It was a sun set tour of three hours in which the ship company picked and dropped us at the hotel and took us in the ocean to enjoy the sun set dinner. There was some entertainment on board with around 300 people on it.

Are there any famous ship ports in your country?

There are several important ship ports in India as our country has a long coastline. The most prominent ones are the Mumbai, Chennai, Vishakhapatnam, Kolkata and Cochin.

What's the difference between travelling in a ship and aero plane?

Travelling in ship is much slower than travelling in air, but the fare is cheaper in ships. One can find more luxuries and space in ships as opposed to an aero plane.

Do the people in your country often travel in boats and ships?

Yes, people in my county often travel in boats and ships as we are not a landlocked country and we have a lot of rivers that flow from one city to the other. The voyage of boat is also cheaper, so many people use this as the transport method.

Online shopping

Do you feel that future of online shopping is bright?

Certainly, today is the era of modern technology and internet has taken over in every field. People are inclining more and more towards online shopping due to its numerous benefits. I think that online shopping has a healthy future.

What are the benefits of online shopping?

There are many advantages of buying things online. The biggest one is that you don't need to roam around markets and different places to buy a product. You can simply order it from any part of the world, and you will get it delivered at your doorstep.

Do you shop online?

Indeed, I like to buy a lot of things from the online shopping websites. There are certain products that are not easily available in the market. For that, I chose online shopping. The other reason I shop online is that it gives me more discounts than things that are available in the market.

Name some of the products that are sold commonly on online platforms.

There are thousands of products that are commonly sold online. Most common ones are clothes and shoes. I have seen a lot of people who buy such things from the online merchants. People also buy mobile phones and other electronic gadgets from online stores.

Do you feel that online shopping is fraud?

No, I don't think so. There might be some websites that do some frauds but most of the renowned platforms are providing genuine products at unbeatable price. There have been some reports of fraud by certain unregistered websites but majority of them are fine.

Tea / coffee

Do you like to drink tea?

I love drinking tea on daily basis. I think it is a part of the Indian culture. It is also believed that tea is the second most consumed drink in the world after water. It is soothing and rejuvenating.

What are the benefits of having tea?

There are number of benefits of consuming tea that have been scientifically proven. Tea contains a lot of antioxidants that provides energy and prevents ageing of organs. Also, it relaxes the mind after a hectic day.

Which drink is more popular in your country, tea or coffee?

I think tea and coffee both are popular in my country but if I have to choose one, then I think that tea is more common. Coffee is also consumed extensively but tea is more popular drink than any other beverage.

Which type of tea is famous in your country?

Our country is famous for its tea plantations. Assam tea is consumed all over the world. Most of the people in my country like oolong tea. This is a black tea that is mixed with milk and sugar to make a traditional Indian tea. With growing health awareness, green tea is also commonly consumed type of tea these days.

Do you like coffee?

I am a coffee and tea lover. I like to consume coffee a couple of times in a week. I like my coffee rich in flavor and with a lot of milk. I generally make latte as it's not that strong and is full of flavor.

Why do people drink tea or coffee?

People drink tea or coffee for several reasons. Tea rejuvenates the mind and provides antioxidants that controls ageing. On the other hand, coffee is a great laxative that helps in digestion. It also contains caffeine that helps to stay active.

Do you often invite people for tea or coffee?

Yes, I do. I like to invite my friends for tea generally in the evening. I think that it is the best way to interact with your friends and you can have a great conversation over tea or coffee.

Do you often like to have tea at home or at cafe?

I prefer to make my tea at home. I also drink it outside when required but most of the times I like it at home. It's one of the easiest things to make. So, I prefer my tea at home.

Smile

Do you often smile?

Yes, I like to smile quite often. It is an activity that gives me energy and positive attitude. I think a smile on face is the greatest trait that a person can have.

Do you like to make people smile?

Yes, if I am given a chance, I would like to make people smile. I am not a very talkative person who could make everyone smile, but I feel that bringing a smile on someone's face is a great deed.

What are the benefits of smiling?

There are many benefits of smiling. The biggest one is that it keeps your mood lighter. It means that you are in good space and can take better decisions. Apart from this, one looks good with a smile on face than a stoned face person.

Do you feel that smiling enhances personality?

Yes, I completely believe in this. I reckon that a person looks different when he smiles. It brings energy within the person and it also influences others. Thus, smile enhances personality.

On what occasions do you smile?

I mostly smile when I hear a joke or when I see a comedy program or movie. I also smile when someone does a foolish thing. Because, I think that reacting strongly to it can be bad, so I just smile off the situation.

Mathematics

Did you study mathematics at school?

I studied mathematics throughout most part of my schooling as it is a compulsory subject in Indian education system. I found it challenging and interesting at the same time.

Did you find it easy or difficult?

I found it to be easy in the early part of my schooling but when I grew up, it became quite a difficult subject for me. I used to score averagely in mathematics in higher schooling.

What are the benefits of learning mathematics?

I think it is very useful for the development of the brain. That's why it has been made a compulsory subject in our education system. Moreover, it helps to develop the analytical and reasoning skills of a person.

Do you feel that mathematics is a useless part of school curriculum?

Not at all, I think that it is one of the most integral part of the education. Without mathematics the study would be so boring and one dimensional. Moreover, it is helpful in most of the higher educational courses as well.

Did you ever fail in mathematics exam?

If I could remember properly then I think that I failed once in my 9th grade class test. The reason I failed was that I could not get time to prepare for the exam as I was down with fever.

Garbage / rubbish

What is the reason behind increasing rubbish these days?

The main reason behind the ever-escalating problem of garbage is population and people's attitude towards hygiene. There has been a huge leap in the demand for the packaged food. This has led to the nuisance of rubbish in the society.

How can we tackle this situation?

There are number of ways through which we can tackle this situation. First, individuals should try to manage garbage at their own level rather than depending upon the government. Secondly, they can keep separate bins for recyclable and non-recyclable waste so that the garbage can be sorted properly.

Do you feel that people are responsible for creating more and more garbage?

To a great extent, yes. I think people are the ones to be blamed for creating garbage everywhere. However, in some cases government must be blamed for poor management of the garbage.

Do you feel that it is the sole responsibility of a government to take care of the garbage?

No, I think there should be collective efforts by administration and common man to tackle this issue. This is one of the most dreadful problems these days that needs to be solved as quickly as possible.

Do you feel that garbage should be recycled?

Indeed, garbage ought to be recycled in a way that we get the maximum return from that. In some countries, government even pays for the waste that you return to them which can be recycled.

Perfume

Do you wear perfume every day?

No, I don't usually wear perfume. I generally apply it when I go out for a dinner or for a special occasion. I have a decent collection of perfumes.

What type of perfumes do you like?

I like pungent smell. I think that a perfume should overpower all the odors that our body has. I also like the bottle of the perfume to be of glass and classy in shape.

Do you feel that wearing perfume has become a trend these days?

It certainly has become a trend to wear perfume these days rather than using it for its intended purpose. I see people buying super expensive perfumes for no reason.

Are perfumes expensive in your country?

There are all types of perfumes that are available in my country. The range starts from as low as 100 rupees and go up to as expensive as you want. So, I won't say that perfumes are expensive in my country. When it comes to the branded perfumes then the prices are more or less the same in most of the countries across the world.

Do the people of your country use perfume on regular basis?

I have seen majority of people using perfumes daily. I think that it completely depends on the individuals. I have also seen some people who do not use perfumes at all.

Borrowing / sharing

Do you like to share your things with others?

I certainly do. I have been taught by my parents from my childhood to share things with people who are needy. It gives me immense pleasure when I share things with others.

Is borrowing a good habit?

It can be both good and bad. I think borrowing something from a sibling or a good friend is a good idea but borrowing loans from bank and other stuff can be lethal sometimes.

Do you feel that sharing is a quality that everyone should have?

Yes, I think that everyone should have this quality. The world would be a great place to live if everyone starts sharing. One should try to share things with the people who need them the most.

Have you ever borrowed something from others?

Yes, I have borrowed many things from my friends and siblings. They always give me the things that I need. I think sharing things with loved ones also enhances the relationships.

Have you shared an expensive thing with your friend?

Absolutely, I have shared some of my expensive things with my friends. One of my best friends had to go on a school trip so he needed my digital camera to click pictures of the tour. So, I did not hesitate to give it to him as he was my best friend. He returned the camera once he came back from the trip.

Bottled water

What are the negative impacts on the environment of using bottled water?

There are many adverse effects of using bottled water on the environment. The major one is the pollution that the plastic bottle causes. It is estimated that the biggest cause of sea pollution in 2018 was from the plastic water bottles.

Do you feel that bottled water is used extensively in your country?

Yes, there is no doubt that bottled water can be found in every corner of our country. Unavailability of clean drinking water in major cities has led to the increased production of mineral water.

Do you use bottled water regularly?

No, I generally drink from the government supply that arrives at our house. We have a water filter attached to the inlet pipe that filters the water that we drink. If I am travelling outside the city, then I prefer drinking bottled water.

Is bottled water good for health?

If we consume bottled water excessively or in daily routine, then it is not good for health. First of all, it contains preservatives that keeps it good to drink for a long time. Moreover, it is generally packed in plastic bottle, which is not the best material for packaging.

Do you feel that bottled water should be banned?

No, I don't think that bottled water should be banned. Instead, government should provide clean drinking water in every city, town and village of the country. The use of bottled water will naturally decrease.

Copyright

Do you feel that copyrights should be abolished?

No, I don't agree with this. I feel that the inventor or the discoverer should keep his/her right of inventing a thing. The copyrights should always be awarded to the inventor.

Why do you think that copyright is necessary?

I think that it is one of the most essential things in a writers, scientists, artists or a discoverer's life. It is important to give the credit of the work to the owner. Copyright is also important to avoid piracy and imitation of the work.

Do you know anyone who owns a copyright of something?

Yes, one of my uncles who is a musician has a copyright to his music album. He produces music and sells it to the film makers.

Do you feel that copyright system in your country is secure?

Yes, there are strict rules and regulations regarding the copyright system in our country. Our system reserves the full right for the work of people and not allow anyone to copy it easily.

Do you think that one day you will be able to have a copyright of something?

Perhaps I would be able to have a copyright of my own. I wish to write a book in future. So, I think that I will surely copyright that book.

Life experiences

Do you feel that we can learn lessons from life experiences?

We can learn many things from life experiences. It's an old saying that experience is the best teacher. A person learns a lot from his/her experiences in life.

Have you learned anything from life experience?

I have learned a great deal of things from my life experiences. I have learned to be patient in life and believe that nothing comes easy. One must work hard in life to attain success.

Do you feel that experience in life is the best teacher?

I do believe that experience in life is the best teacher. One should always learn from bad and good experiences of life.

Have you ever faced a bad experience in your life?

Yes, I have faced a bad experience in my life once. I was involved in an accident and it took me some time to recover.

Do you feel that life will be smooth if one has only good experiences?

I think that there are ups and down in everyone's life. It is important to celebrate small achievements in order to keep life smooth. Life can be smooth with all sorts of experiences.

Influence of television

Do you feel that television has a negative influence on kids?

Television is very addictive and no doubt that it has had a negative influence on the life of kids. The biggest negative point is that kids become lazy and can learn vulgar things from it.

Is television dangerous for school going kids?

I won't say that television is dangerous. I think that some channels and aspects are dangerous, but school kids can also learn a great deal of things from TV.

Do you feel that watching television in excess impacts our health?

Watching television for long hours have proven negative effects on the health of a person. It is related to weak eyesight as well as migraine issues.

Has television influenced you in anyway in your life?

Without a doubt T.V. has influenced me in a positive way. I have learned great deal of things from it over the past so many years.

Do you feel that people will continue getting influenced by television in future as well?

I think more and more people will be influenced by television in future as well. The number has been growing from the past few years and it will continue to grow.

Retirement and old age

What sort of problems do people face at older age?

343

People face numerous problems at older age. They face health related issues. Some old aged people also face loneliness as not all members in the family have time for old people.

Have you ever thought about the day when you retire?

No not yet. I have not given it the slightest of the thought. I think that I am young and there are many years to go before I retire.

Do you agree that the most difficult part of life is the old age?

It certainly is the most difficult part according to me. The reason is that the person is not at his/her full strength and there are many problems that come with old age. I think that it is very difficult to be in that position.

Do you feel that a person becomes more dependent in old age?

Yes, a person becomes lot dependent in old age just like kids. They need help in more tasks than in young age. I have seen my grandparents asking for help for smallest of the tasks.

Do you think that retirement age should be increased to 65 years for government services?

No, I don't think that retirement age should be increased than the current limit. Ours is a huge nation and population is also high. If the retirement age bar is raised than youngsters will find difficulty in getting jobs.

Eating habits

Do you feel that poor eating habits contributes to poor health?

Poor eating habits leads to many health issues. People can get a chronic disease and become fat. Poor eating habits also makes a person lazy.

Do you think that eating habits needs to be in place in order to maintain good health?

Yes, most of the scientists claim that good health is associated with good diet. Having a controlled diet is more important than doing exercise.

What are your eating habits?

I like to eat heavy breakfast as it allows me to stay energetic for the whole day. After that I take normal lunch and light dinner.

What should we eat in order to stay healthy?

We should eat non oily food. Also, one needs to have fruits in daily routine. We should prefer homemade food over fast food in order to stay fit.

Do you feel that one should eat nutritious diet?

344

Yes, one should always eat nutritious diet. There are many healthy options available to us. Taking nutritious diet has many advantages. It gives all the minerals and vitamins required for the smooth functioning of the body.

Universities

Are universities greedier these days?

Certainly, they are much greedier these days. Universities have become money minting machines. Most of the universities are not concerned about the wellbeing of the student.

Is it difficult for a poor kid to study at university?

It has become almost impossible for a poor kid to study at a university. The fee structures have shoot up greatly and no scholarship programs are available for them.

Are universities losing importance in terms of educational quality?

As the number of new universities is growing, there has been deficiency in the quality of education they provide. I think that very few universities are there who impart quality education.

Do you think that universities concentrate more on theory rather than practical knowledge?

These days in our country the level of education has gone down and most of the universities are focused on theory knowledge. However, there are old universities that have not lost any importance and still concentrate on practical studies.

Is college a better place to study than university?

I can't say that college is the better place to study than a university. Both type of institutions has its own merits. Although it is altogether a different environment to study in college as compared to a university.

Work and life balance

How many hours do people generally work in your country?

People generally work for 8 – 10 hours in a day in my country. Some people work even longer than this. In most of the government sectors, the timings are fixed.

Do you think that people these days are able to maintain a balance between work and personal life?

In most of the private companies, people are not able to make a balance between work and personal life. The companies put so much pressure on their employees and expect them to work long hours for the benefit of their company.

How many hours one should work in a day ideally?

Ideally, one should work for not more than 8 hours in a day. I think one needs to strike a balance between life and work. So, I believe that 8 hours work in a day is perfect.

Do you feel that work is worship?

I don't feel that work is worship. Although work is crucial in life, but it should not be seen as worship. Work should be considered work.

Was work life better in the past?

I can agree as well as disagree with this. There was no pressure in the past which is a good thing. These days there are more perks in terms of salary, which is good too. So, work life had advantages in past as well as in present.

News

How do you get news?

I get news from several sources. Mainly I read news through internet on my phone. I also get news from my friends and family members.

Is getting news important?

It is crucial to get regular updates on news. One should know what is going on in and around the country. It increases the knowledge of a person.

Do you feel that most of the news present on internet is not reliable?

I feel that most of the news is true but there are some articles and websites that spread fake propaganda. But most of the news is reliable.

Is it true that news editors intentionally try to make the news spicy?

Yes, there are some news editors who try to make news spicy by adding unnecessary news and fake news in the newspapers and television media.

How often do you read news?

I read news every day for at least 10 minutes. I don't think that I have missed a single day from the past few years. I think it is crucial to stay updated through news.

Island

Have you ever been to an island?

Yes, I have been to an island named Sri Lanka. It is an island country located in the southern side of India. I went there last year with my family and had a great time there.

Why do you think that islands are different from inlands?

Islands are very different from inlands. One can enjoy beaches around the islands and the weather is also different in islands than inland.

Is there any special island in your country?

Yes, there is a very special island in our country. The name of the island is Andaman and Nicobar Islands. It is in the far east side of India. It is one of the most beautiful parts of our country.

Speak about an island you wish to visit in future

If I am given a chance, then I would like to visit Maldives. Maldives is one of the most gorgeous island cluster in the whole world. It is situated in the south west of India. The flight takes about three hours to reach there.

Is there any difference in weather in islands than mainland?

Yes, I have been to a couple of islands and I have felt that the weather over there is more pleasant throughout the year. It might be different on some islands that I have not visited but I have generally heard that in most of the islands the weather remains pleasant all year round.

Make-up

Do you do make-up?

Yes, I do makeup. I feel that it makes my looks perfect. I feel more presentable and attractive when I apply make-up.

Do you feel that make-up increases confidence of a person?

Yes, it escalates the confidence of a person because one feels more attractive. Also, if there are any imperfections, it is concealed by make-up. Hence it increases the confidence of the person.

Do you use any expensive cosmetics?

I use inexpensive cosmetics in my daily routine, but I do have one concealer that is expensive. I feel that the cosmetics should be branded but it doesn't matter whether they are expensive or not.

Is there any person you know who does a lot of make-up?

Yes, one of my aunts does a lot of make-up. She puts on make-up all the time. She is very conscious of her looks, so she always remains tip top.

Are there any side effects of applying cosmetics on face?

There are side effects of applying excessive make up on the face especially. I think branded and herbal cosmetics are fine but local cosmetics can cause a great deal of problems.

Tiredness

Do you get tired?

Yes, I get tired when I work for long. I generally don't get tired in my daily routine but on some days I really get tired.

What do you do when you get tired?

I relax when I get tired. My best way to get rid of tiredness is by spending time at home. I relax by sleeping more and listening to my favourite songs.

Why do people get tired?

People get tired due to several reasons. The main factor is working over-time. They also get tired when they travel more.

Is there any thing that makes you tired?

I think working more than my capacity makes me tired. I also get tired when I play sports on weekends.

Speak about a situation when you got tired

I remember one day when I really got tired. I went to Dubai last year and had to walk in the world's largest mall for more than five hours. At that time, I really got tired.

Forest

Have you ever been to a forest?

Yes, I have been to a forest area in Himachal Pradesh a couple of times. The name of the forest is Chail. It is a wildlife sanctuary that is preserved by the government and is open for everyone to visit.

What is the importance of forests in our life?

Forests are very important for us. Forests purify the nearby areas and acts as the habitat to thousands of bird and animal species.

Do you feel that preserving forests should be the number one priority?

It should the number one priority for the governments around the world. Google maps revealed that forests in many areas of the world are continuously cleared for timber and furniture. If the forests are cleared at this rate, then it will create serious issues in the environment.

Is the government of your country doing anything to preserve forests?

I have read that government of our country is putting many efforts in preserving and maintaining the forests around the country. There have been many cases of crack down on the forest mafia.

Is there any forest area near your hometown?

There is a huge forest reserve adjoining my hometown. It is a preserved and bordered forest area that is regulated by the local government. Its name is Sukhna Sanctuary.

Beach

Do you feel that beaches are getting polluted day by day?

There is no doubt in this fact that beaches are getting polluted day by day. Although there have been some measures taken by government recently to control the littering on beaches.

What are the disadvantages of living near a beach?

I think that there is no such disadvantage of living near the beach but in case of a high tide, there can be some flooding in the nearby areas.

Do you know anyone who lives near the beach?

Yes, one of my cousins lives in Goa. He lives by the beach. He owns a house and a small hotel there.

Have you ever seen a beach area?

I have been to a couple of beach areas in the past. I have seen beaches in Goa as well as in Andaman and Nicobar Islands.

Do you like beaches?

I relish visiting the beach areas. I simply like to sit by the beach and enjoy the nature. I love the sound of the waves.

Oceans

Have you ever sailed in an ocean?

I have sailed in the ocean once when I visited Andaman and Nicobar Islands. We took a ferry to Havelock Island and enjoyed our day there.

Is there any ocean near your country?

Our country is surrounded by ocean on three sides. 40 % of India's boundary is surrounded by different oceans.

Do you feel that people are polluting oceans more than ever before?

It is a sad scenario these days. People don't care about the environment and are polluting the seas more than ever before. The main source of ocean pollution is plastic.

Can oceans be a threat?

Oceans can be threat during earthquakes. One such earthquake happened in south east Asia and caused humungous waves known as Tsunami that took lives of thousands of people.

Supermarket

How often do you go to a supermarket?

I go to a supermarket every 15 days. I like to shop for groceries myself. I generally visit Reliance Mart in my local area.

Which is your favourite supermarket?

My favourite one is Reliance Mart. It is the biggest supermarket in my hometown. Not only this, it is also the best in terms of cost and variety.

What do you usually buy from the supermarket?

I normally buy all sorts of stuff from the supermarket. I buy perfumes, soaps, cremes, milk, fruits and any other things that are required.

Do you think that supermarkets have destroyed the local businesses?

Supermarkets have certainly destroyed local business up to a certain extent. Supermarkets have more variety and better rates than the local shops. So, more and more people prefer to buy from the supermarkets than local shops.

What type of supermarkets are located nearby your residence?

There are all sorts of supermarkets located near my residence. There are international brands like Walmart and Metro. On the other hand, there are Indian brands like Reliance and Birla supermarkets as well.

Street market

Have you bought something from street market?

Yes, I have bought many things from the local street markets. Once I bought a sling bag from a street market. It was very cheap and was of good quality.

Is there any street market nearby your house?

There are street markets everywhere in India. This is how the society works in India. There are temporary markets that are organized at certain locations near my house on selected days of the week.

What sort of things are generally sold in the street markets?

All sorts of things are sold in the street markets. Vendors sell dairy products, vegetables, fruits, spices, toys and daily need products at the street markets.

Do you feel that the quality of products in the street market is not good?

Sometimes the quality of products sold in these types of market is not up to the mark. However, some vendors sell quality things to their customers.

Do you feel that street markets should be banned?

No street markets should not be banned as it is run by people who can't afford to pay the rent of shops or own shops for that matter. I think everyone has the right to sell things so the street markets should be allowed to run but should be managed by the government for smooth operation.

Visiting relative and friends

How often do you visit your relatives?

I visit my relatives regularly. I love to meet my relatives, especially cousins. I have cordial relations with most of my relatives, so I often visit them.

Do you go on your friend's family functions?

Yes, if I am invited then I surely go to my friend's family functions. Recently I was invited to attend marriage of my friend's brother and I enjoyed the occasion very much.

Have any of your relatives invited you to his/her home recently?

Yes, my uncle and aunt recently invited me recently to a dinner. I went there with my parents and brother. We had a fun time together.

How often do your friends invite you to their homes?

My friends invite me regularly to their homes. Although I don't have lots of friends but the few friends that I have always invite me on weekends.

For what purpose do you visit your relatives and friends?

I visit their homes to meet them and play with them or simply for family gatherings. Recently I was invited to join a friend's gathering at one of my friend's house.

Places to play

Where did you play as a child?

I used to play in the park nearby my house. I also played in my friend's house a lot. I remember that I also played in our school ground in recess time.

Are there places in your hometown where kids can play?
There are countless public parks and a lake area where kids can enjoy
themselves. There are few sports centers made by government in certain
areas where kids can play.
Do you feel that places to play have changed over the years?
The play areas have changed drastically as compared to the past. In the
past kids used to enjoy in the parks more than anywhere else. These days
kids like to be indoors and play indoor games.
Where do most of the kids of today's era like to play?
Most of the kids in this era like to play in their homes on video games. They
don't relish going out of their houses and play outdoor sports.

Time management
How do you manage your time?
I manage my time by planning the day beforehand. This way I can get free
time for activities apart from studies and work.
Do you feel that time management is necessary in life?
Time management is the most essential thing in life. People who manage
their time are more successful than others. Time management allows the
proper utilization of 24 hours.
Do you think that a lot of people these days don't value time?
Yes, most of the people in this era don't value time. I often see people
reach late at certain occasions in our country. They don't take the value of
their time seriously.
Are people of today's generation managing time properly?
Some people of today's generation manage time properly because it's the
need of hour. So, I feel that many people are managing the time properly.
Do you feel it is necessary to make a timetable to manage time properly?
Yes, making a timetable allows you to manage your tasks in an efficient
way. People can prioritize their activities according to their schedule.

Sun
What is the importance of sun in our life?
Sun gives us light and it also gives us life. If there was no sun, then there
would be no life possible on this planet. Plants grow due to sun light and
sun is the most important aspect of this solar system.
Do you often bathe in sunlight?

Yes, I sit in the open and absorb sun light in winters. I feel warm and relaxed when I bathe in sunlight. I only do it in winters though.

Do you feel that today's people have less access to sunlight?

With the growing number of skyscrapers and other infrastructure, sunlight is not reaching all places. People living in cities often complaint about having pain in joints which occurs due to the deficiency of Vitamin D which is absorbed from sunlight.

How do you feel when its sunny?

Sunny day is the best day for me. On some occasions I also like grey sky or gloomy days. But I love when the sun is out and is at its full glow. I feel energized and clear in my mind. If the day is not sunny, I can feel depression.

Do you feel that sun will ever die?

I don't know. Perhaps one day everything will end but I don't know about sun. I have read somewhere that sun also has a life expectancy and one day it may end.

Sunglasses

Do you wear sunglasses?

Yes, I love wearing sunglasses. It saves me from sun's glare. Sun can get very hot in summers, so sunglasses provides much cooler feeling to me and my eyes.

What kind of sunglasses do you wear?

Wayfarer and Aviators are my favourite kinds of glasses. I like to wear brown and blue colour glasses.

For what purpose people wear sunglasses?

There are two main reasons for wearing sunglasses. The first one is that it protects our eyes from sun's glare and UV rays. The other reason is fashion, people wear sunglasses to look smart.

Do you prefer branded or local sunglasses?

I like Ray Ban and HRX brand the most. I think that one should only wear branded sunglasses as local brands can affect the eyes. Those glasses will not protect your eyes against ultraviolet rays.

Do you feel that wearing sunglasses has become more of a fashion than utility?

It certainly has become more of a fashion statement for some people. Although most of the individuals wear it for the intended purpose.

Pen and pencil

What is the difference between using pen and pencil?

Pen and pencil are very different from each other. Anything written by pen is not easy to rub, on the contrary if you write anything by pencil, it can be rubbed and corrected easily. Moreover, pencils are cheaper whereas pens are costlier.

Is it better to use pencil instead of pen?

I am personally a big fan of using pencils over pen. Pencils are better as one can easily make correction by using an eraser. Pencils are cheap and can write on most of the surfaces with ease.

What did you use as a child in school, pen or pencil?

I remember vividly that we used pencils as kids. Pens were only allowed to use in the higher grades. However, I have always relished pencils for any writing work.

Do you feel that pen is mightier than sword?

Indeed, pen is mightier than sword. Writers in the past have brough spectacular reforms in society through their writings. There have been numerous transformations and revolutions through many writers in the previous time.

What is the difference between the pencils of the past as compared to one's available today?

I think the main difference is in the quality due to improved technology. Nowadays, there are pencils that don't require sharpening. These pencils can be used by refilling lead refills and no sharping tool is required. Also, there are different shapes and sizes available in pencils these days.

Do you use same kind of pen as you did in the past?

No, these days I use ball and gel pens. In my childhood, I mostly used the pens with nib and ink tanks.

Cakes and desserts

On what occasions do people cut cakes?

People generally cut cakes on occasions such as wedding parties, birthday and anniversary celebrations. It has now become a trend in some societies to cut cake to celebrate most of the occasions.

Is there a tradition of cutting cake in your country?

Yes, there is a widespread custom of cutting cake in weddings as well as birthday parties. People nowadays buy expensive and fancy cakes for their near and dear ones.

What is the significance of cutting cake?

Most people cut cake when they achieve something, or they are happy. I think that the significance of cutting cake is quite clear. Sweets are generally consumed in celebrations. Cake is a sweet food so that's why people cut it to celebrate different occasions.

What sort of desserts do you like?

I like cakes, traditional sweets, ice cream and anything made from chocolate. I usually don't eat a lot of desserts, but I have them when I feel happy or satisfied.

Are desserts good for health?

Yes, if one takes desserts in a controlled amount or occasionally, then deserts are not harmful. Although eating desserts on regular basis can have bad impact on body and health.

On what occasions do people eat desserts in your country?

People eat desserts on every occasion, I think. In Indian society desserts are a part of the meal. People like to have at the end of the meal on regular basis.

Do you make desserts?

Yes, I can make a couple of simple desserts. One of them is sweet curd. It is one of the simplest desserts to make and is very healthy to eat in summers. You just need to whisk some curd and then add some finely crushed sugar in it.

Numbers

Do you have a lucky number?

Yes, I do. I like number 7 the most. I don't know the reason behind the liking, but this number looks better than others. If I have to choose something, I always look for a number 7 connection.

OR

No, I don't have a lucky number. I like all the numbers. I don't believe in superstitions much, so I feel that I don't have a lucky number.

Are you superstitious about numbers?

No, I am not at all superstitious about numbers. I believe that all the numbers are same and there is no need to treat any number in a special way.

Do you remember any important number from your past?

Not really. I can't remember any important number from my past. I am not a believer of special numbers, so I can't recall any important number from my past.

Are you good at remembering phone numbers?

Yes, I remember many phone numbers of my family and friends. I learn the numbers easily than any other type of text.

OR

No, it is very hard for me to remember phone numbers. Although I remind some numbers of my family members and friends, but I can't memorize a lot of numbers.

Breaks

Is it important to take short breaks from your job on daily basis?

It is vital to take short breaks from work on daily basis. I think little breaks can help maintain concentration and interest in the job.

Do you feel that one should take a long break at least once in a year?

Without a doubt. It is essential for everyone to get away from work for at least once in the whole year. In my opinion, people should take a couple of weeks' off and go for a holiday with family.

Do you often take breaks from your study/work?

Yes, I take breaks from my study and work whenever I feel bored. I try to take short breaks every other month and a long one at least once a year.

What is the importance of taking breaks in life?

Taking break rejuvenates a person physically as well as mentally. It is essential to take breaks every now and then. Taking breaks allow you to break the monotony.

What should one do in breaks?

These days the life is too hectic. I personally feel that one should go to new places and explore the area and food. One can also go to mountains to feel peace and calm environment. People should also use their breaks in learning new things such as learning new languages or cuisines.

How do you spend your breaks?

I usually travel to a new place to spend my breaks. I like travelling so I pack my bags and go to faraway places for a week and enjoy the place. Sometimes I also utilize my breaks to learn some things that I don't know.

Running / walking

Do you run in your daily routine?

No, I don't run in my daily routine. However, I jog and walk when I am free in the evening.

Do you feel that running is helpful for the body?

Indeed, running is the best exercise. Our most of the body parts move while running so it is the best way to trim weight.

Do you believe that people walk less these days than the past?

Yes, people walk less as compared to the past. Previously there were not many resources, so people preferred to travel by foot. Nowadays, technology has made people lazy than before.

Do you often walk to nearby places or you use a vehicle?

I prefer walking to nearby places than taking a vehicle. Even though I use vehicle for far away places, but I generally walk to nearby places.

How much distance do you walk each day?

I walk about 10000 steps in a day. I keep a track on my phone every day. The average distance that I travel on foot is 10000 steps. World Health Organization suggests that a person must walk at least 8000 steps in a day to remain fit.

Are there facilities for pedestrians in your country?

Yes, there are facilities for the pedestrian in many cities around my country. The newly developed areas are now coming up with amenities like walking and cycling tracks along the roads.

Wild animals

Which is your favourite wild animal?

My favourite wild animal is Giant Panda. It is an animal that is mostly found in China. It mostly eats bamboo shoots and leaves. It is a very peace-loving animal.

Do you feel that wild animals are safe in forests?

Certainly, forests are the safest place for wild animals. Forest is the natural habitat of wild animals. Hence, they should be living there without interference from humans.

Do you believe that some species of wild animals will become extinct in the future?

I am afraid to say yes. There are some species in our country like the Bengal Tiger. Its population is declining at a rapid pace. If some corrective measures are not taken, then their population can be in danger.

Do you feel that government is taking enough steps to take care of the wild animals?

Yes, in some cases I have seen that government has taken active steps in making people aware about the species that are on the verge of extinction. Also, the government has taken keen interest in the maintenance of the wildlife sanctuaries all over the country in the past few years.

What are the most common wild animals in your country?

Monkey, Leopard and Lion are one of the most common wildlife animals in my country.

Do you reckon that wildlife is important for the survival of our planet?

Without a doubt, wildlife is crucial for the smooth running of our planet. Having a healthy wildlife ensures the proper balance in the life cycle of most of the species living on earth.

Scenery

Have you ever seen a wonderful scenery in your life?

I have seen many wonderful sceneries in my life. I live in the north part of my country, so mountains are never too far. There are numerous gorgeous spots which I have visited multiple times.

How do you feel when you see a beautiful scenery?

I feel humbled and refreshed. I always thank God when I see scenery. I also like to capture some photos of the scenery and relish them afterwards.

Is there a scenic spot in/near your hometown?

Yes, there is a lake in the east part of my hometown. The lake has lush green mountains on the back of it along with green areas all around. My hometown is surrounded by Shivalik Hills from one side, so we are never short of scenic spots in and around our hometown.

Do you often like to visit such places?

Yes, I do like to spend some time in these places. I feel close to nature and, I feel calm and rest that I don't get in the city life. I visit these places a couple of times every month.

Have you ever drawn a scenery in your life?

I have drawn many sceneries in my life. I remember in school time when we were taught to make scenery on a drawing sheet. I must have drawn it hundreds of times.

Voice

What type of voice do you like?

I like loud and clear voice. I feel that anyone who has a clear and crisp voice can attract many people.

Can anyone change his/her voice?

Yes, there are many comedian and mimicry artists that change their voice in order to make people laugh. They can imitate famous actors and politicians.

Do you feel that everyone should have same type of voice?

Not at all, I believe that beauty lies in diversity. If everyone will have same voice, then it would become very difficult to recognize different people on phone. It will create a world of confusion.

Have you ever talked to a person who has an unusual voice?

Yes, one of my friends has a very unusual voice. I think he has some issue with his throat. His voice is very crumbly, and one can hardly understand him speak.

Is it important to raise voice against evils in society?

Yes, it is essential to raise your voice against the evils in society. These days most people are busy in their life and they hardly find time to give opinion in important matters. However, I feel that one should take out time and raise voice against evils and injustice.

Haircut

How often do you get your hair cut?

I get my hair cut every week. I like to see my hair in good shape, so I regularly visit a barber for my hair cut.

OR

I don't cut my hair, so I never go to a barber for a haircut.

Do you like to have different haircuts every now and then?

No, I don't like to experiment with my looks. I try to stay the same. I get same haircut every time so that it doesn't affect my appearance.

OR

Yes, I like to do experiments with my haircut. I like to follow haircuts of celebrities and sportspersons. So, I change my haircut according to the trend.

From where do you get your hair cut?

I get my hair cut from a salon in my city. It is one of the oldest and best salons of my town.

OR

I cut my hair myself. I have proper kit to do so.

Do you feel that hair cutting is a special art?

Indeed, hair cutting is one of the most difficult arts around the world. It is very difficult to cut hair according to one's need. One must be very trained and smart to be a hair stylist.

Do you know anyone who is a hair stylist?

Yes, one of my school friends is a hair stylist and is working with a leading salon. She's taken the training of 6 months and now she is a certified hair stylist.

Which is your favorite type of hair cut?

I like plain haircut that balances my looks. I don't like to have fancy haircut at all.

Plan

Do you often plan your day?

Yes, I always plan my day. I like to plan my day in a proper manner. I note down the things that I want to achieve in the day and review those things at the end of the day.

Do you plan before taking a holiday?

Absolutely I plan a lot of things before taking holidays. I search about the weather of that place and pack my clothes accordingly. I also browse the best hotels and landmarks before visiting the holiday destination.

Do you plan your weekends?

No, I usually don't plan my weekends. But if I have some plan to go out with my friends and family members then I do plan for it.

Do you feel that planning is important in life?

Planning is very important in life. One should always plan about the future and obstacles that can come in the way. Planning leads to success and better opportunities.

Have any of your planning failed in the past?

Yes, some of my plans didn't work in the past. I planned to learn guitar and bought one for the same reason. But due to busy schedule, I couldn't learn it.

Have you ever planned a surprise party for someone?

Yes, I have planned a surprise party for my brother a few years ago. I surprised him by arranging a party at our home. He was very happy with this surprise and gave me a gift in return.

Languages

Is it important to learn more than one language?

It is very helpful to know more than one language. It is scientifically proven that a person who knows more than one language has better learning capabilities than a person who only knows one language.

How many languages do you know?

I can read, write and speak Hindi, Punjabi and English.

Do you feel that a person learns more from different languages?

A person can learn more about the cultures and tradition from different languages. One can understand more literature and history by reading multiple languages

Have you ever attempted to learn a foreign language apart from English?

Yes, I tried to learn Spanish a few months back but couldn't learn that. Although I learned few basic phrases and words but couldn't learn beyond that due to the shortage of time.

Are there language schools in your city?

There are several language schools in my city. Many people from my city go to abroad for study and work. So, there are an array of institutes that teach foreign as well as local languages.

Do you feel that there should be single language in the entire world?

I wish it was possible. If there will be a single language in the world then it would become so easy to communicate with everyone. There will be better understanding between people across the nations and less conflicts will be there.

Spending time alone

Do you like to spend some time alone?

Yes, I like to spend time alone as it gives me peace and calm environment. I am a peace lover, so I regularly go to some places and spend some quality time alone.

What are the benefits of spending lone time?

In my case, the main benefit of spending lone time is that I can think about myself and I can work on my future without any distractions.

How do you spend your time when you are alone?

I mostly listen to music or I read books. Sometimes I also write about my life experiences and daily happenings.

Do you know someone who spends a lot of time alone?

Yes, one of my childhood friends like to spend some time alone every day. He goes to temple and sits there for 1 hour every day. He does it on daily basis and loves it very much.

Do you feel that spending more time alone is not good?

Sometimes spending more time alone can be dangerous. People can start to get depressed and can get frustrate.

Jeans

How many jeans do you buy in a year?

I buy three to four jeans in a year. I like Levis Brand.

How many pairs of jeans do you have?

I must be having around 7 or 8 pairs of jeans. I like to buy jeans every now and then. It is my favourite type of bottom wear.

What are the benefits of wearing jeans?

There are many benefits of wearing jeans. Number one, it doesn't get dirty easily and it is also quite durable. You don't need to wash jeans regularly. Moreover, it can pair up with any kind of shirt.

Do you feel that jeans look very informal?

There are certain types of jeans that look quite informal. Some people wear jeans that are funky in colour and has threads hanging from all sides. On the contrary, there are jeans that look decent too. Despite that jeans do look a bit informal.

Are jeans a good-looking piece of clothing?

Absolutely jeans are a good-looking attire. Nowadays it has become a widespread fashion. People all over the world prefer jeans over other stuff.

What colour of jeans do you like the most?

I mostly like all shades of blue and black when it comes to jeans.

Science

Is it necessary to learn science at school?

It is very crucial to learn science at school because science is the basis of our life. We learn most of the practical things from science. Science gives us holistic knowledge of past, present and future.

Do you feel that science is a useful subject?

It is a very useful subject. With science we can conquer most of our fears. With science we have reached the moon and came back safely. With science we have busted many myths of the past.

Is science the way forward?

Science is definitely the way forward. We can use science as the binding factor between different countries, cultures and societies. Science can be used to enlighten people about the nature and its principles.

Do you feel that science is 100 % true?

I do believe that most of the scientific discoveries and theories are true. Although there can be some theories that can be regarded as false but most information on science till date has proven right.

Did you like science as a subject at school?

I liked science as a subject very much. Although my grades were not that great in science, but I liked the things that I learned from different science subject's physics, chemistry and biology.

Laughter

Do you often laugh?

Yes, I often laugh. I think it is good to laugh at small things as it keeps your mood good and helps you to stay away from stress.

What are the benefits of laughing?

There are proven benefits of laughing. Science says that our blood flow through the body parts increases when we laugh. Also, some chemicals are released within our body that helps a person to remain calm and happy.

Do you watch laughter shows?

Yes, whenever I get a chance, I like to watch laughter shows. There are many laughter shows that are telecasted on television. The best one is The Kapil Sharma Show.

Why do you think that laughter is important in life?

Laughter is like a therapy. It is very important to have laughter in life. One should laugh whenever he/she gets a chance.

Do you like to make others laugh?

Yes, I like to make people laugh. If I see someone depressed, then I like to make them laugh by cracking a joke or making some fun out of the situation.

Water sports

Do you relish water sports?

Yes, I like water sports but the ones that are not dangerous. I like mild risky activities like riding a jet ski. It is a simple scooter kind of a vehicle that runs in water. This type of activity is generally held in sea areas.

What type of water sports you have participated?

I have only attempted jet ski a couple of times. I don't like other activities like para sailing and deep ocean diving. I have a fear of deep water and heights.

Are water sports good for fun

Water sports are great for fun. Most of the people in my county doesn't live by the beach areas so they like to enjoy water sports and they consider that activity as fun.

Are water sports common in your county?

Yes, water sports are quite common in my country but only in coastal areas. Most of the people in my country live inland. There you hardly find water sports. But in coastal areas it is famous.

What type of water sport you would like to do in future?

If I get a chance to try any type of water sport, then it would be snorkeling. In this activity you don't go deep down the ocean. You float at the top and discover beautiful coral reefs in shallow waters.

PART FOUR

Important Vocabulary for IELTS Speaking

1. Absolutely – unquestionably / undeniably
2. Abundance – enough resources / plenty
3. Access – admittance / entree
4. Accolades – honors / awards / praises
5. Accomplish – achieve / complete / finish
6. Accumulate – amass / gather / collect / hoard
7. Acquire – obtain / get / gain
8. Admire – respect / like / appreciate
9. Adore – love / admire
10. Adrenalin rush – a sudden surge in energy in a person
11. Adroit – expert / skillful
12. Advent – beginning / arrival / start
13. Adverse – hostile / opposing
14. Affection – liking / fondness
15. Ageing – getting old / mature
16. Aggressive – violent / destructive
17. Alarming – disturbing / upsetting
18. Alien – unknown / unfamiliar / strange
19. All walks of life – from every background / from all backgrounds or age groups
20. Allied – associated / related / connected
21. Allure – attract / appeal
22. Almighty – enormous / massive / huge
23. Alternatives – replacements / substitutes
24. Amass – accumulate / collect
25. Ambitious – determined / striving
26. Amenities – facilities / services
27. Ample – enough / plenty / sufficient
28. Amusement – laughter / enjoyment / delight
29. Analytical – logical / investigative / diagnostic
30. Ancestors – decedents / dynasties
31. Anxiety – nervousness / concerns / worry
32. Anxious – nervous / worried / concerned
33. Apolitical – a person who is not political
34. Apparels – attires / clothes

35. Appealing – attractive / interesting / tempting
36. Aptly – appropriately / fittingly / suitably / rightly
37. Archipelago – is a collection of small islands in an ocean
38. Ascend – arise / rise
39. Aromatic – fragrant / perfumed
40. Array – collection / selection
41. Aspect – feature / facet / characteristics
42. Assault – attack / beating
43. Association - connotation
44. Assortment – variety / collection / range / mixture
45. Assure – promise / guarantee / pledge
46. Astonish – surprise / amaze / astound
47. Attire – clothing / dress / outfit
48. Authentic – true / reliable / dependable
49. Autobiographies – memoires / a self-written life journey
50. Awe – wonder / admiration / respect
51. Awestruck – impressed / enthralled / overwhelmed
52. Backdrop – at the back / background
53. Bamboozle – confuse / deceive
54. Bane – curse / misery
55. Banter – teasing /mockery / joking
56. Barely – just / hardly / scarcely
57. Barricades   barriers / hurdles / blockades
58. Bearable – manageable / tolerable / endurable
59. Beverage – drink / hot drink / cold drink
60. Biographies – profiles / memoirs
61. Blueprint – plan / drawing / design / proposal
62. Bond – promise / pledge / oath
63. Boon – benefit / advantage / bonus
64. Boredom – dullness / monotony
65. Breakdown- failure / collapse
66. Breathtaking- magnificent / spectacular
67. Briefly- fleetingly / momentarily
68. Brittle- fragile / breakable
69. Browse- look / glance

70. Bruise- discoloration / shiner
71. Bulk- majority / loose
72. Bump- collision / smash
73. Bustling- lively / busy
74. Buzz- crowd / chaos
75. Bygone – past / previous
76. Cakewalk – easy / very easy
77. Candid – straight forward / frank
78. Catapulted – threw / hurled
79. Chaos – disorder / confusion
80. Charity – aid/ contribution
81. Charming – attractive / appealing
82. Cherish – appreciate / relish
83. Chores – errands / task
84. Chronologically – historical / sequential
85. Circulation – flow / movement
86. Cited – quoted / mentioned
87. Close quarters – from a close perspective
88. Coastal – seaside / beach
89. Coastline – shoreline / seashore
90. Cognitive – reasoning / intellectual
91. Colonized – populated / settled
92. Commemorate – honor / memorialize
93. Commendable – admirable / worthy
94. Commercialization - development
95. Commit – pledge / promise
96. Commute – travel / shuttle
97. Compact – compressed / condensed
98. Complimentary – free / courtesy
99. Comprise – include / encompass
100. Concession - discount
101. Conscious – aware / mindful
102. Consequences – negative outcome
103. Conceal – hide/ cover
104. Conservation – preservation / maintenance

105. Considerable – substantial / significance
106. Consoled – comforted / supported
107. Constantly – continuously / repeatedly
108. Constellations – gatherings / group
109. Contented – satisfied / pleased
110. Convenience – suitability / ease
111. Converse – opposite / contrary
112. Conviction – belief / opinion
113. Coral reefs – food for marine life
114. Courage – bravery / valor
115. Courtyard – yard / garden
116. Cozy – warm / snug
117. Cram – fill up / pack
118. Cramming – packing / stuffing
119. Cramps – pains / contractions
120. Creek – narrow river / stream
121. Cremate – burn / incinerate
122. Criticism – disapproval / condemnation
123. Cruel – harsh / hard
124. Crunch – critical situation
125. Cuisines – foods / cookeries
126. Curb – control / limit
127. Cure – treatment / therapy
128. Curious – interested / inquisitive
129. Customs – duties / levies
130. Daunting – intimidating / scary
131. Decay – falloff / decline
132. Dedicated – devoted / keen
133. Deed – action / act
134. Delicate – gentle / mild
135. Delicious – tasty / palatable
136. Departed – left from somewhere
137. Dependent – reliant on
138. Depress – reduce / dampen
139. Designation – title / name

140. Desperate – anxious / worried
141. Desperately – badly / urgently
142. Deteriorate – worsen/ decline
143. Determined – strong minded / resolute
144. Detrimental – harmful / damaging
145. Devote – dedicate / offer
146. Dilemma – difficulty / problem
147. Diminishing – lessening / fading
148. Disaster – tragedy / adversity
149. Disintegrating - crumbling
150. Distinctive – different / distinguishing
151. Distracted – unfocussed / sidetrack
152. Diverse – varied / assorted
153. Diversions - changes / deviations
154. Diversity – variety / range
155. Dreadful – terrible / awful
156. Drowsiness – sleepiness / lethargy
157. Dumping – removal / discarding
158. Duplex – double storied house or complex
159. Durable – long lasting / hard wearing
160. Dwarf – short in height
161. Dwell – reside / live
162. Dynamic – lively / active
163. Dynasty – reign / family
164. Eagerly – keenly / excitedly
165. Earthen – clay / mud
166. Echoes – repeats / resonances
167. Efficient – effective / well-organized
168. Elated – overjoyed / delighted
169. Elevate – raise / lift
170. Embarrass – shame / humiliate
171. Embedded – fixed / rooted
172. Eminent – famous / renowned
173. Emissions – releases / discharges
174. Emphasized – highlighted / stressed

175. Empower – authorize / allow
176. Endurable – manageable / tolerable
177. Engage – involve / occupy
178. Enhance – improve / augment
179. Enlarge – increase / expand
180. Enroll – register / join
181. Ensure – safeguard / guarantee
182. Enthusiasm – eagerness / interest
183. Enticing – tempting / alluring
184. Equivalent – equal / comparable
185. Eradicate – eliminate / destroy
186. Erudite – very knowledgeable / expert in a subject or skill
187. Escalate – intensify / heighten
188. Essential – vital / important
189. Establish – found / start
190. Eternal – everlasting / unending
191. Ethics – morals/ beliefs
192. Etiquettes – manners / protocols
193. Euphoric – overjoyed / elated
194. Eventually – finally / ultimately
195. Evolution – development / growth
196. Evolved – changed / advanced
197. Exaggerated – overstated / inflated
198. Except – excluding / bar
199. Excess – extra / additional
200. Excitement – enthusiasm / eagerness
201. Excursion – trip / outing
202. Execute – perform / implement
203. Executed – accomplished / performed
204. Exhaust – consume / drain
205. Exile – outcast / refugee
206. Existence – presence / survival
207. Expect – suppose / assume
208. Expedition – excursion / trip
209. Expenditure - spending

210. Explore – travel / discover
211. Exposure – contact / experience
212. Extensive - widespread
213. Extensively – widely / broadly
214. Extraordinary – unusual / unexpected
215. Exuberant – excited / energetic
216. Fabulous – wonderful / marvelous
217. Façade - front
218. Facet - aspect
219. Fascinate – captivate / attract
220. Fauna - wildlife
221. Features - characteristics
222. Fellow – associated / related
223. Feminine – female / womanly
224. Firm – stable / fixed
225. Flashy – showy / gaudy
226. Flaunt – exhibit / display
227. Flawless – perfect / faultless
228. Flock – group / herd
229. Flora - vegetation
230. Fluffy – cottony / furry
231. Foodie – a person who likes food
232. Forbid – ban / prohibit
233. Forgive – pardon / excuse
234. Forthcoming – approaching / upcoming
235. Fortunate – lucky / privileged
236. Fragile – delicate / brittle
237. Frequency – occurrence / rate
238. Frequently – often / regularly
239. Frustrated – irritated / unsatisfied
240. Fulfilment – completion/ execution
241. Gadgets – devices / appliances
242. Generous – lavish / plentiful
243. Genre – type / kind
244. Genuine – honest / sincere

245. Gesture – sign / signal / hand movements
246. Gigantic – huge / enormous
247. Glittering – sparkling / dazzling
248. Gloomy – dull
249. Grievance – complaint / protest
250. Groceries - foodstuffs
251. Guilty – shamefaced / embarrassed
252. Gust – breeze / strong winds
253. Gymnasium – fitness center
254. Habitat – home / territory
255. Handful – a few
256. Hardcore - dedicated
257. Harmony - agreement
258. Harsh - strict
259. Haste – speed / swiftness
260. Heatstroke – issues arising from extreme hot environment
261. Hectic – frantic / chaotic
262. Heritage – inheritance / legacy
263. Hesitant – uncertain / cautious
264. Highlands – hilltops / uplands
265. Hire – rent / lease
266. Hit the sack – go to sleep / go to bed
267. Hoist – lift / elevator
268. Holistic – overall / rounded
269. Horizon – skyline / limit
270. Hospitality – friendliness / warmth
271. Humble - polite
272. Humid – moist / sticky
273. Humorous – funny / entertaining
274. Humungous – huge / great
275. Hygiene – cleanliness / sanitation
276. Hymns – songs / chants
277. Iconic – major / famous
278. Ideology – philosophy / thought
279. Idle – indolent / free

280. Idol – star / favorite
281. Illiterate – uneducated / unschooled
282. Imitation – fake / mock
283. Immense – huge / vast / enormous
284. Impact – effect / influence
285. Impeccable – perfect / flawless
286. Imperial – grand / majestic
287. Impose – execute / enforce
288. Impression - imprint
289. Imprisoned – confined / captive
290. Inaugurate – initiate / install
291. Incentives - motivations
292. Inclined – tending / persuaded
293. Incredible - unbelievable
294. Inculcate – teach / instruct
295. Incurred – experienced / suffered
296. Indeed – certainly / really
297. Indigenous – native / original
298. Indispensable – essential / crucial
299. Induce – encourage / persuade
300. Industrious – hardworking / diligent
301. Inevitable – unavoidable / predictable
302. Inferior – lesser / lower
303. Inflation – rise / increase
304. Infrastructure - structure
305. Ingredients – elements / components
306. Inhale – gasp / huff
307. Inherit – receive / succeed to
308. Injurious – harmful / damaging
309. Innate – inborn / characteristic
310. Inscribed - adorned
311. Insecurity – uncertainty / diffident
312. Insights – visions / understanding
313. Insomnia – sleeplessness
314. Inspect – examine / check

315. Inspire – motivate / encourage
316. Instance – example / illustration
317. Instant – on the spot / immediate
318. Instrumental – contributory
319. Integral – essential / vital
320. Integration – combination / incorporation
321. Intent – determined / committed
322. Intentionally – purposely / deliberately
323. Interaction – contact / communication
324. Interfere – hinder / inhibit
325. Intimidate – threaten / frighten
326. Introvert – shy / reserved
327. Invade – attack / occupy
328. Invent – discover / create
329. Joyous – jolly / festive
330. Kitchenette – kitchen / pantry
331. Knack – ability / skill
332. Landlocked – surrounded by land / blocked in
333. Landmark – milestone
334. Lane – path / track
335. Laxative - purgative
336. Leaps and bounds
337. Lenient – soft / merciful
338. Lentils – curry food
339. Lethal – deadly / fatal
340. Lethargic – lazy / sluggish
341. Liabilities – obligations / charges
342. Likewise – similarly / equally
343. Literally – actually / factually
344. Littering – throwing waste
345. Long-lasting – lifelong / enduring
346. Loyal – faithful / trustworthy
347. Loyalty – faithfulness / trustworthiness
348. Lure – trap / entice
349. Magnificent – wonderful / brilliant

350. Majestic – royal / grand
351. Mandatory – compulsory / obligatory
352. Maneuver – movement / operation
353. Manifesto – policy / strategy
354. Manned – operated / staffed
355. Manuscripts – documents / copies
356. Marine – sea / aquatic
357. Martyr – sufferer for a cause
358. Marvelous – amazing / wonderful
359. Marvels - geniuses
360. Masculine – male / manly
361. Massive – huge / enormous
362. Medicinal – remedial / therapeutic
363. Melodious – musical / harmonious
364. Menace – threat / danger
365. Merchandise – produce / stock
366. Merchants – wholesalers / dealers
367. Mere – simple / sheer
368. Merrymaking – celebration / partying
369. Mesmerized – fascinated / awestruck
370. Metabolism – digestion / absorption
371. Minimal – slight / negligible
372. Minutest – smallest / miniature
373. Miraculous – unbelievable
374. Miscellaneous – various / mixed
375. Mist – fog / vapor
376. Momentum – thrust / energy
377. Monotony – dullness / boredom
378. Monument – memorial / shrine
379. Myriad – many / innumerable
380. Myth – legend / saga
381. Mythology - tradition
382. Negligent - careless
383. Noble – decent / moral
384. Noteworthy – significant / notable

385. Nuisance - annoyance
386. Obesity - overweightness
387. Occasionally – rarely / irregularly
388. Offspring – children / decedents
389. Often – frequently / repeatedly
390. Optimistic – positive / hopeful
391. Optimum – best / finest
392. Overly – excessively / exceedingly
393. Overtaken – passed / outdone
394. Palatable – edible / pleasant
395. Panic – terror / fear
396. Parallel – equivalent / similar
397. Partial – incomplete / limited
398. Patience – tolerance / endurance
399. Patrol - tour
400. Pedestrians - walkers
401. Penal – severe / strict
402. Perception – insight / awareness
403. Persistent - determined
404. Pessimistic – negative / doubtful
405. Phenomenal – extraordinary / remarkable
406. Pinnacle – highpoint / peak
407. Pleasure – desire / wish
408. Plight - dilemma / difficulty
409. Plume – trail / cloud
410. Ponder – think about / consider
411. Posh – noble / superior
412. Posture - position
413. Potential – probable
414. Potholes – holes / dips
415. Precedent – example / model
416. Precious – valuable / costly
417. Predators – killers / hunters
418. Predict – forecast / foresee
419. Preference – fondness / favorite

420. Premises – buildings / locations
421. Preserve - reserve
422. Prevail – overcome / conquer
423. Prevalent – dominant / widespread
424. Prior – previous / former
425. Priority – importance / significance
426. Prominent - famous
427. Promote – endorse / sponsor
428. Prone – disposed to / inclined to
429. Protest – objection / complaint
430. Publish – print / put out
431. Random – accidental / chance
432. Rapid – fast / quick
433. Rapidly – quickly / swiftly
434. Rare – occasional
435. Recite – perform / rehearse
436. Reckless – irresponsible / thoughtless
437. Reckon – calculate / count
438. Reconciliation – settlement / understanding
439. Refrain - restrict
440. Regulated – planned / controlled
441. Rejuvenate – revive / refresh
442. Rejuvenating – reviving / refreshing
443. Releasing – to leave / freeing
444. Relieve – dismiss / discharge
445. Relish - enjoy / delight
446. Rely – depend upon / count on
447. Remarkable – extraordinary / amazing
448. Remedy – medication / therapy
449. Renowned – famous / well-known
450. Rescue - save
451. Respiratory – breathing
452. Restrict – limit / confine
453. Revenge – retaliation / vengeance
454. Revere – admire / respect

455. Revive – come around / recover
456. Rigorous – hard / difficult
457. Rituals – rites / ceremonies
458. Roam – travel / wander
459. Rushed – hurried / quick
460. Sachet – packet / pouch
461. Sacred – holy / blessed
462. Sanctuary – national preserve / national park
463. Savor – taste / smell
464. Scarcity – shortage / insufficiency
465. Scary – terrifying / frightening
466. Scenario – situation / set up
467. Scorching – roasting
468. Sculptures – statues / figures
469. Sedatives - tranquillizers
470. Segments – sections / parts
471. Segregated – separated / isolated
472. Seize – grab / take hold of
473. Seldom – rarely / occasionally
474. Serene – calm / peaceful
475. Several – numerous / some
476. Severity – cruelty / strictness
477. Shatter – smash / destroy
478. Significance - importance
479. Sinful – bad / evil / wicked
480. Sitcom – series of TV programs
481. Skip – hop / or to leave a step
482. Skyrocketed – shoot up / rise steeply
483. Skyscrapers – high rise buildings / towers
484. Snatch - fetch
485. Snorkeling – swimming / diving
486. Soothing – comforting/ calming
487. Sore – tending / painful
488. Souvenir – memento / reminder
489. Spacious – airy / large / roomy

490. Span – distance / length
491. Species – classes / types
492. Sporty – athletic / muscular
493. Stationary – motionless / still
494. Steer – maneuver / to move
495. Stiff – rigid / firm
496. Stone face – no reaction at all
497. Stray – lost / wandering
498. Stress buster – a thing that gets rid of stress
499. Striking – outstanding / prominent
500. Strive – struggle / try
501. Stroll - wander
502. Subscriptions – contributions / payments
503. Subsidiary – minor / secondary
504. Substantial – considerable / significant
505. Subtle - delicate
506. Succulent – moist / tender
507. Superb – excellent / outstanding
508. Superstitions – delusions / fantasies
509. Supplements – additions / complements
510. Suppress – overpower / conquer
511. Surf – waves / sea
512. Survive – last / endure
513. Suspect – doubtful / suspicious
514. Sustainable – bearable / maintainable
515. Tariff – price / rate
516. Temperate – moderate / mild
517. Tender – loving / caring
518. Terrace – walkway / porch
519. Terrain – land / territory
520. Thick and thin – happiness and sorrows
521. Timid – nervous / fearful
522. Traits – personalities / qualities
523. Tranquil – calm / serene
524. Transition – change / conversion

525. Tremendous – marvelous / great
526. Trigger – start / activate
527. Trivial – small / minor
528. Turf – lawn / grass
529. Twigs – branches / brushwood
530. Typhoon – storm / cyclone
531. Unanimous – common / undisputed
532. Underneath – under / below
533. Undoubtedly – certainly / unquestionably
534. Uninterrupted – continuous / non-stop
535. Unpredictable – random
536. Unwrap – open / undo
537. Up to the mark
538. Utilize – use / employ
539. Vanish – disappear / die out
540. Verdict – decision / judgement
541. Versatile – multipurpose / handy
542. Version – form / type
543. Viable – practical / feasible
544. Vibes – feelings / vibrations
545. Vibrant – lively / exciting
546. Victim – prey / target
547. Vigil – watch / wake
548. Vigilance – watchfulness / observance
549. Vital – important
550. Vividly – brightly / vibrantly
551. Vouch – promise / vow
552. Voyage – journey / trip
553. Wardrobe – clothing / attire
554. Weird – strange / odd
555. Wicked – good / great
556. Window shopping
557. Wisdom – understanding / insight
558. Witness – observer / bystander
559. Woods – forests

560. Wreckage – debris / remains
561. Yester years – past years / recent years

PART FIVE

Tips for IELTS Speaking Test and Format

Important tips for the IELTS Speaking interview

A day prior to the interview

It is important that you have read this book thoroughly till the day prior to your interview. On the day before exam it is advised that you should not practice a lot of speaking. Reading of this book should also be avoided. Reading should be done before that. Don't mark anything as important or common. Read the whole book carefully and take out ideas for your speaking test.

Sleep on time a day before the interview. If you sleep well, you will be energized for the test day. It is important to be active on important days. This helps you to perform better.

On the test day

Reach the exam center at least 40 minutes before your speaking slot. You will also receive an acknowledgement via email. Just take a printout of that and take it along with original passport and a photocopy of it on the exam day.

Don't read any book or try to practice anything on the day of speaking test. It is important to stay focused and blank before the interview.

In the interview (one on one)

These days in many IDP centers, speaking is done through webchat. But in this section, I am going to give you tips regarding the conventional type of speaking test. The one on one IELTS Speaking test is taken by one examiner in an enclosed cubical or a test room.

In this type of a test, the examiner will ask you questions, and you must answer them one by one. There are some things that you need to remember before going in the exam. The do's and don'ts are as follows:

Do's

- Reach the exam center at least 40 minutes before the speaking test slot
- Take along acknowledgement, original passport and copy of passport at the time of exam
- Drink a full glass of water before the start of exam (ask anyone there, they will be happy to help you)
- Dress formally for the speaking test
- Knock before you enter the speaking test room

- Ask for a permission to sit
- Greet the examiner with a smile
- Listen to the questions carefully
- Always answer a bit loud and with clear tone
- Make eye contact with the examiner (this increases your confidence)
- Use formal language to communicate (Avoid using slangs)
- Ask the examiner to repeat the question politely if you don't understand it
- Prepare notes for the Cue-card Topic
- Stop speaking when examiner tells you to stop

Don'ts
- Never wear accessories like earrings or metal studs (for boys)
- Never reach late for the exam (it will rush you and your thoughts)
- Don't start your answer before the question is completed
- Don't keep your hands on the table while speaking
- Don't use memorized phrases and topics
- Don't wear a watch in the exam as it will distract you
- Don't take too many pauses
- Don't use a lot of hand movements and gestures
- Don't repeat the question before giving the answer
- Don't smile too much at the time of speaking (just be natural)
- Don't finish your answer mid-way
- Avoid using repetitive vocabulary and words
- Don't rush in giving your answers
- Don't stop the cue card topic before time
- Don't ask the examiner about the interview at the end (simply say thank you and goodbye)

How to answer General round questions – First Round

Sometimes candidates go over the top in answering the general round questions. These questions are very easy but can be deceptive as well.
It is crucial to cover the while aspect with minimal of explanation. You should not answer these questions in detail. Only a few lines are required.
Try to answer the general questions in three to four lines. Don't stretch your answer too much as it will deviate you from your topic.
This round lasts for about 5 minutes. In these 5 minutes the examiner has a quota of at least 10 – 15 questions that he/she ask you.
So be precise and accurate in your answers to fetch higher band score. As you are only speaking three or four lines for each answer, you don't have a lot on your plate. You can't go wrong in your answers.
If you are answering in this length, then there are rare chances of you to make any grammatical error if you are prepared well.
The speaking interview is divided in such a way that all the three rounds weigh equally in terms of band score.
So, you can try to get full marks in the first round as the questions will also be not that tricky and the answer length required is also not too long.

Cue-card Topic – Second Round

In this round the examiner will ask you to speak on a topic for about 2 minutes. You must speak for 1 minute and 30 seconds minimum and not more than 2 minutes.
You are also given a piece of paper, a pen and one minute to prepare some notes on the Cue-card Topic.
There is a certain way to prepare the topics that will help you to score good in this round. You need to be good in your grammar and use of vocabulary in this round. Moreover, it is integral to follow the timing in the second round.

How to Prepare Cue-card Topic

Suppose my topic is – Speak about your visit to a Mall
So, I know that there are lot of aspects associated with malls. So, my first job should be to write everything that is associated with mall. As you get only a minute to prepare for your topic, you can't write a long story.
However, you can make bullet points that will help you while speaking the topic.

Bullet Points for this Topic are as follows:

- My city
- Many malls
- Favourite one
- About the visit
- Why
- With whom
- When
- What I did
- Shopping
- Movie
- Hungry
- Food
- Came back

These points can be easily recalled and written under one minute. If you have read the whole book, then you can simply recall the idea and not the whole text.

Recalling ideas is very easy than memorizing 300 odd topics for your exam. Even if you have read a certain topic once, you will still remember a lot of it in idea's sense.

IELTS Speaking Test Format

Format   Part 1: The examiner will introduce him or herself and ask you to introduce yourself and confirm your identity. The examiner will ask you general questions on familiar topics, e.g. home, family, work, studies and interests. This section should help you relax and talk naturally.

Part 2: The examiner will give you a task card which asks you to talk about a particular topic, including points to include in your talk.
You will be given one minute to prepare and make notes. You will then be asked to talk for 1-2 minutes on the topic. You will not be interrupted during this time, so it is important to keep talking. The examiner will then ask you one or two questions on the same topic.

Part 3: The examiner will ask you further questions which are connected to the topic of Part 2. These questions are designed to give you an opportunity to discuss more abstract issues and ideas.

Timing   11-14 minutes

Marks   You will be assessed on your performance throughout the test by certificated IELTS examiners. You will be marked on the four criteria: fluency and coherence, lexical resource, grammatical range and accuracy, pronunciation. Scores are reported in whole and half band.

Made in the USA
Monee, IL
19 April 2021